SeX Inc.

SeX Inc.

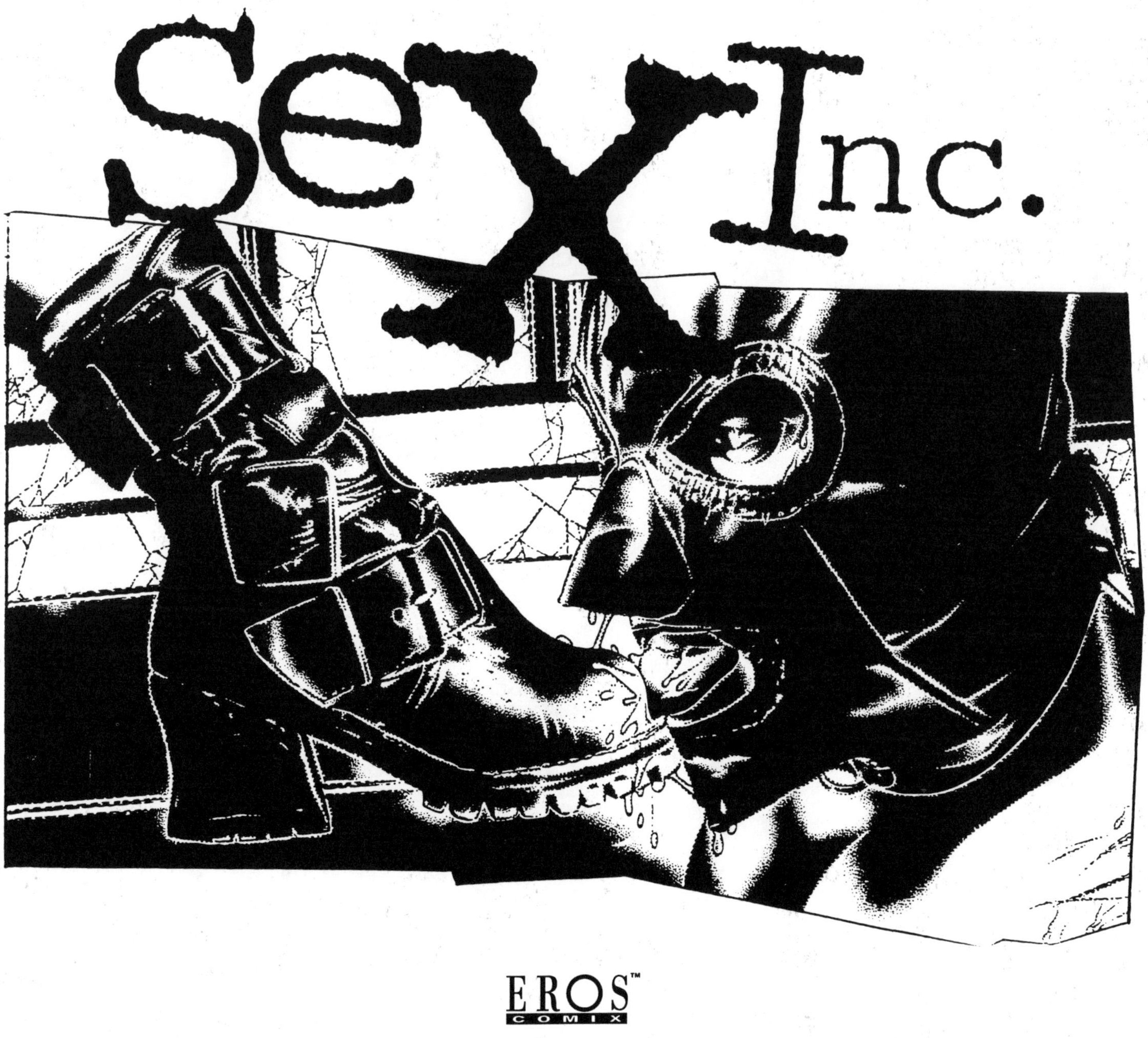

EROS™
COMIX

EROS COMIX™
P.O. BOX 25070
SEATTLE, WA 98125

EROS COMIX™ AND STARNET COMMUNICATIONS PRESENT:
SEX INC.

CREATED BY NICO AND RICHARD GALLO
ARTWORK BY NICO
STORY BY STEPHANIE HALLEY
EDITED BY EZRA MARK
ART DIRECTION BY LINUS CHALK
PUBLISHED BY GARY GROTH AND KIM THOMPSON

SPECIAL THANKS TO:
MIKE T., JEFF T., CRAIG C., BRAD S., JAY J., JOHN A.,
JASON K., PAUL C., BOB, ROXY M.R., VERONICA, HONEY
G.H., TERRY C., PHIL G., JAY B., SYDNEY, ANDRE T.

SEX INC. APPEARS AT: **WWW.SIZZLE.COM** AND
WWW.REDLIGHT.COM
CHECK OUT THE EROS WEBSITE:
HTTP://WWW.EROSCOMIX.COM.

FIRST EROS COMIX™ EDITION: APRIL, 1998

ISBN: 1-56097-320-X

PRINTED IN U.S.A.

Gal*ileo*: an enormous computerized entity capable of self-awareness

Sex Inc.

PART ONE

www.sizzle.com/world

In the year 2117 the prostitutes of Sex, Inc. attempt to make their living in the urban decay of a collapsed world.

Confronted with the limitless fetishes and fantasies of a desperate and enslaved public, the girls attempt to fulfill every fantasy while pursuing Sex, Inc.'s personal goals.

Every man, woman and child was meant to access second century.

WWW OVER21

America erotic girls advertising etal

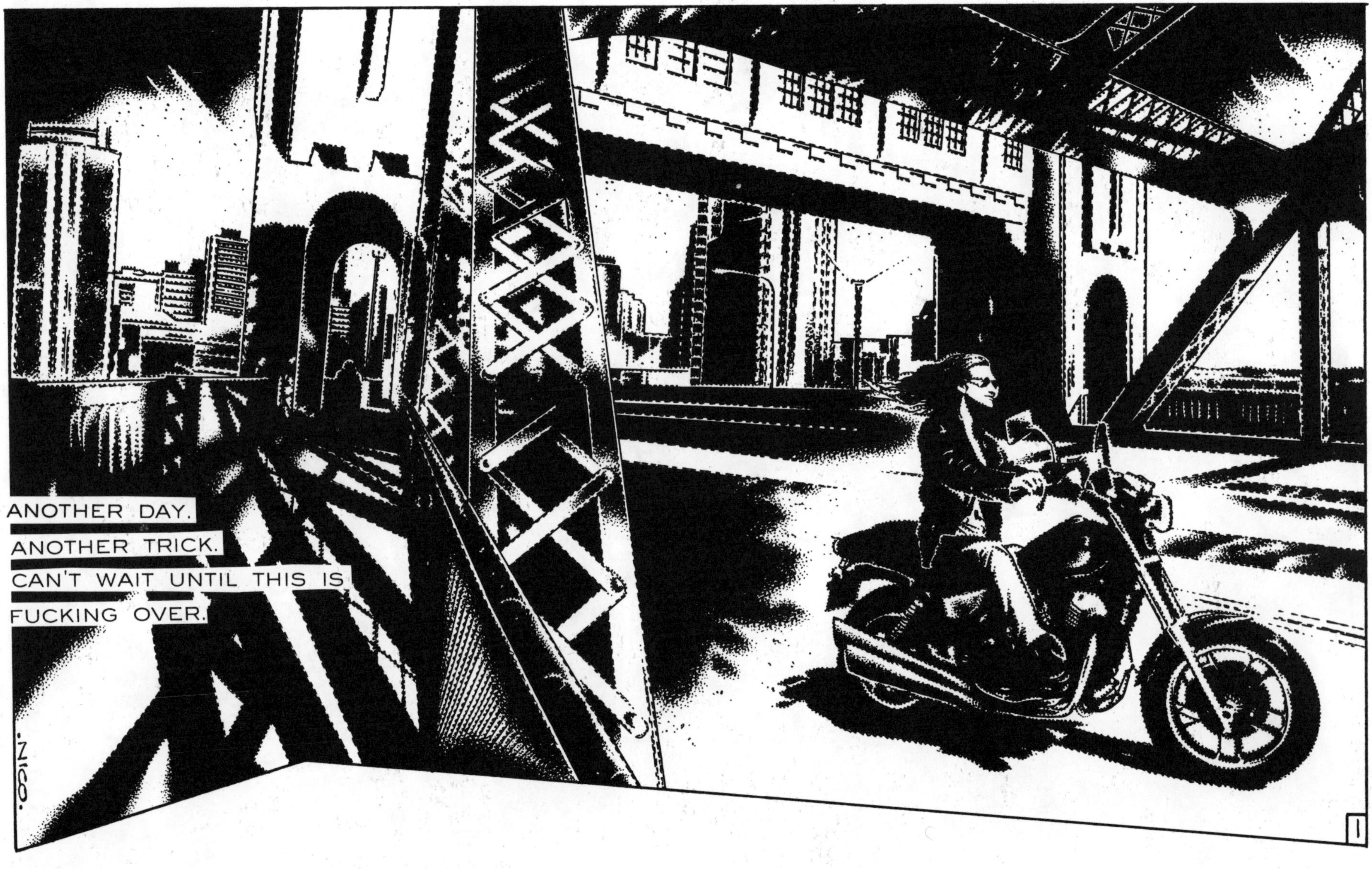
ANOTHER DAY.
ANOTHER TRICK.
CAN'T WAIT UNTIL THIS IS
FUCKING OVER.
NICO.
1

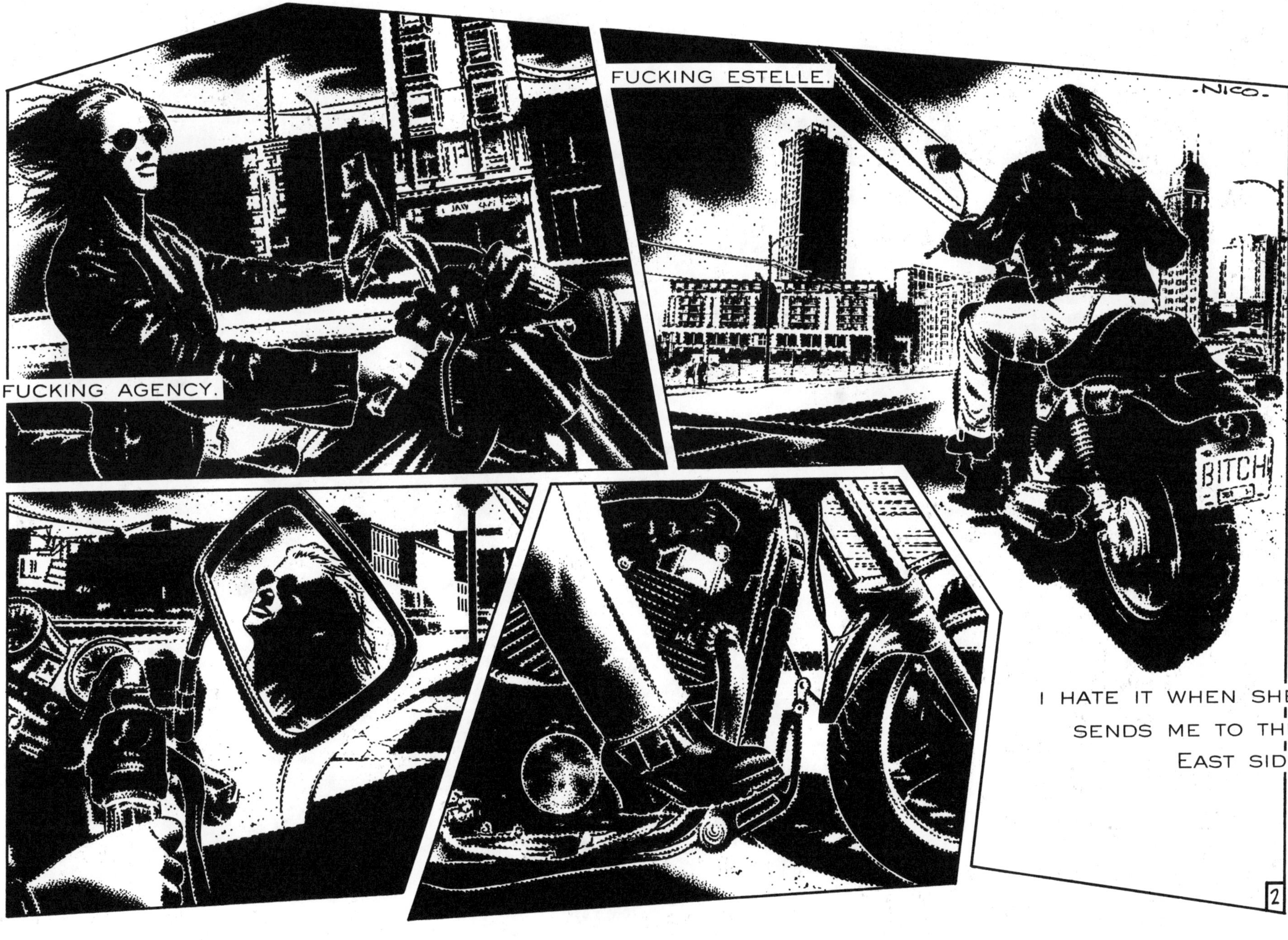
FUCKING AGENCY.
FUCKING ESTELLE.
-NICO-
BITCH
I HATE IT WHEN SHE SENDS ME TO THE EAST SIDE.

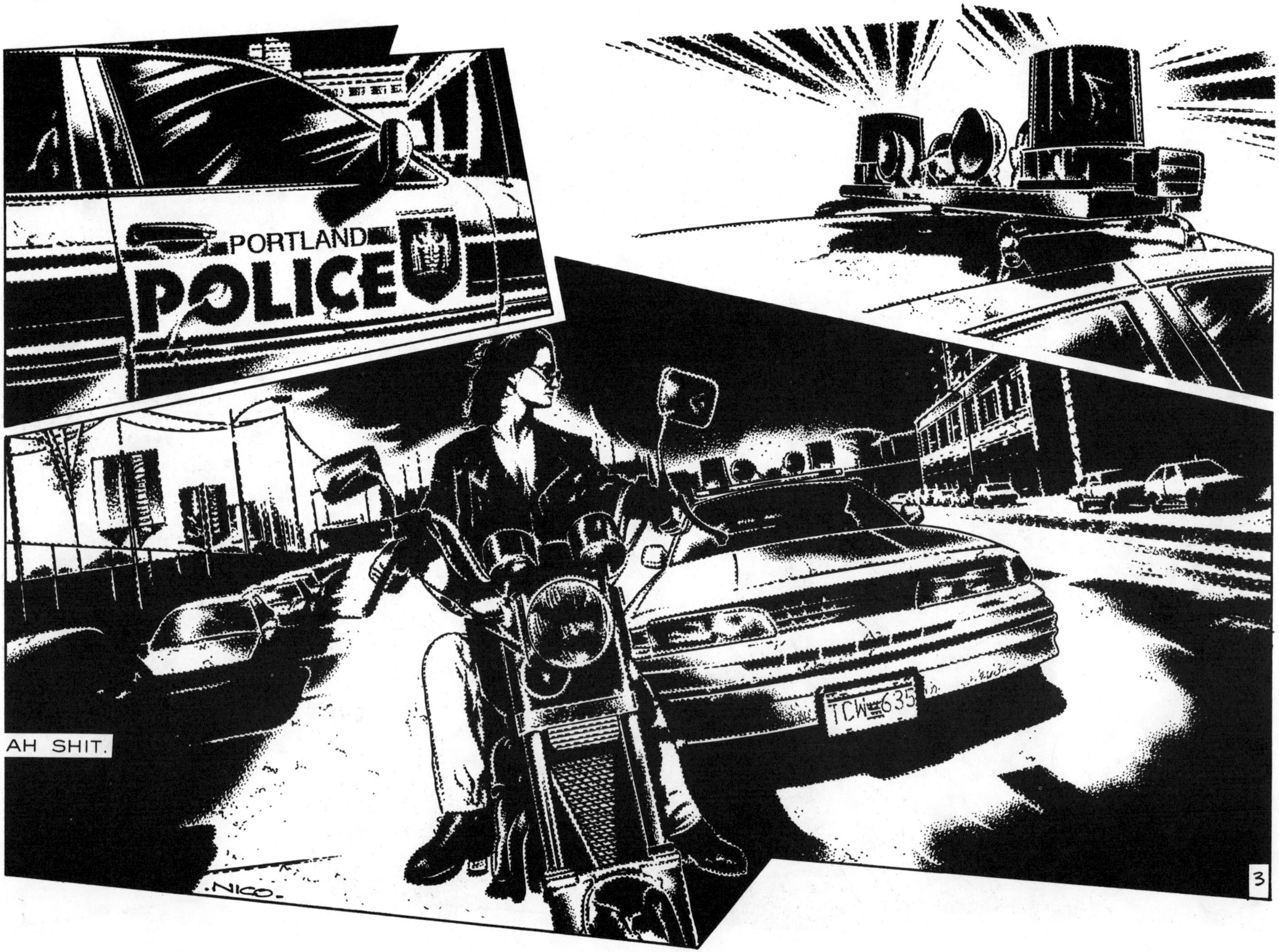
PORTLAND
POLICE
TCW 635
AH SHIT.
NICO

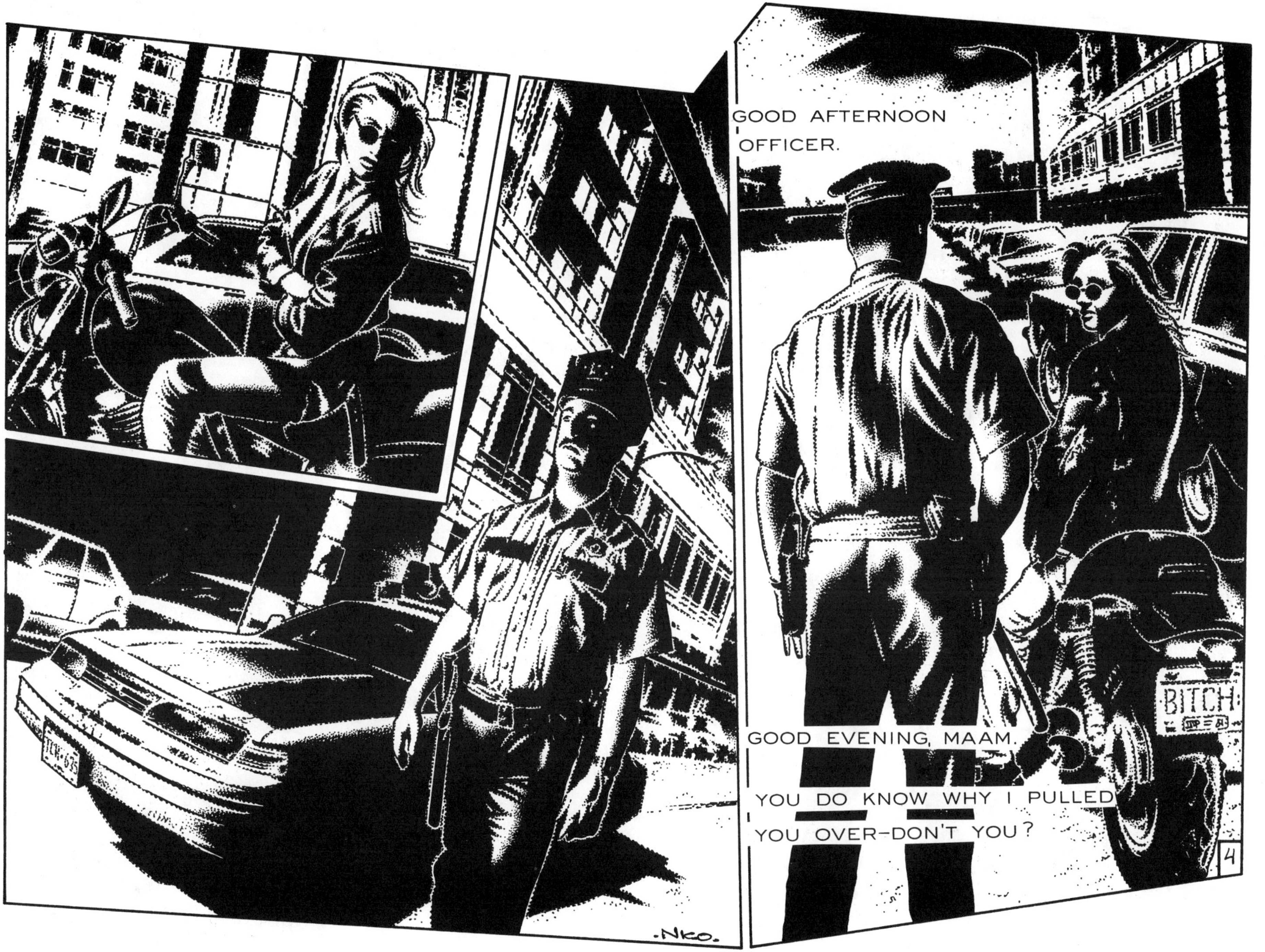
GOOD AFTERNOON OFFICER.
BITCH
GOOD EVENING, MAAM.
YOU DO KNOW WHY I PULLED YOU OVER-DON'T YOU?
.NKO.
4

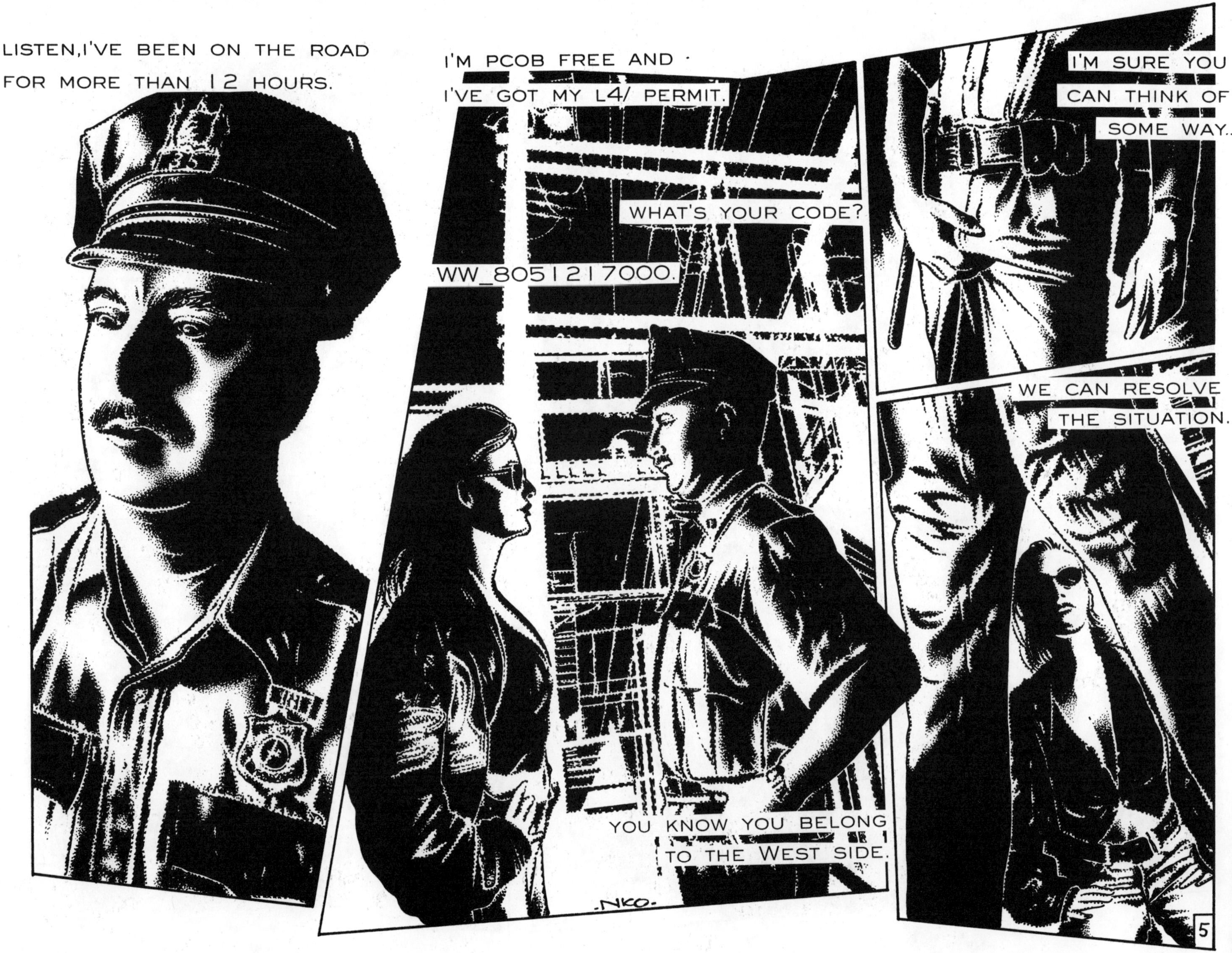
LISTEN,I'VE BEEN ON THE ROAD FOR MORE THAN 12 HOURS.
I'M PCOB FREE AND I'VE GOT MY L4/ PERMIT.
WHAT'S YOUR CODE?
WW_80512170000.
YOU KNOW YOU BELONG TO THE WEST SIDE.
I'M SURE YOU CAN THINK OF SOME WAY...
WE CAN RESOLVE THE SITUATION.
NKO
5

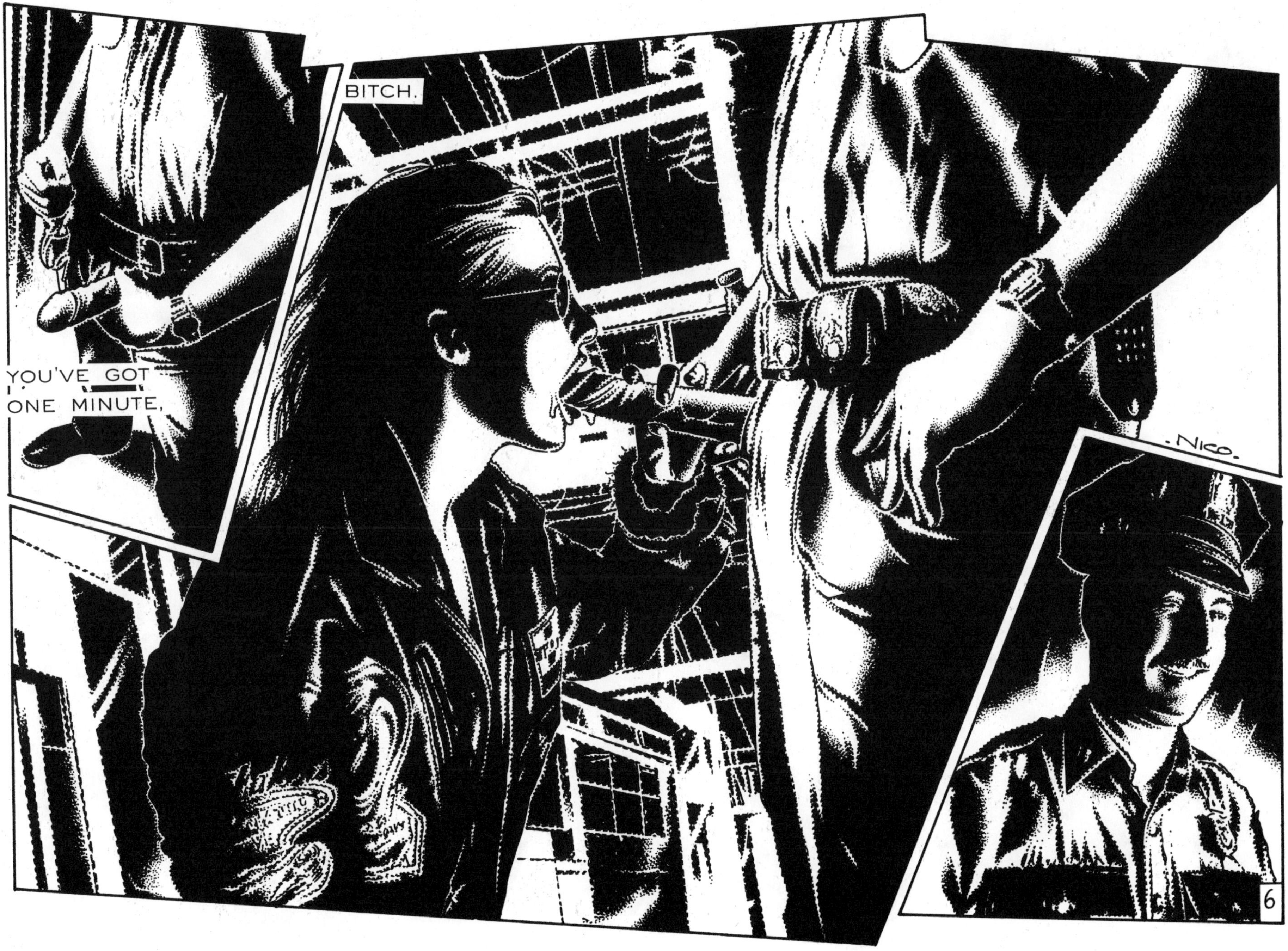
YOU'VE GOT ONE MINUTE,
BITCH.
.NICO.

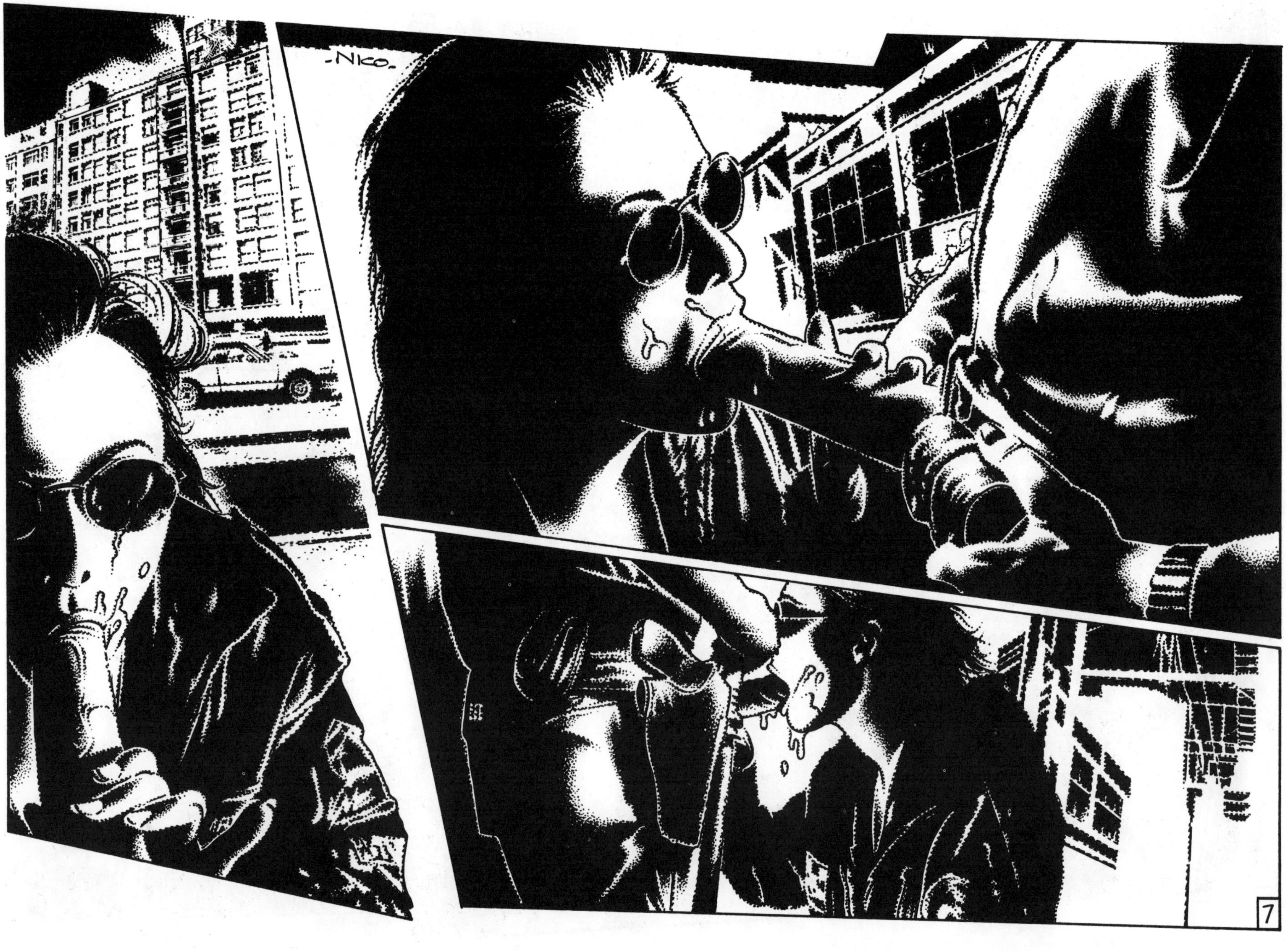
-NIKO-

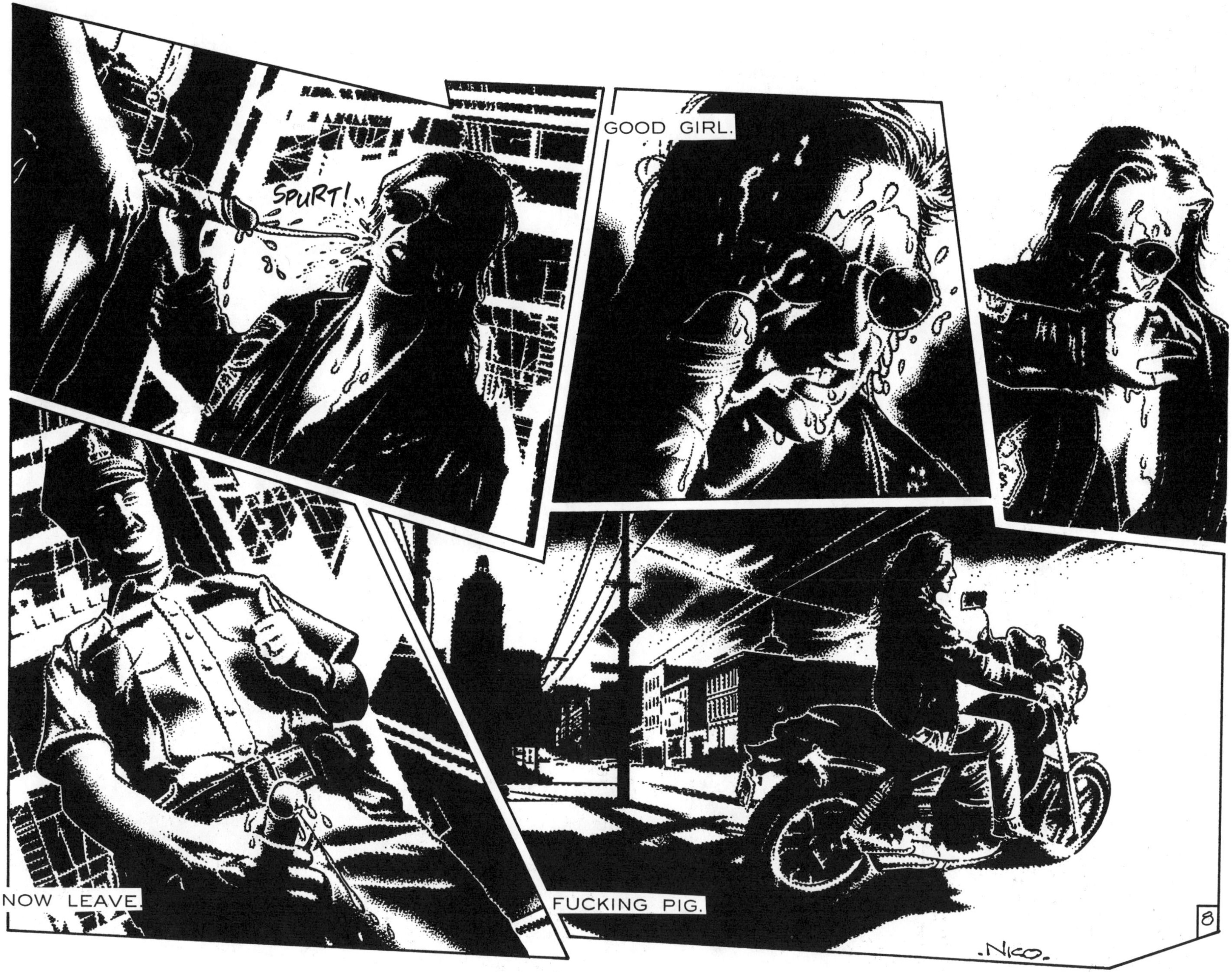
SPURT!
GOOD GIRL.
NOW LEAVE.
FUCKING PIG.
8
NICO

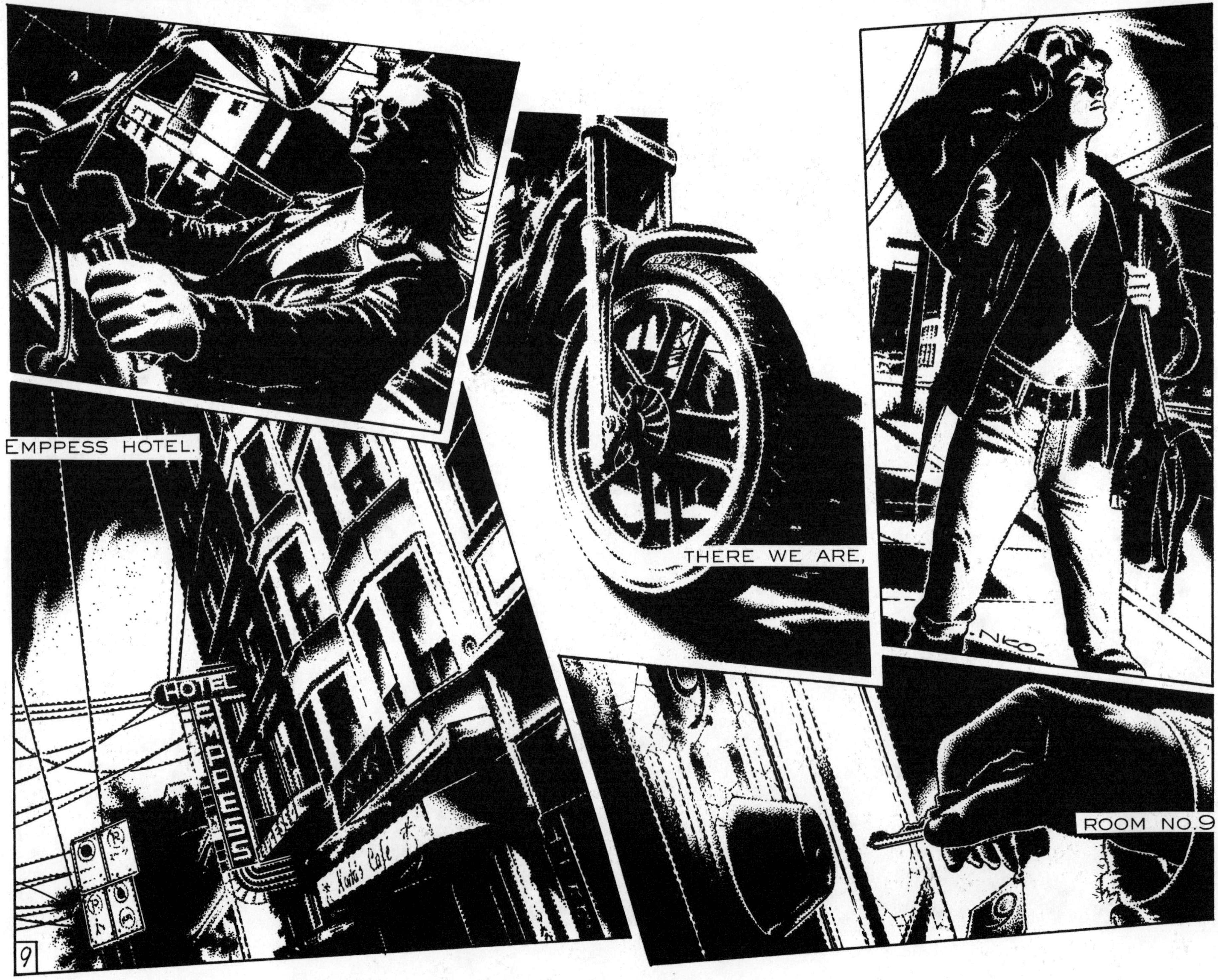
EMPPESS HOTEL.
HOTEL
EMPPESS
THERE WE ARE,
ROOM NO.9

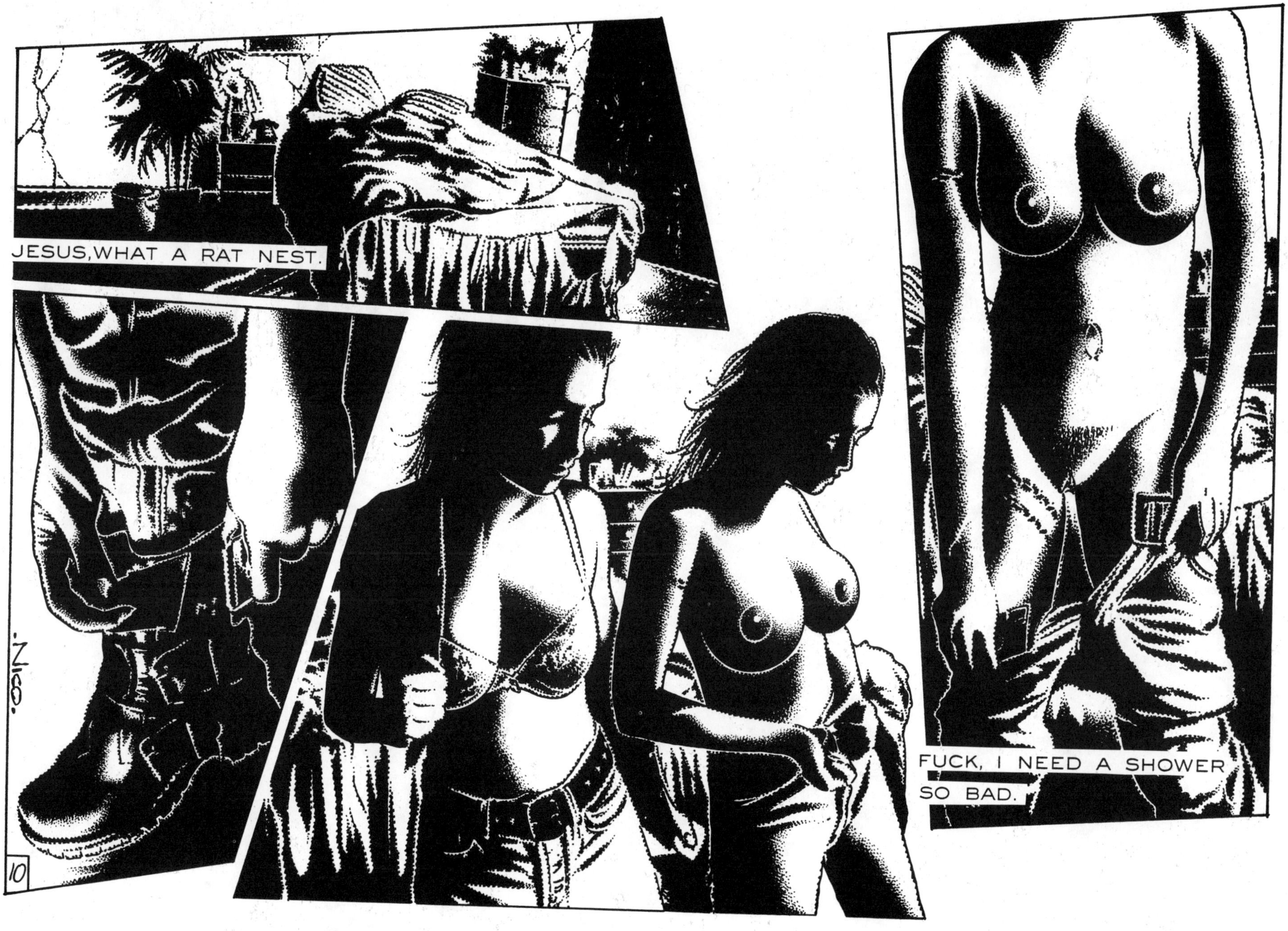
JESUS, WHAT A RAT NEST.
FUCK, I NEED A SHOWER
SO BAD.

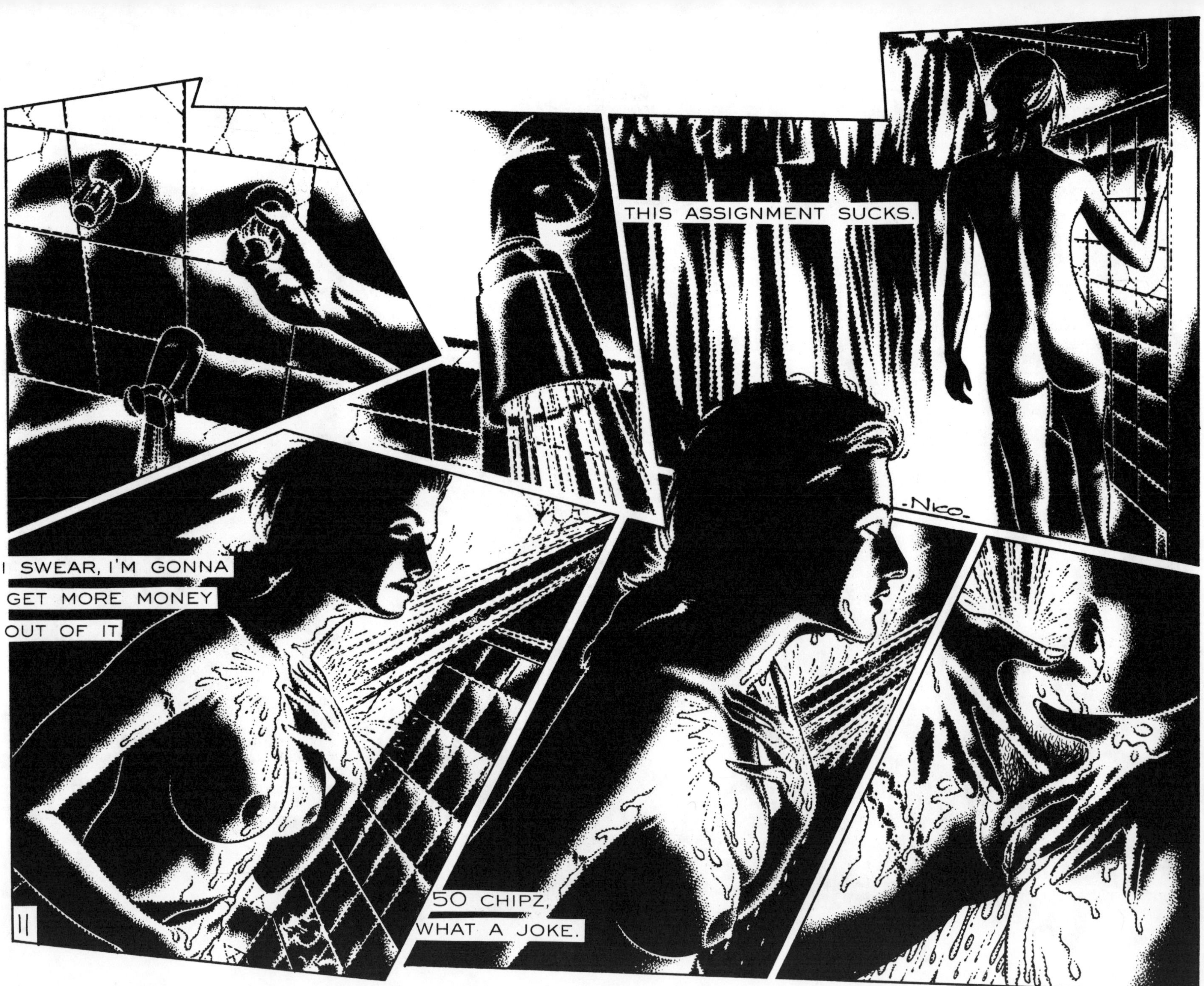
THIS ASSIGNMENT SUCKS.
I SWEAR, I'M GONNA GET MORE MONEY OUT OF IT.
50 CHIPZ, WHAT A JOKE.

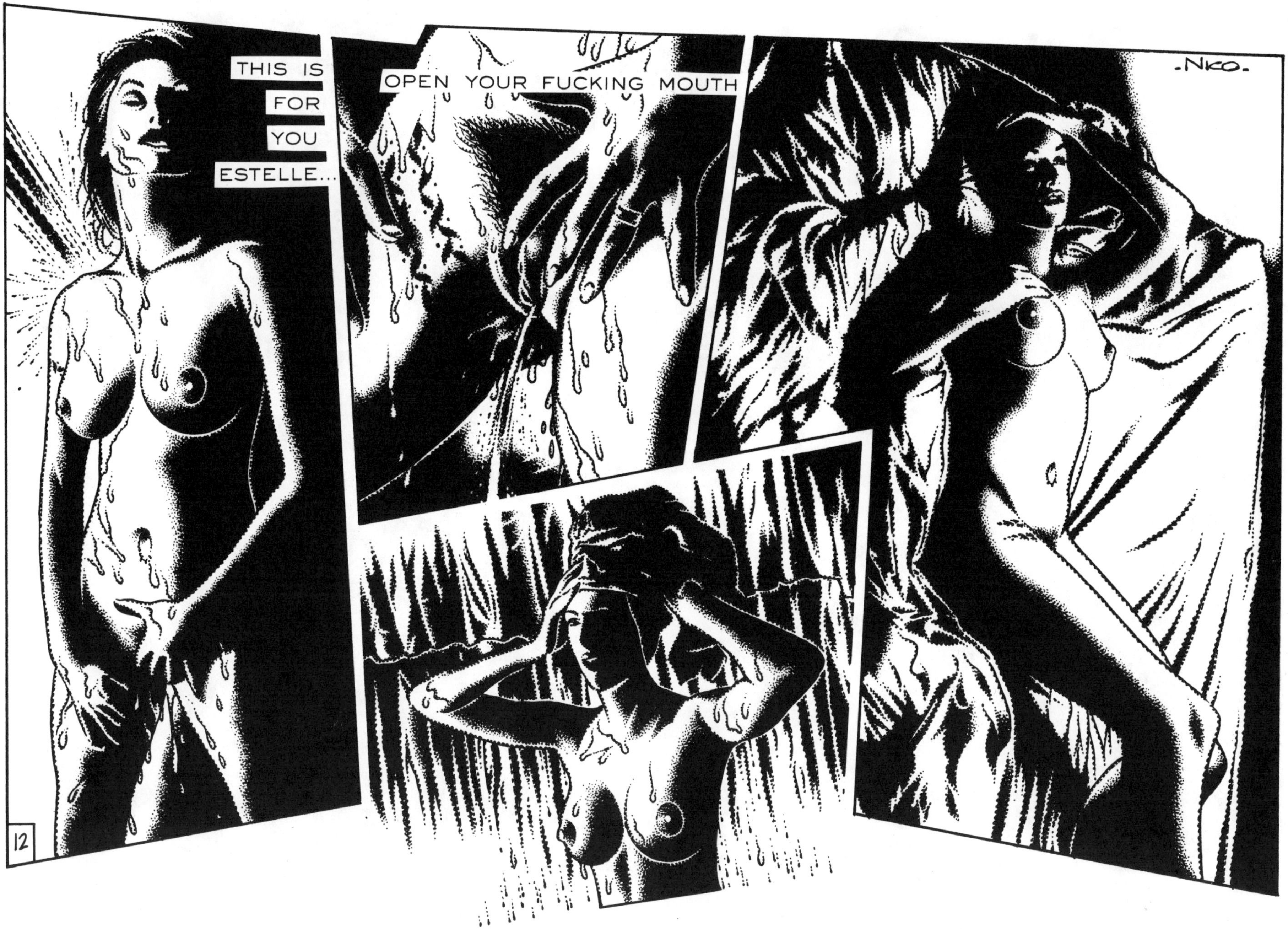
THIS IS
FOR
YOU
ESTELLE...
OPEN YOUR FUCKING MOUTH
-NICO-
12

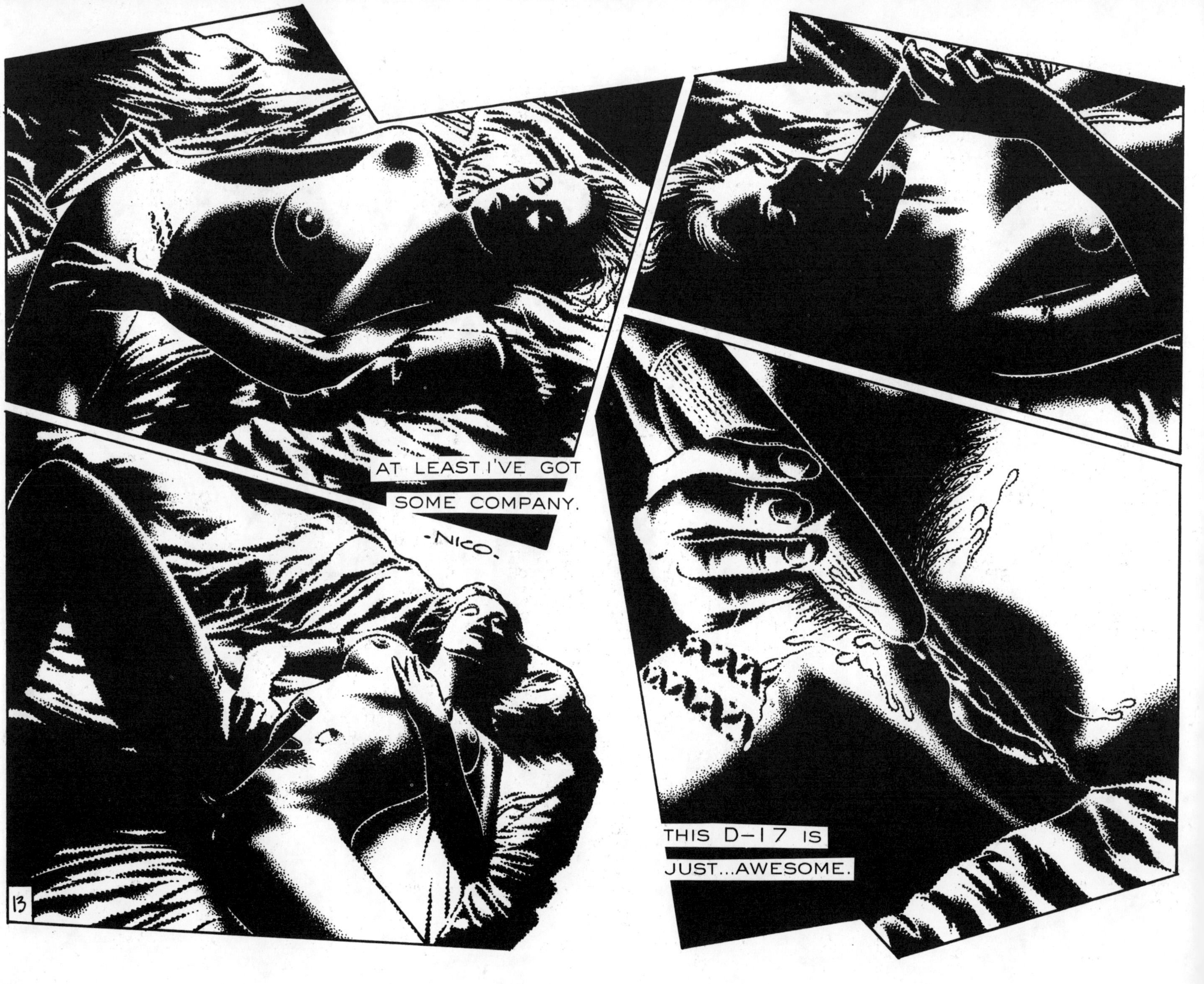
AT LEAST I'VE GOT
SOME COMPANY.
-NICO-
THIS D-17 IS
JUST...AWESOME.

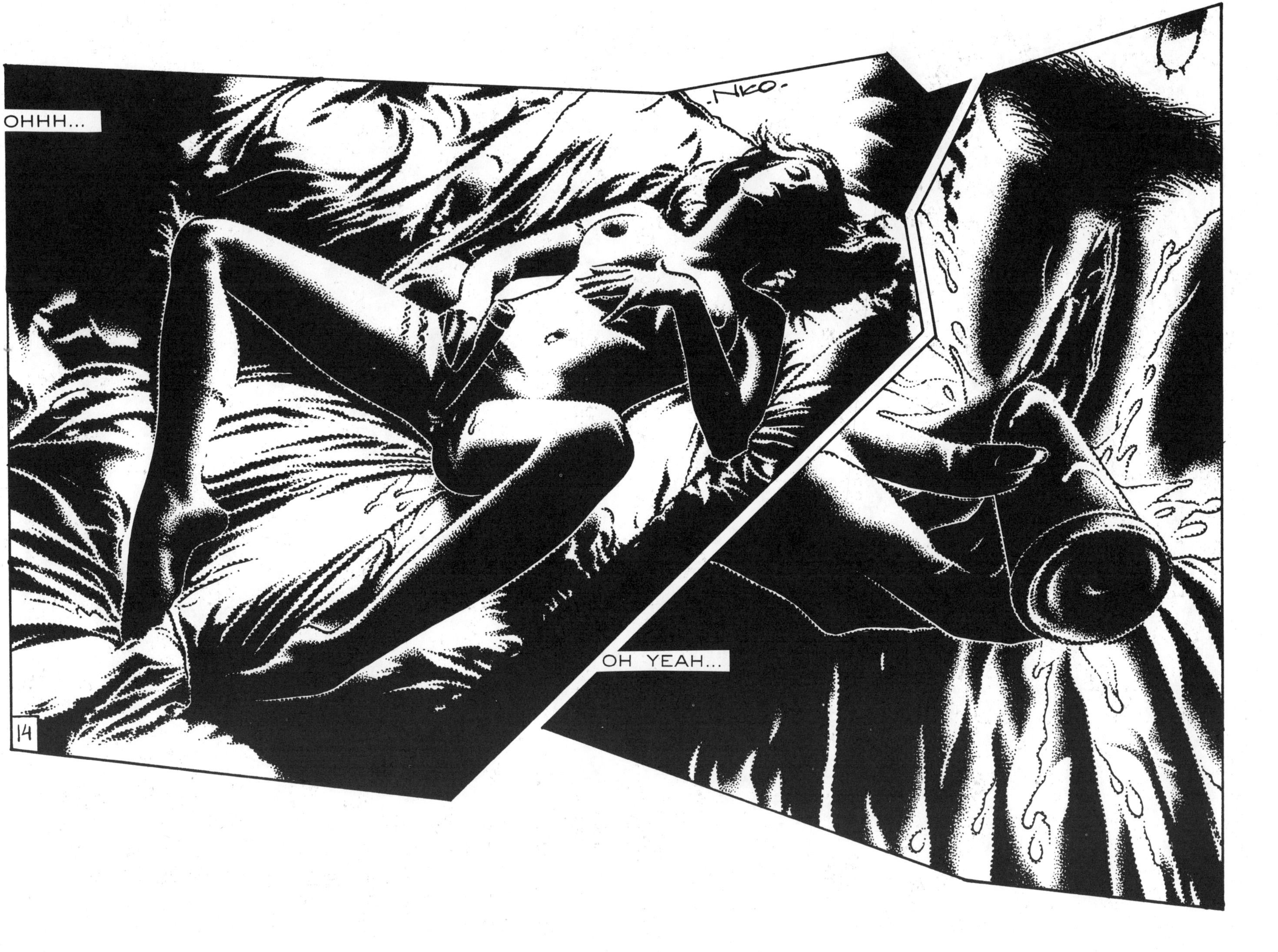
OHHH...
OH YEAH...

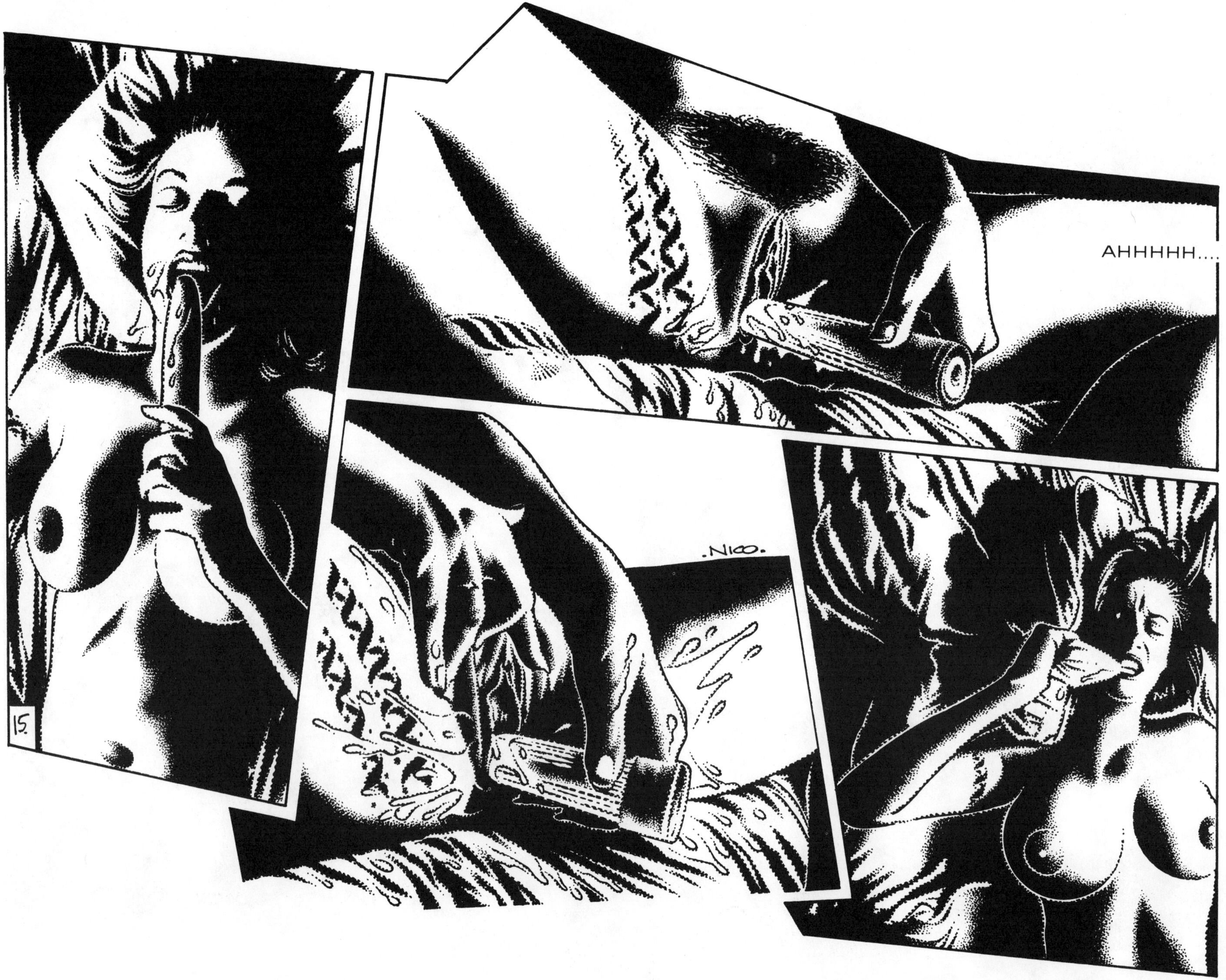
AHHHHH....
.NICO.
15.

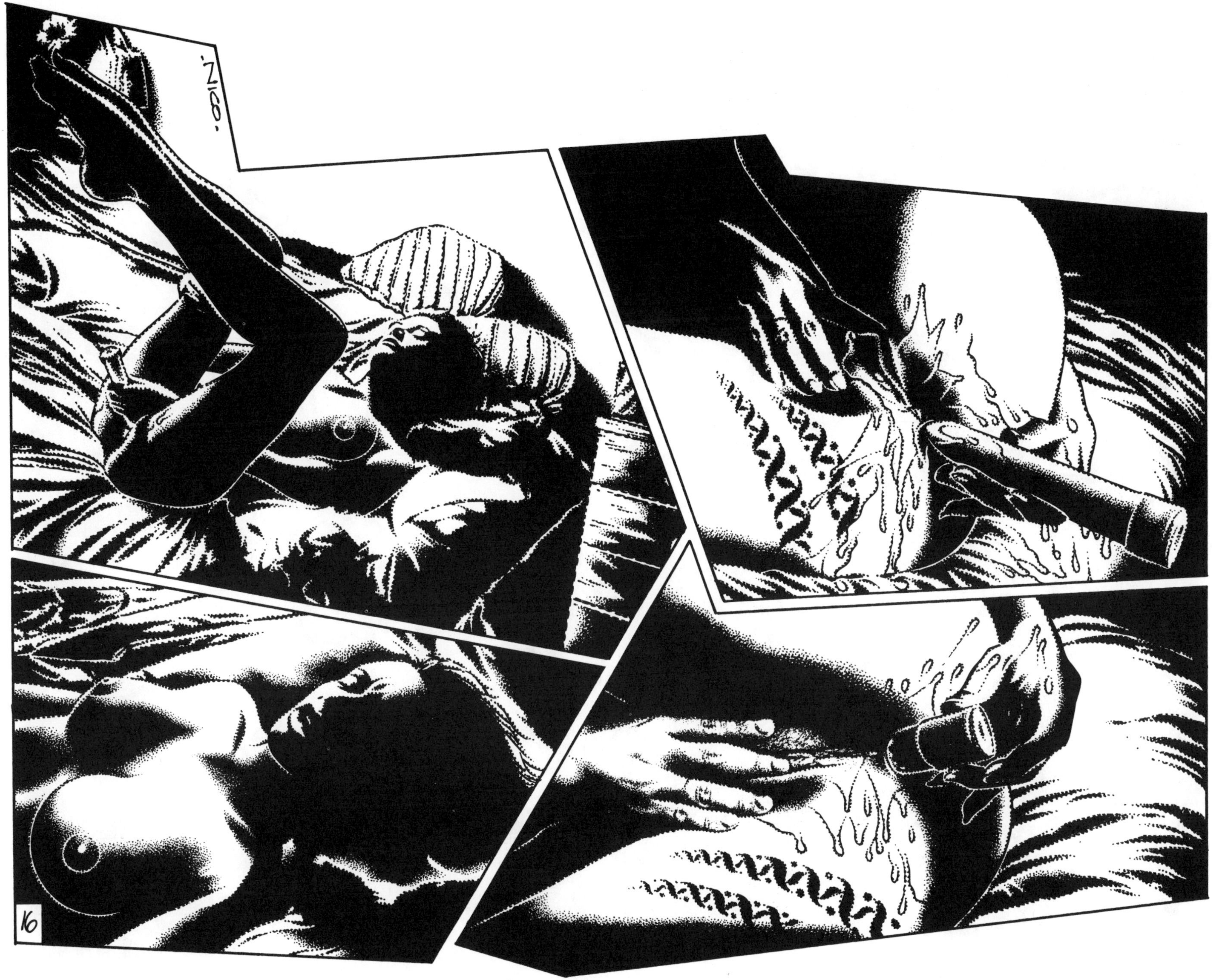

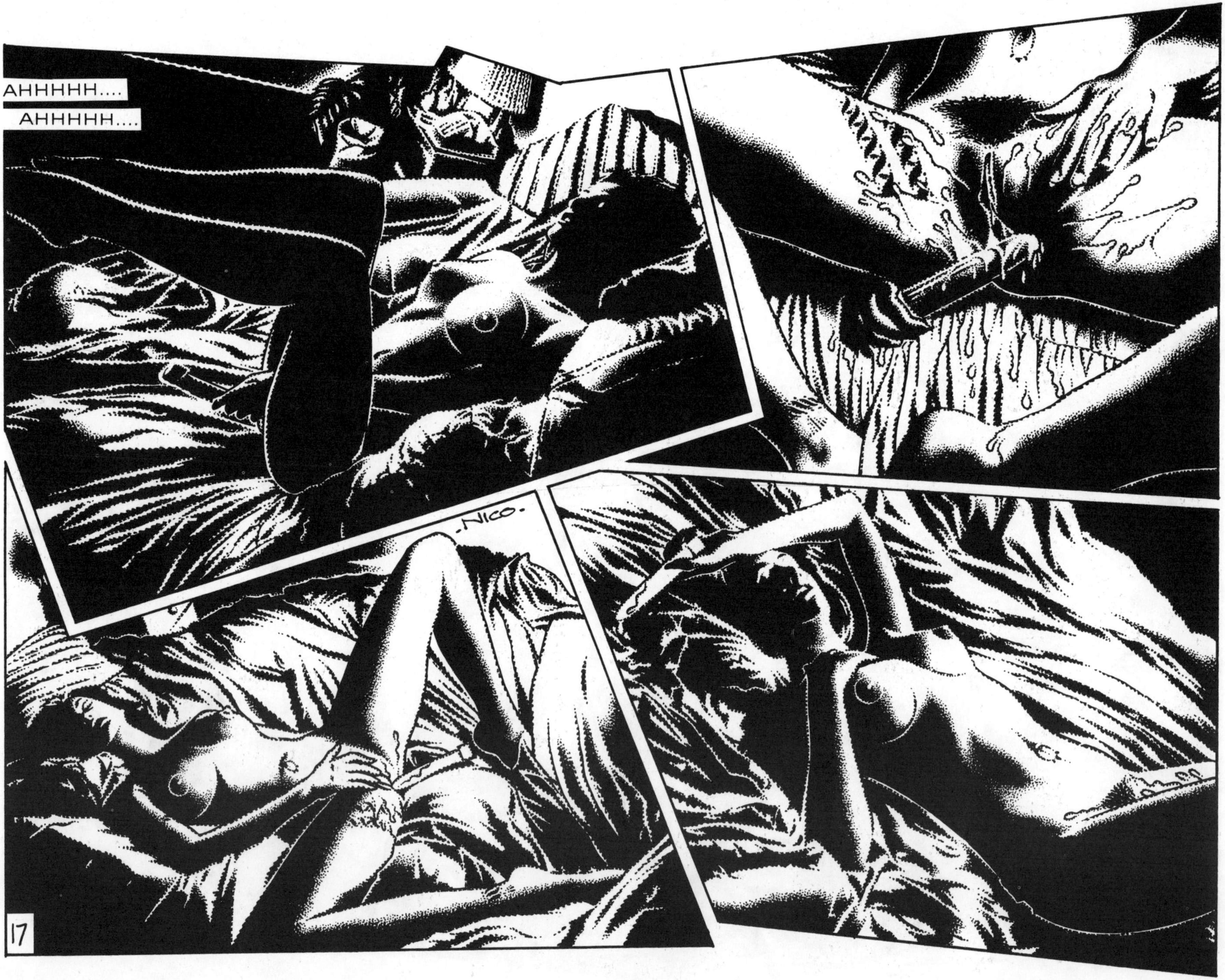
AHHHHH....
AHHHHH....
NICO

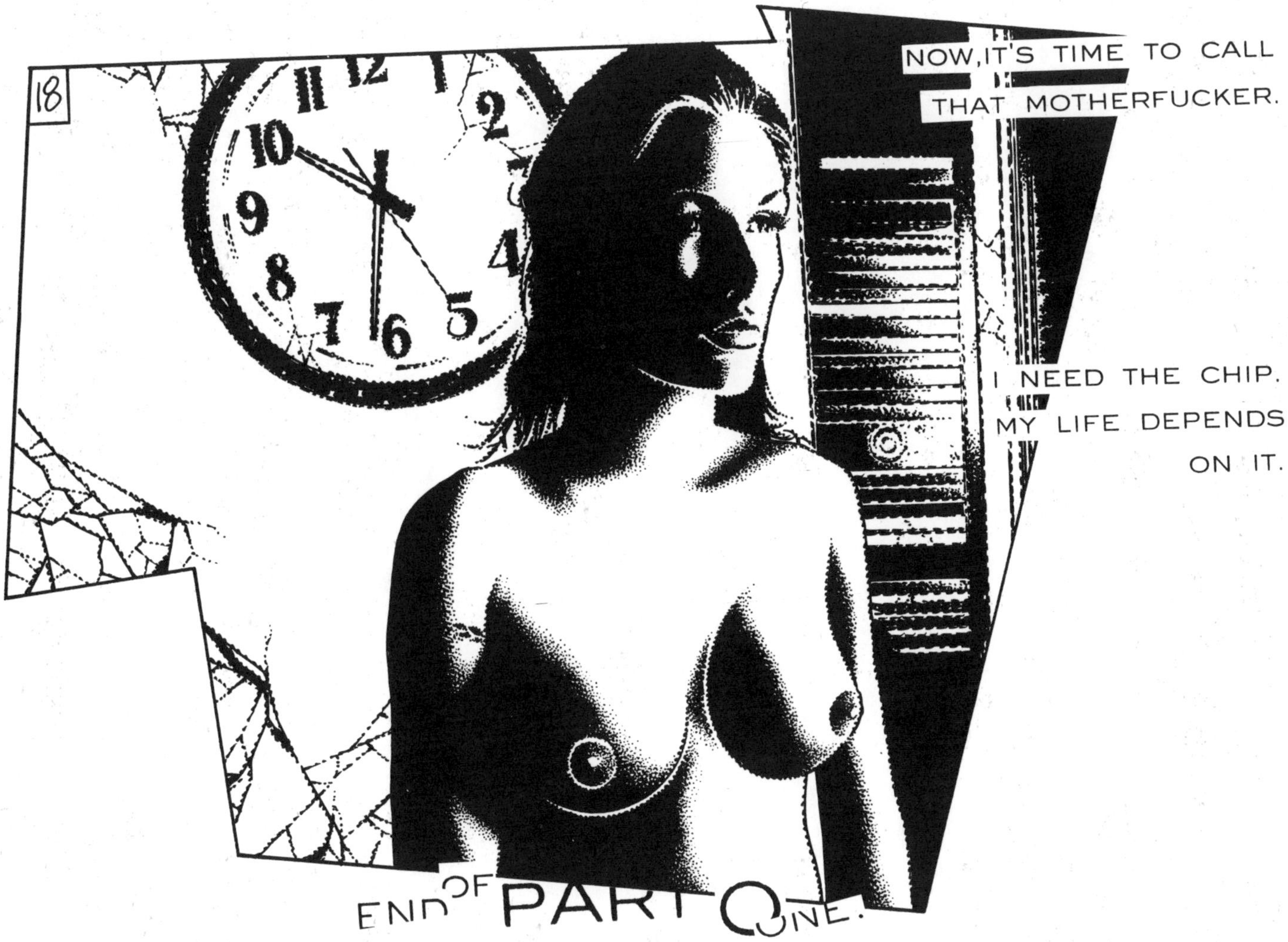
18
NOW, IT'S TIME TO CALL THAT MOTHERFUCKER.
I NEED THE CHIP. MY LIFE DEPENDS ON IT.
END OF PART ONE.

Sex Inc. PART TWO

The Pan-American government(Est. 2085) has been overthrown during a bloody civil war (circa 2105).

The next twelve months saw another two hundred and ninety million people die as a direct result of complications.

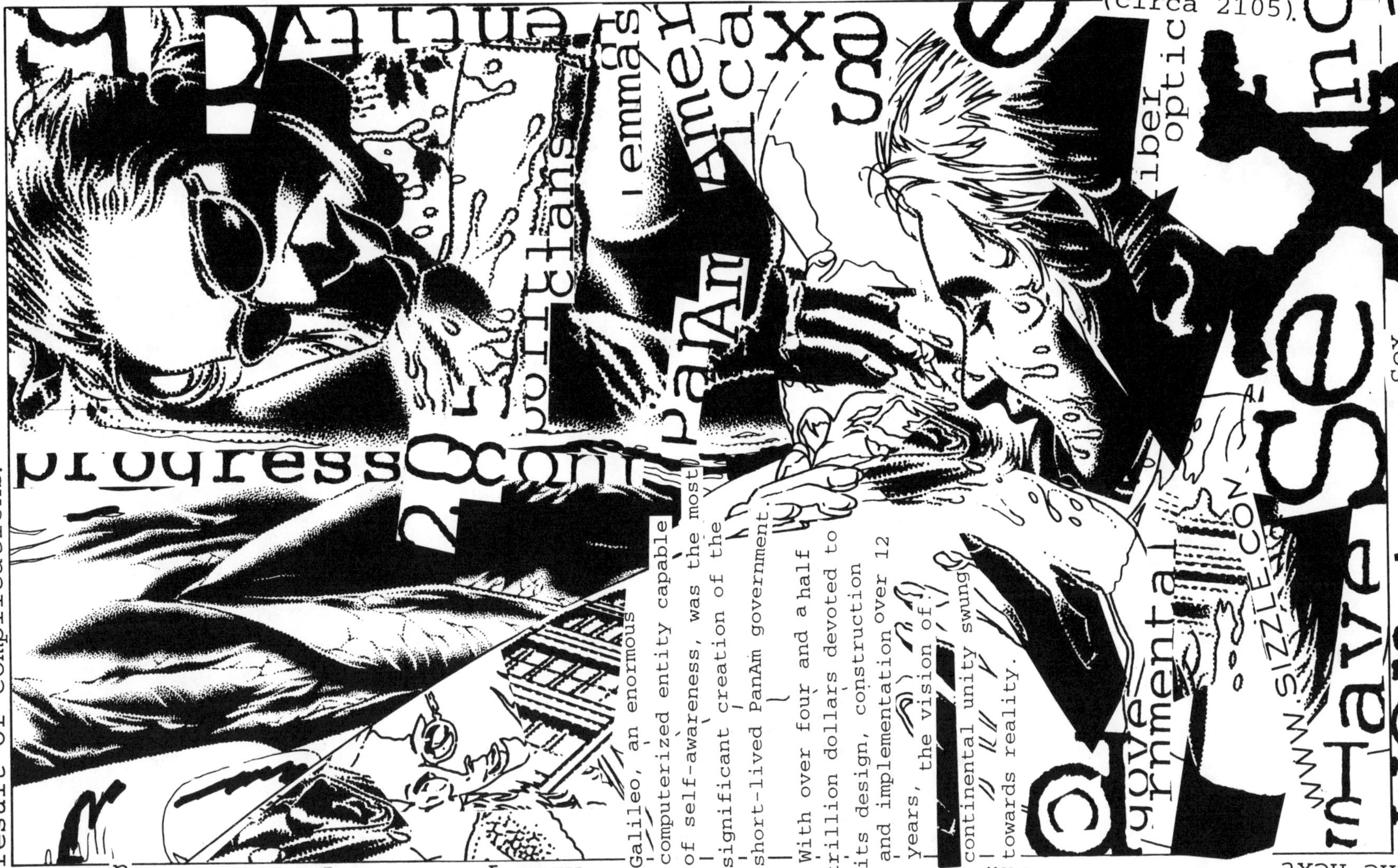

progress
politicians
entity
PanAm
America
fiber optic
Sex Inc.
governmental
www.sizzlecon
have
word

Galileo, an enormous computerized entity capable of self-awareness, was the most significant creation of the short-lived PanAm govenment.

With over four and a half trillion dollars devoted to its design, construction and implementation over 12 years, the vision of continental unity swung towards reality.

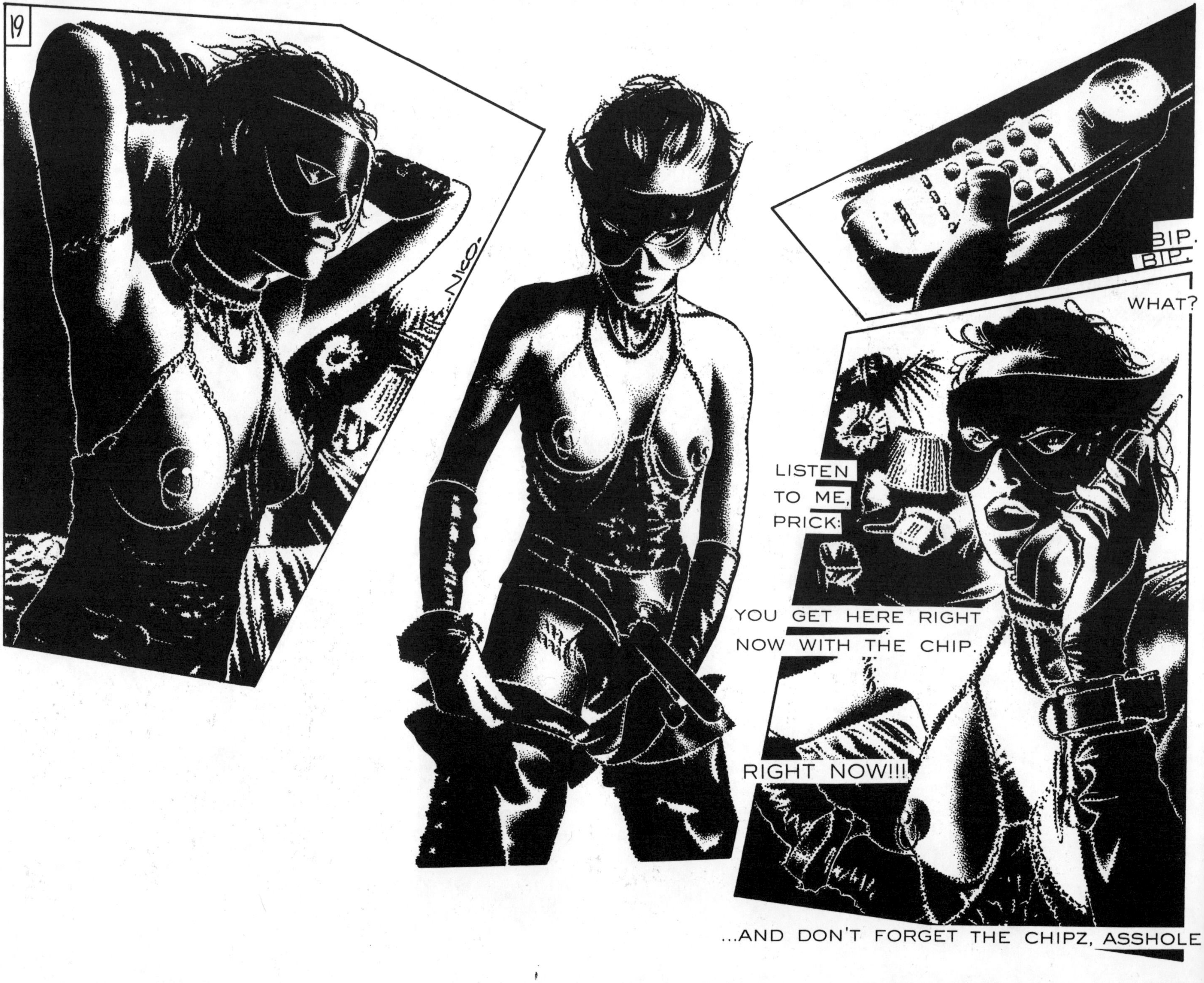
19
NICO
BIP.
BIP.
WHAT?
LISTEN TO ME, PRICK:
YOU GET HERE RIGHT NOW WITH THE CHIP.
RIGHT NOW!!!
...AND DON'T FORGET THE CHIPZ, ASSHOLE

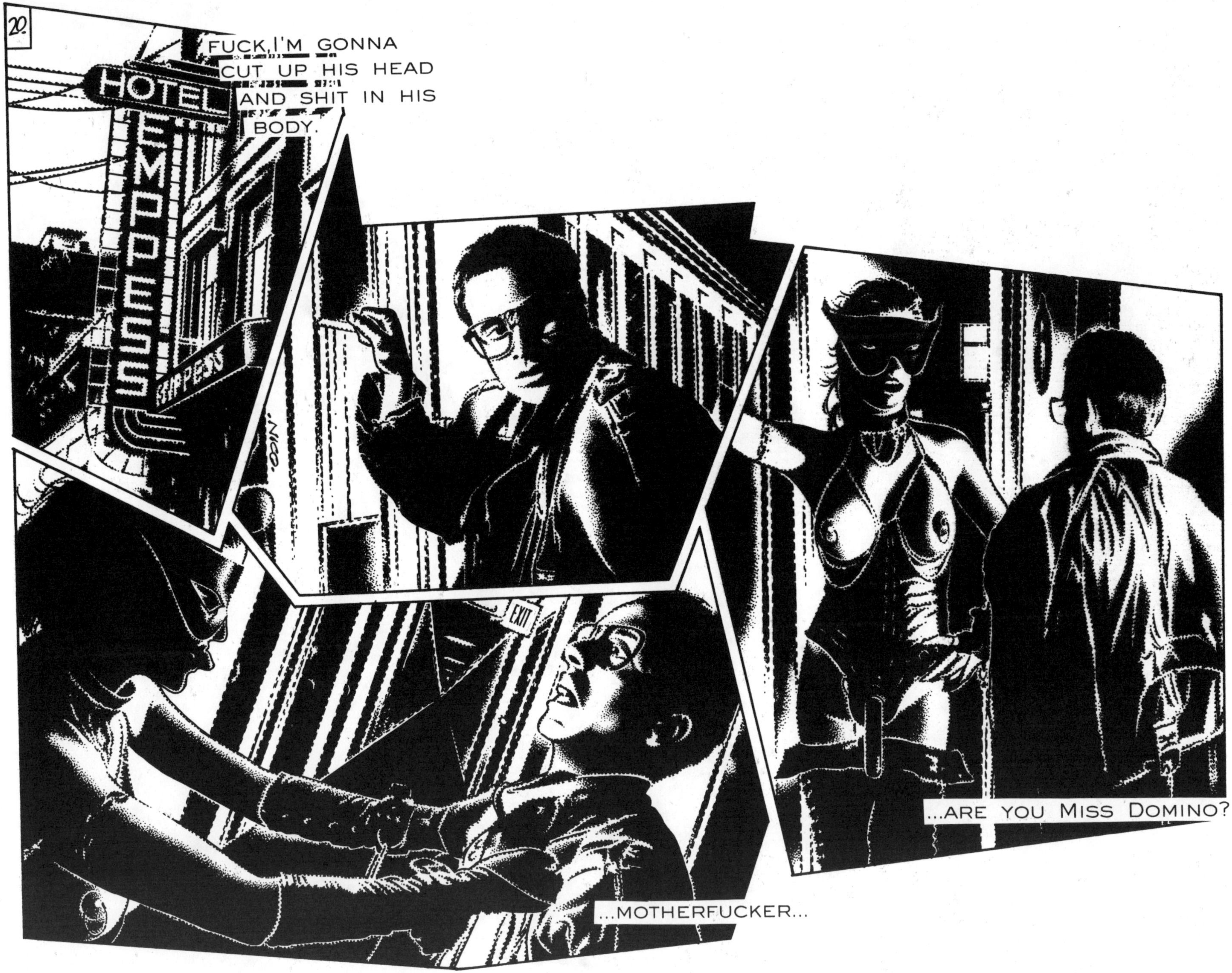
FUCK, I'M GONNA CUT UP HIS HEAD AND SHIT IN HIS BODY.
HOTEL EMPRESS
EMPRESS
NICO
EXIT
...MOTHERFUCKER...
...ARE YOU MISS DOMINO?

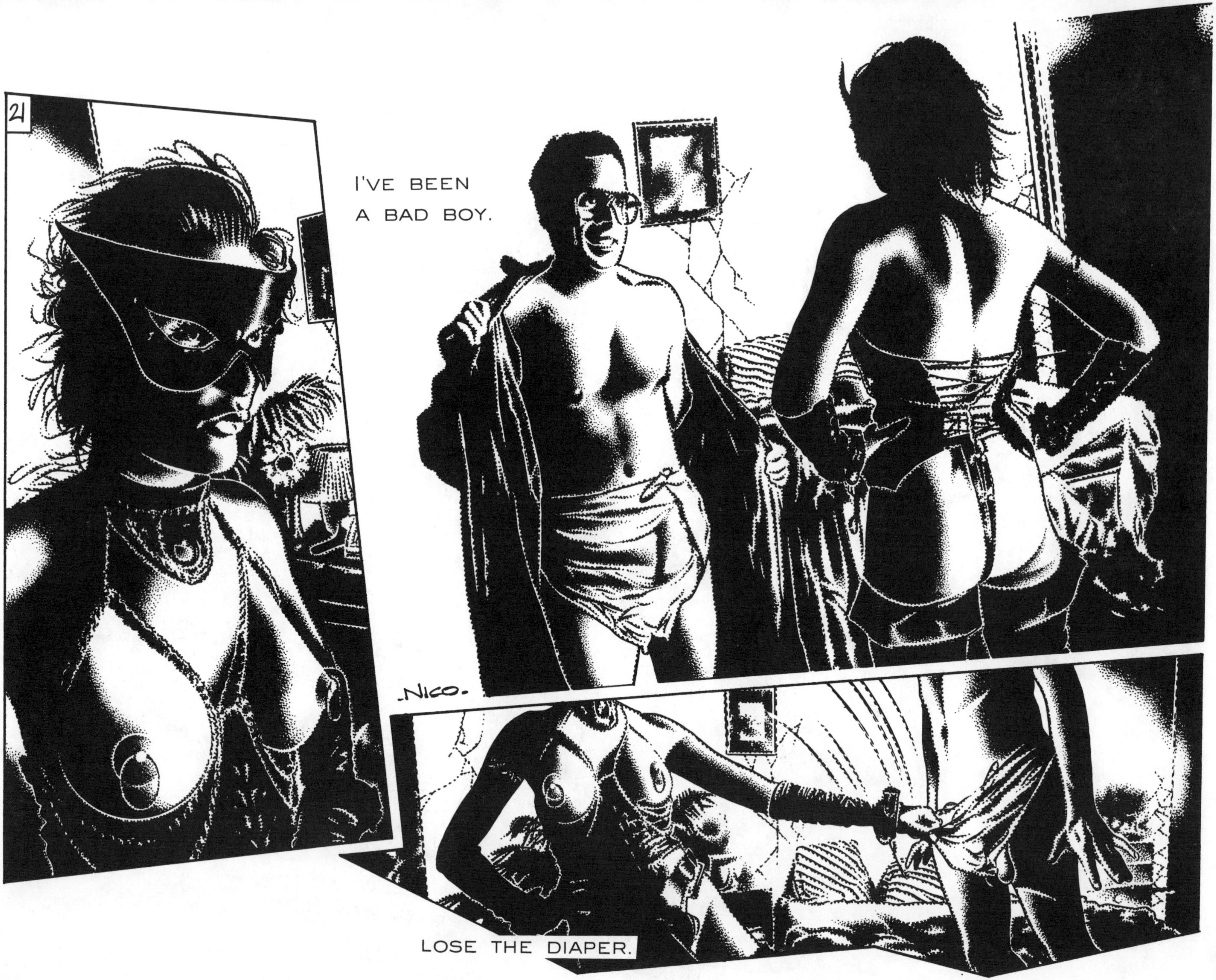
21
I'VE BEEN
A BAD BOY.
NICO
LOSE THE DIAPER.

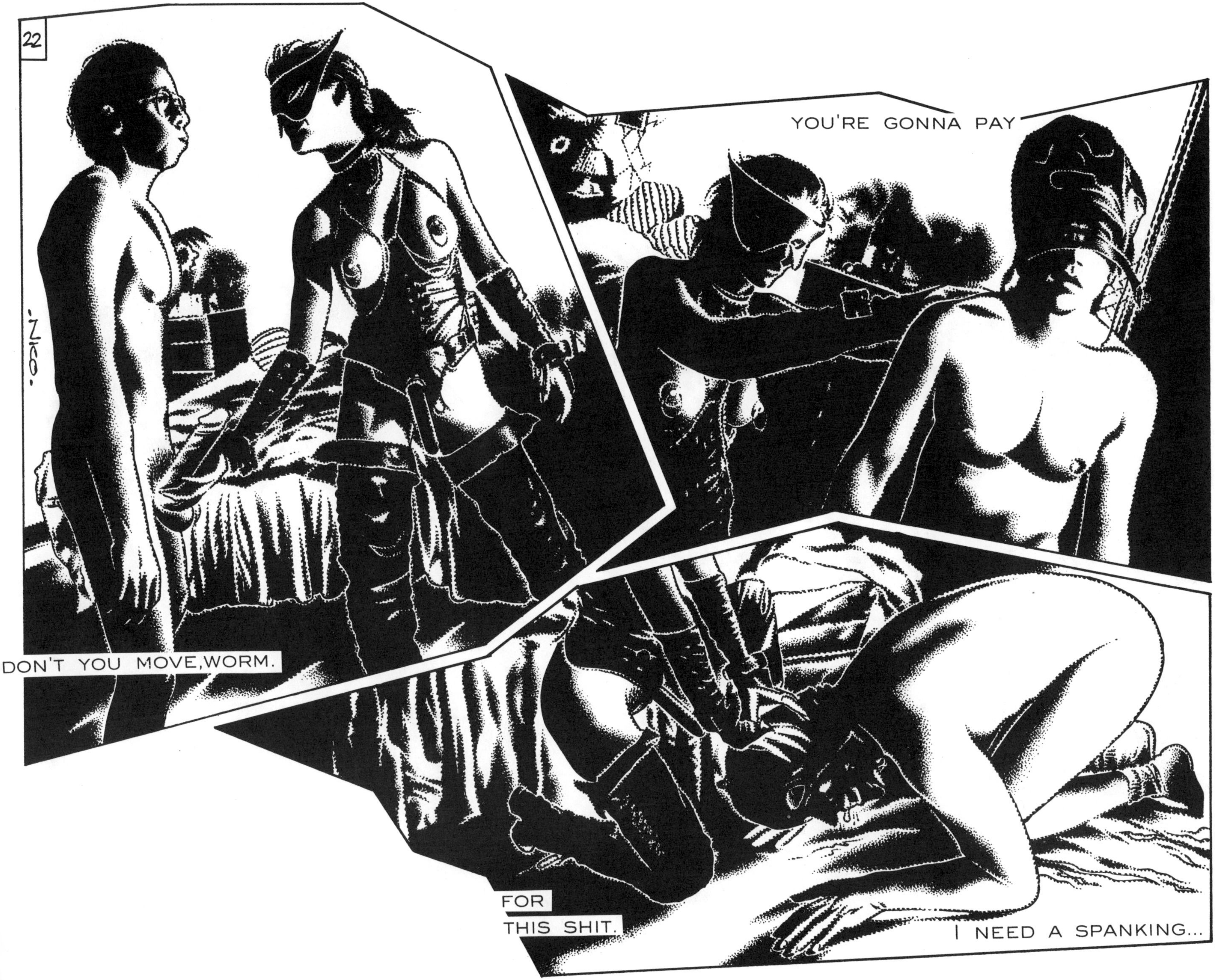
22
DON'T YOU MOVE,WORM.
YOU'RE GONNA PAY
FOR
THIS SHIT.
I NEED A SPANKING...

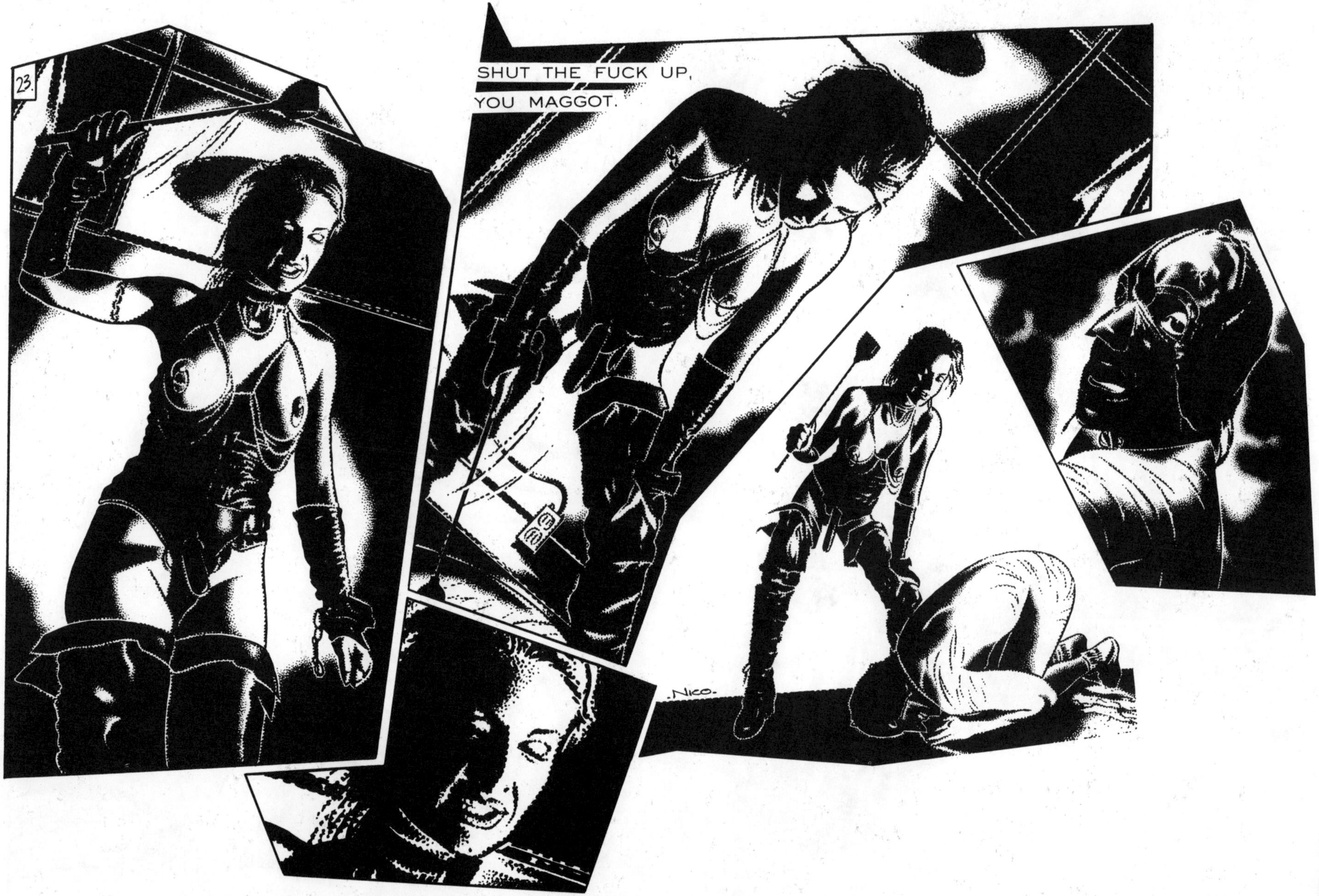
23.
SHUT THE FUCK UP,
YOU MAGGOT.
NICO.

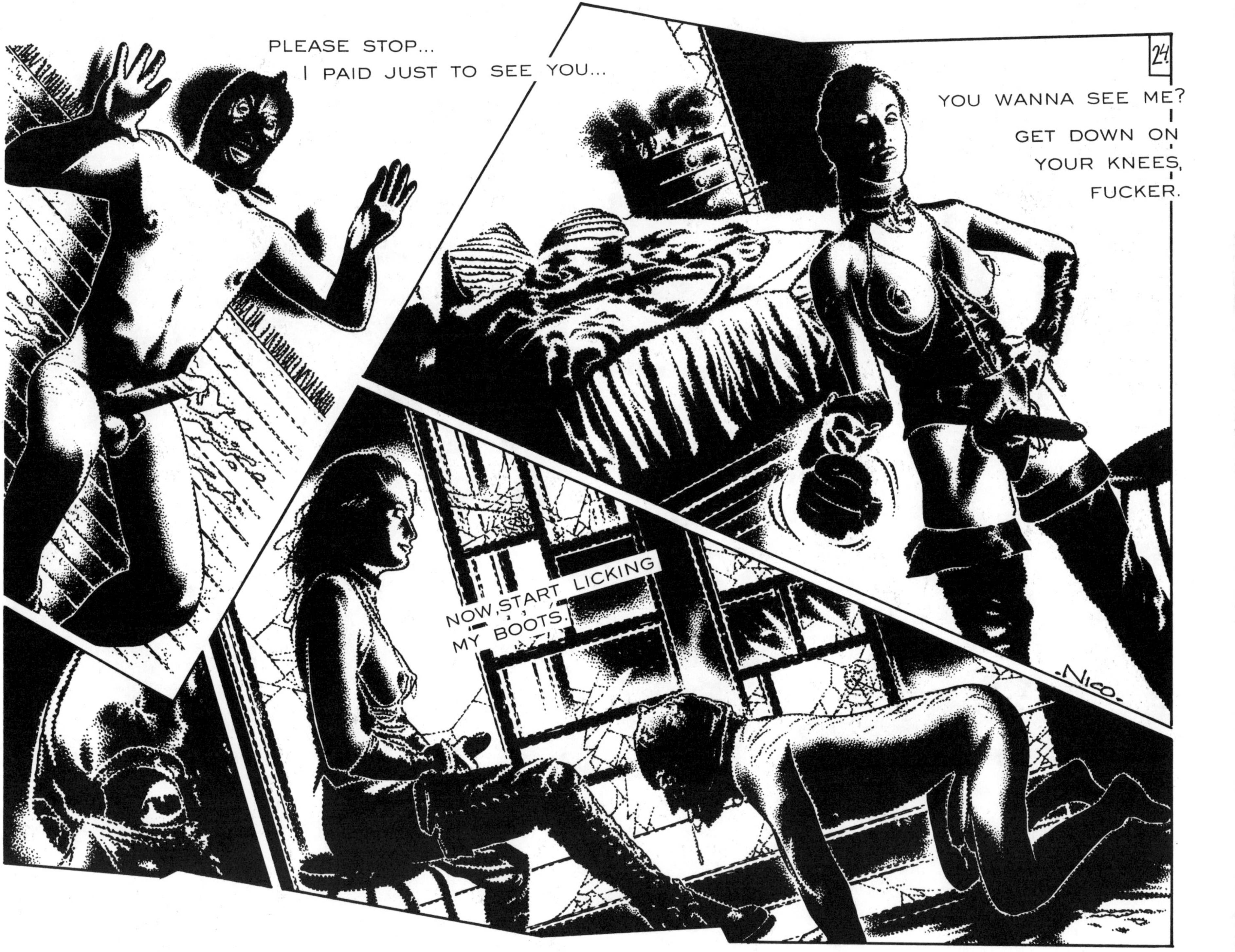
PLEASE STOP...
I PAID JUST TO SEE YOU...
YOU WANNA SEE ME?
GET DOWN ON YOUR KNEES, FUCKER.
NOW, START LICKING MY BOOTS.
Nico

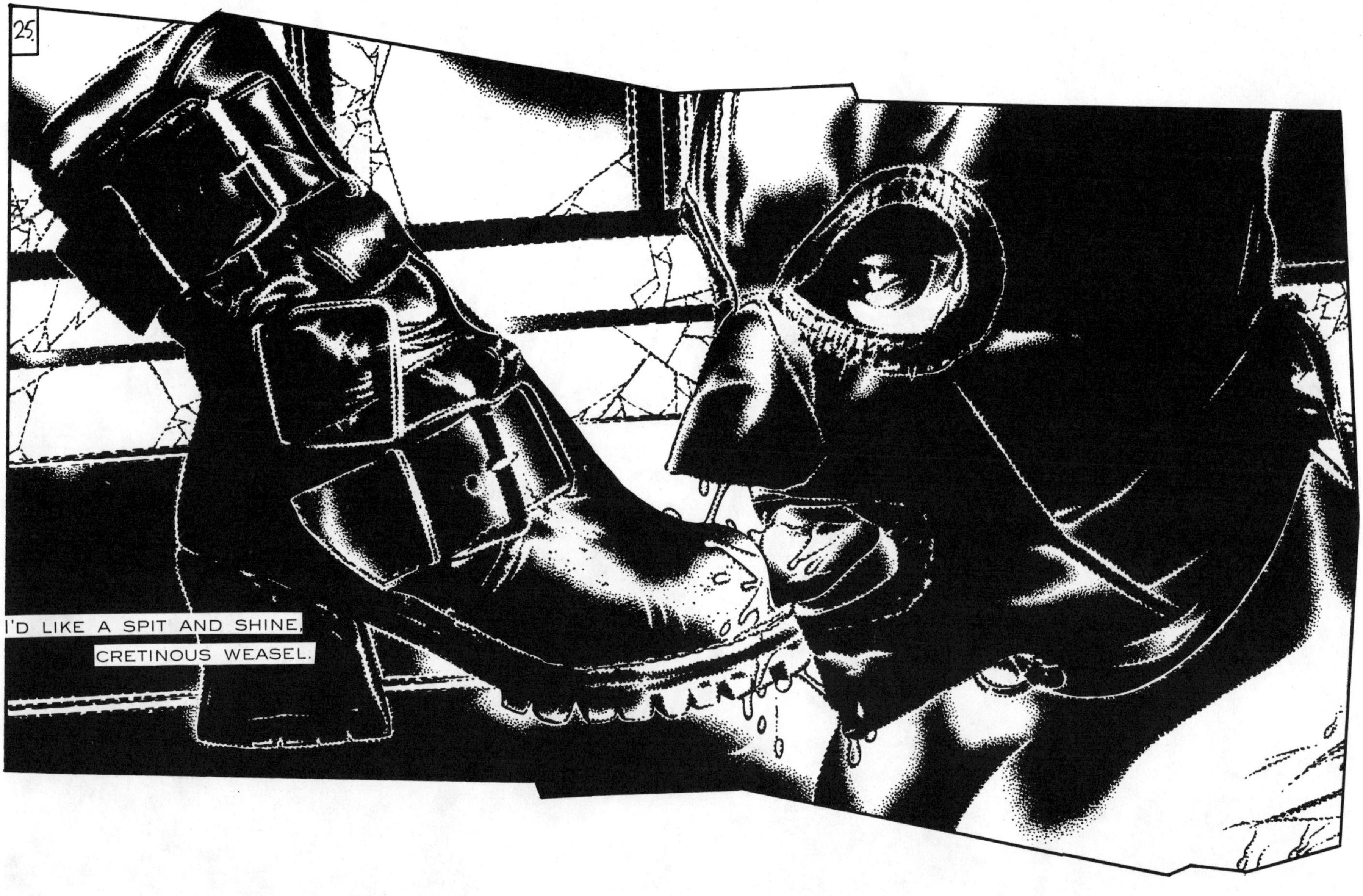
25.
I'D LIKE A SPIT AND SHINE,
CRETINOUS WEASEL.

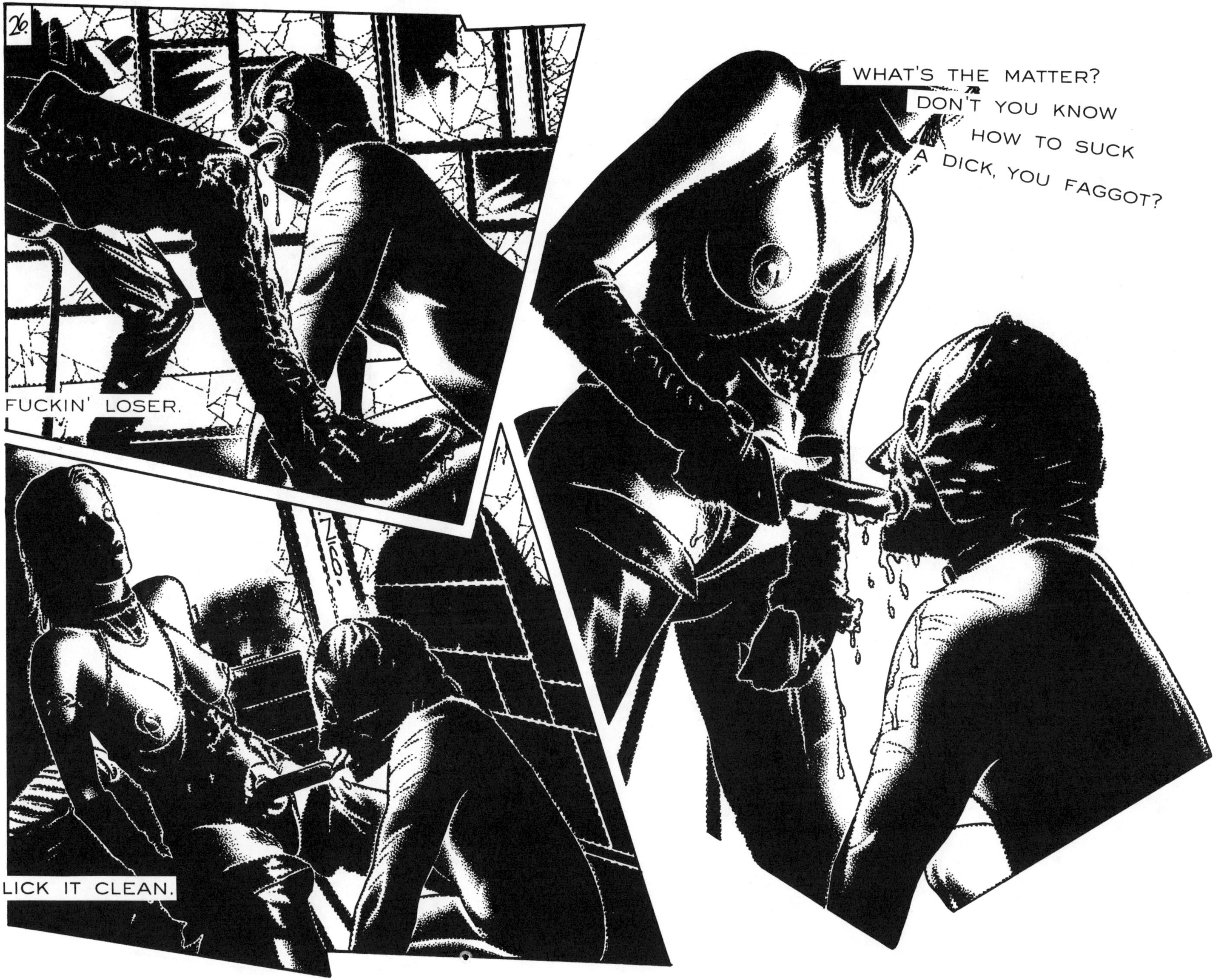
FUCKIN' LOSER.
LICK IT CLEAN.
WHAT'S THE MATTER?
DON'T YOU KNOW
HOW TO SUCK
A DICK, YOU FAGGOT?

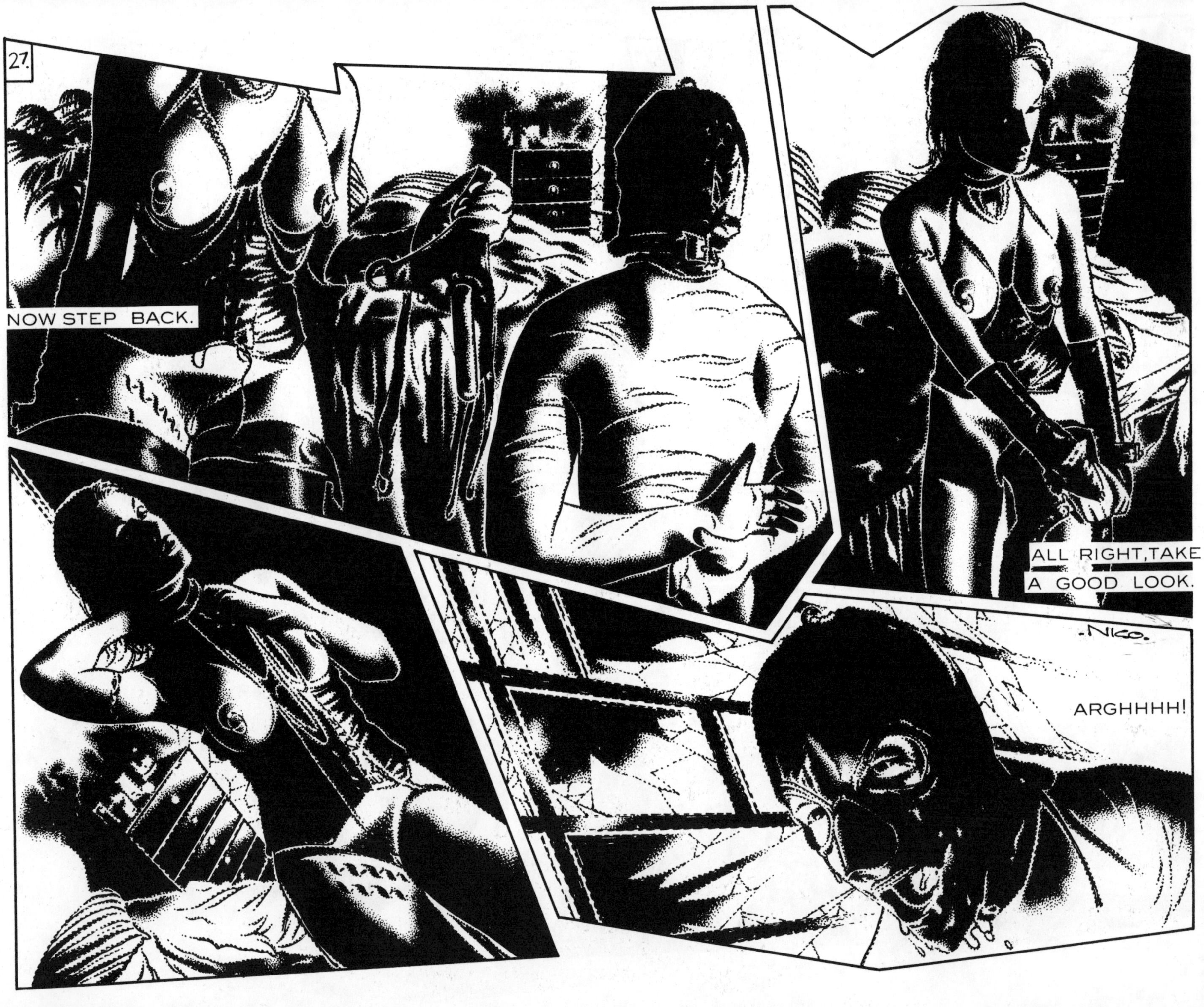
NOW STEP BACK.
ALL RIGHT,TAKE A GOOD LOOK.
ARGHHHH!

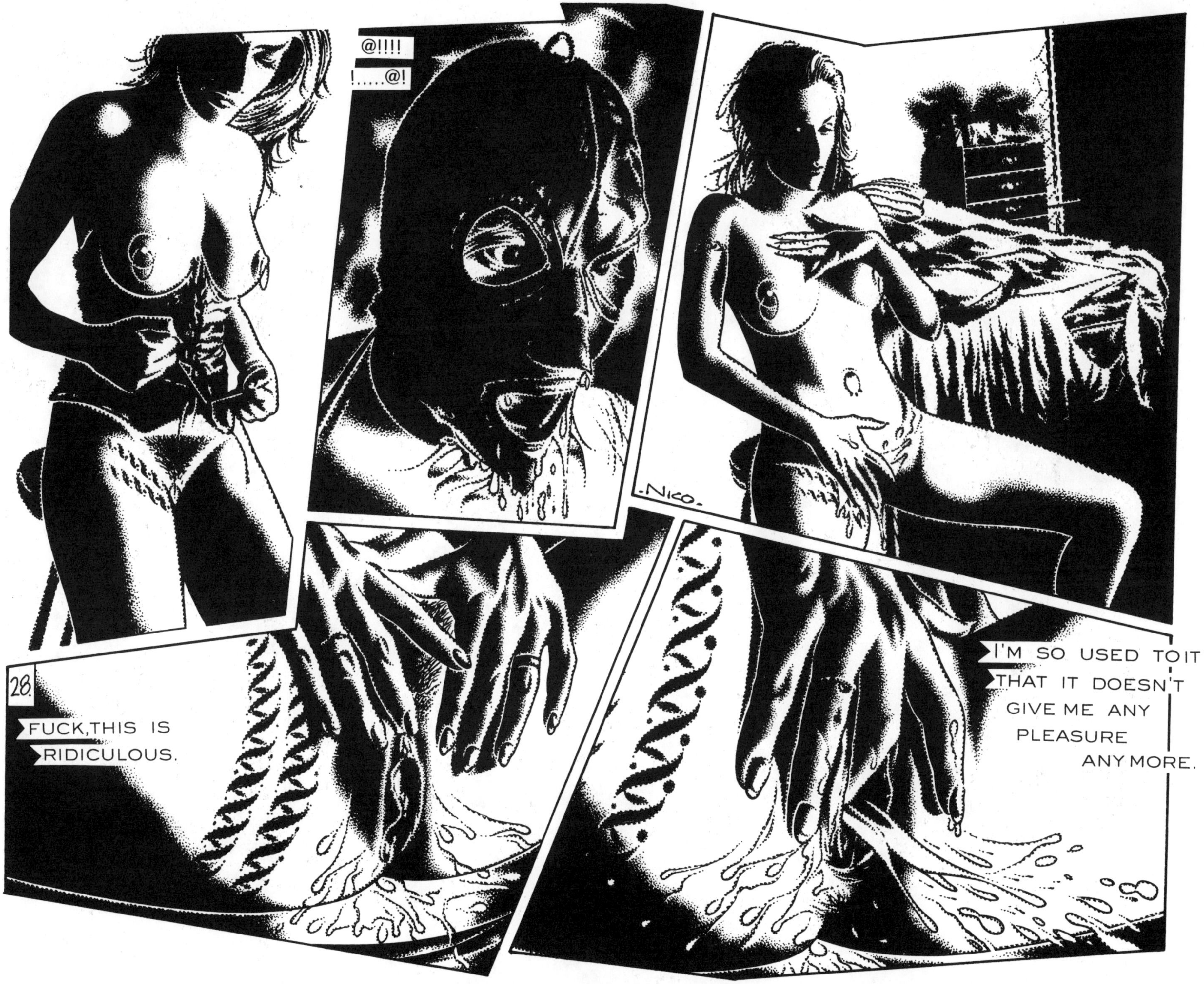
@!!!!
!.....@!
NICO
28.
FUCK,THIS IS
RIDICULOUS.
I'M SO USED TO IT
THAT IT DOESN'T
GIVE ME ANY
PLEASURE
ANYMORE.

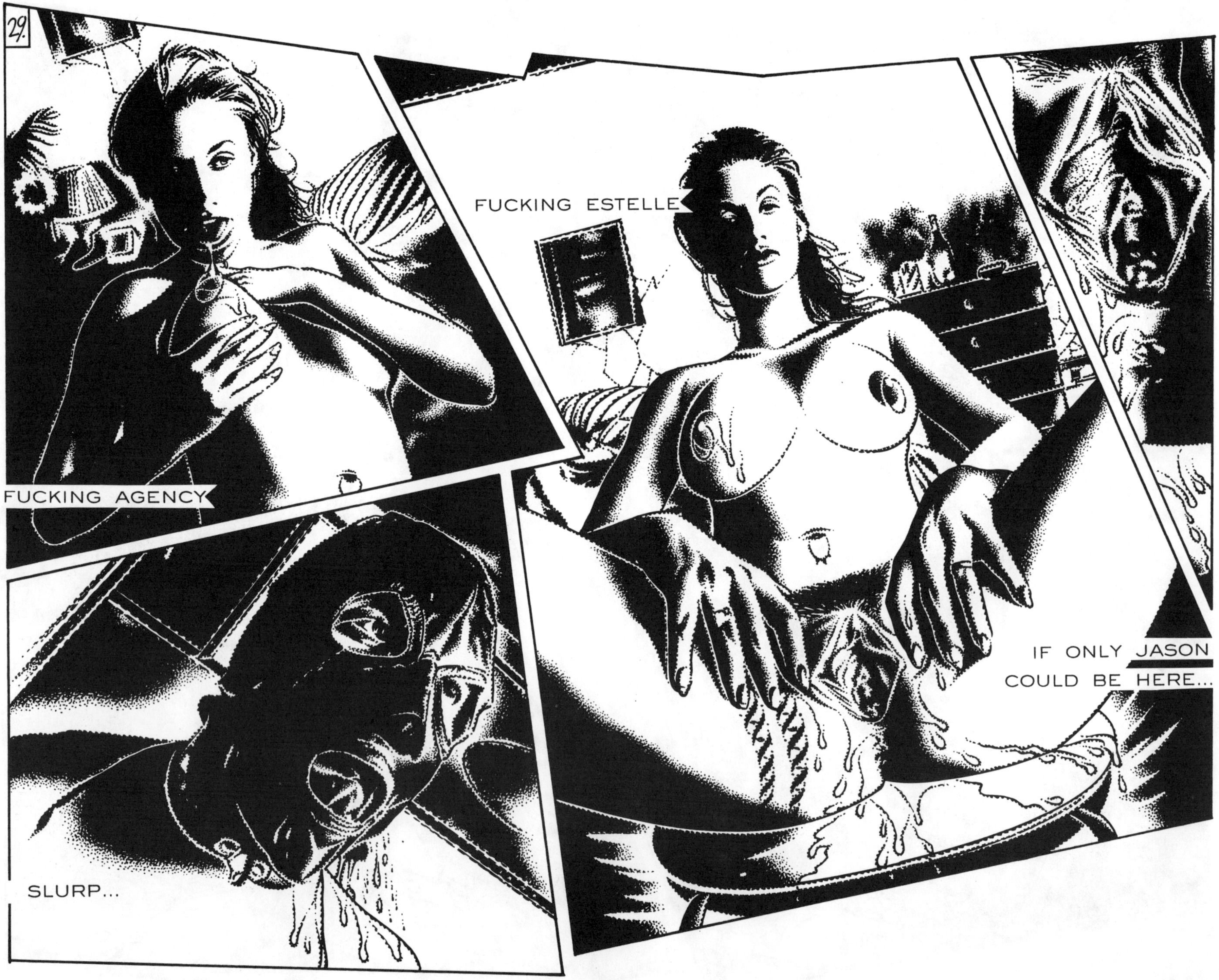
FUCKING AGENCY
SLURP...
FUCKING ESTELLE
IF ONLY JASON
COULD BE HERE...

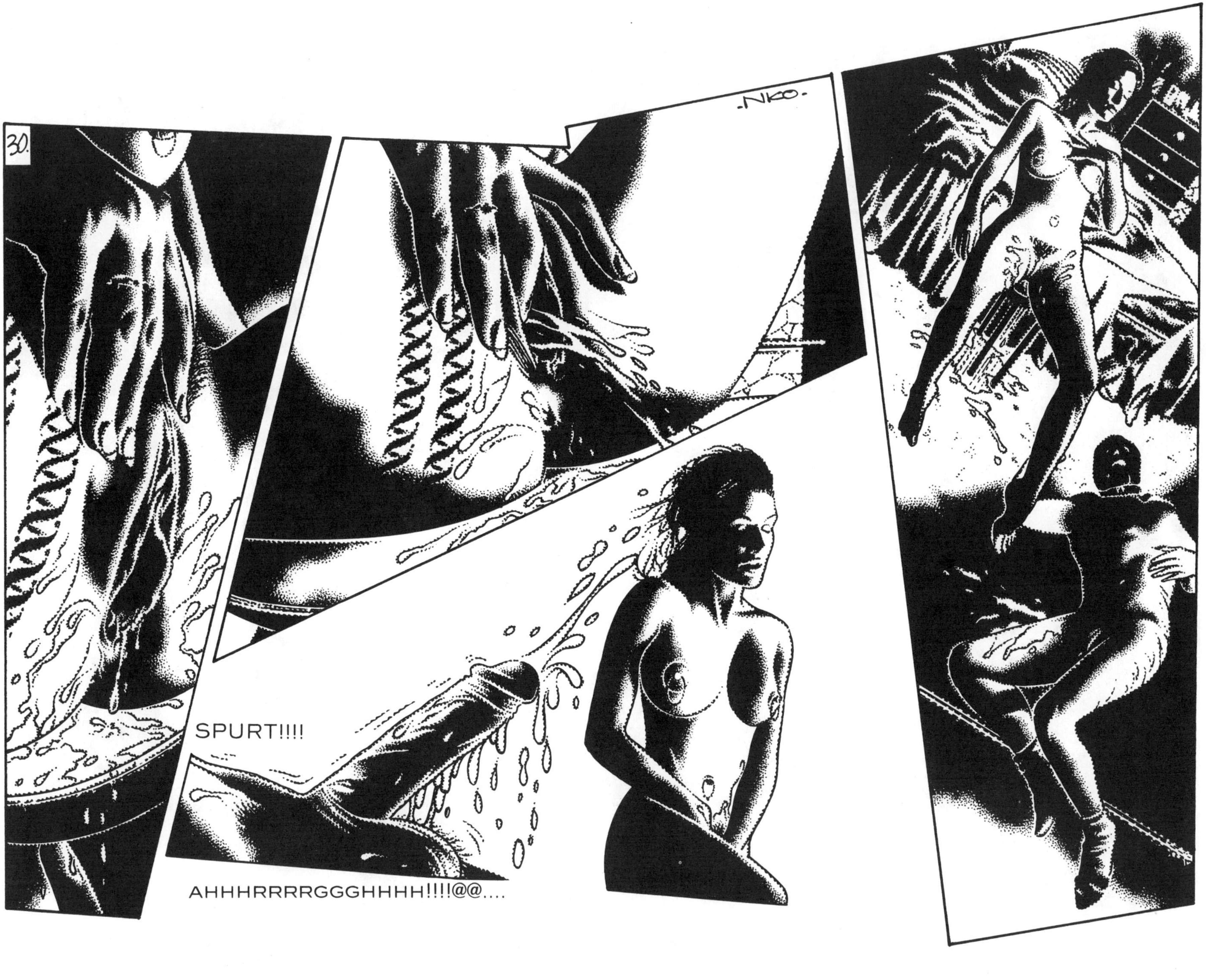
30.
-NKO-
SPURT!!!!
AHHHRRRRGGGHHHH!!!!@@....

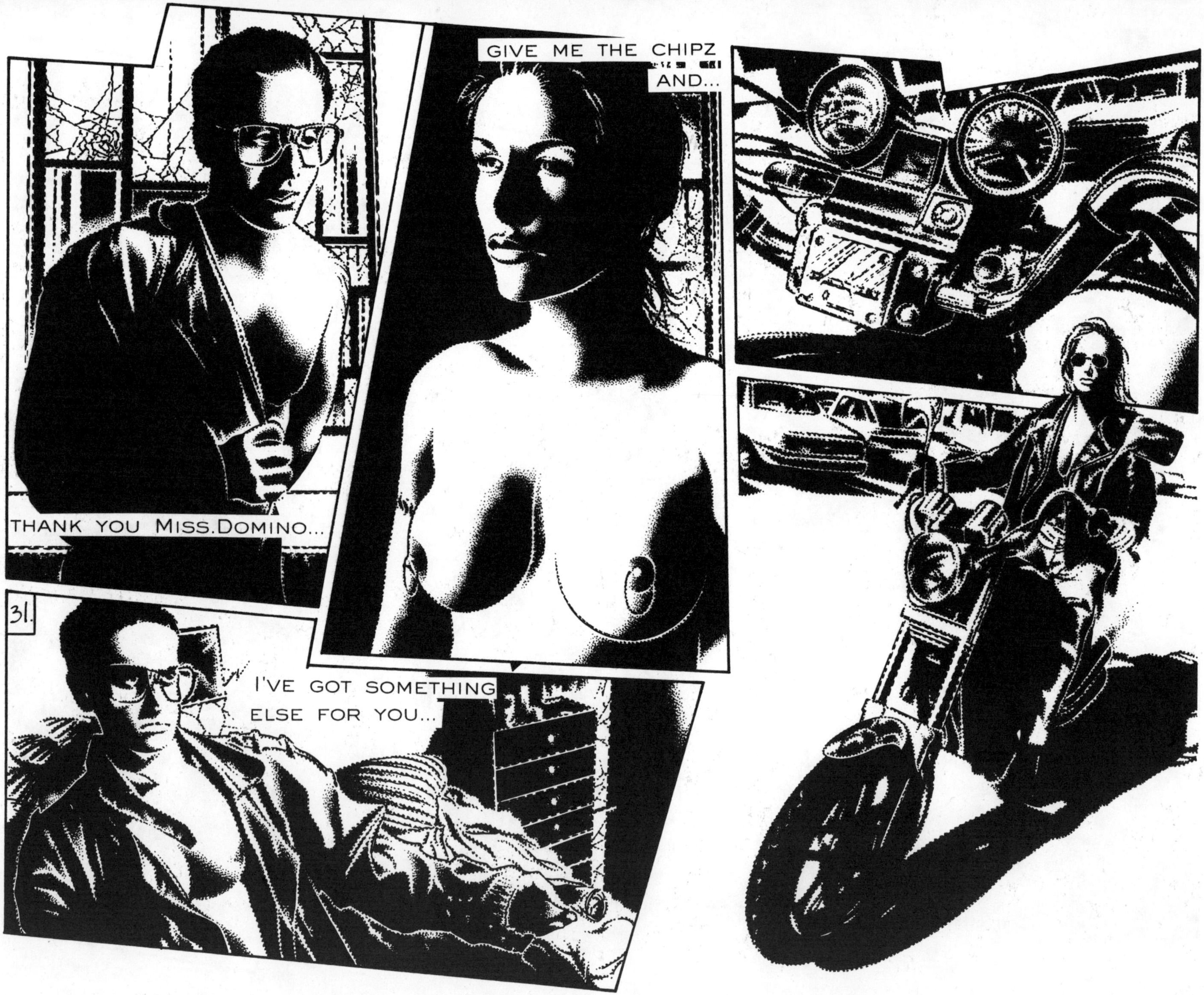
THANK YOU MISS.DOMINO...
GIVE ME THE CHIPZ
AND...
31.
I'VE GOT SOMETHING
ELSE FOR YOU...

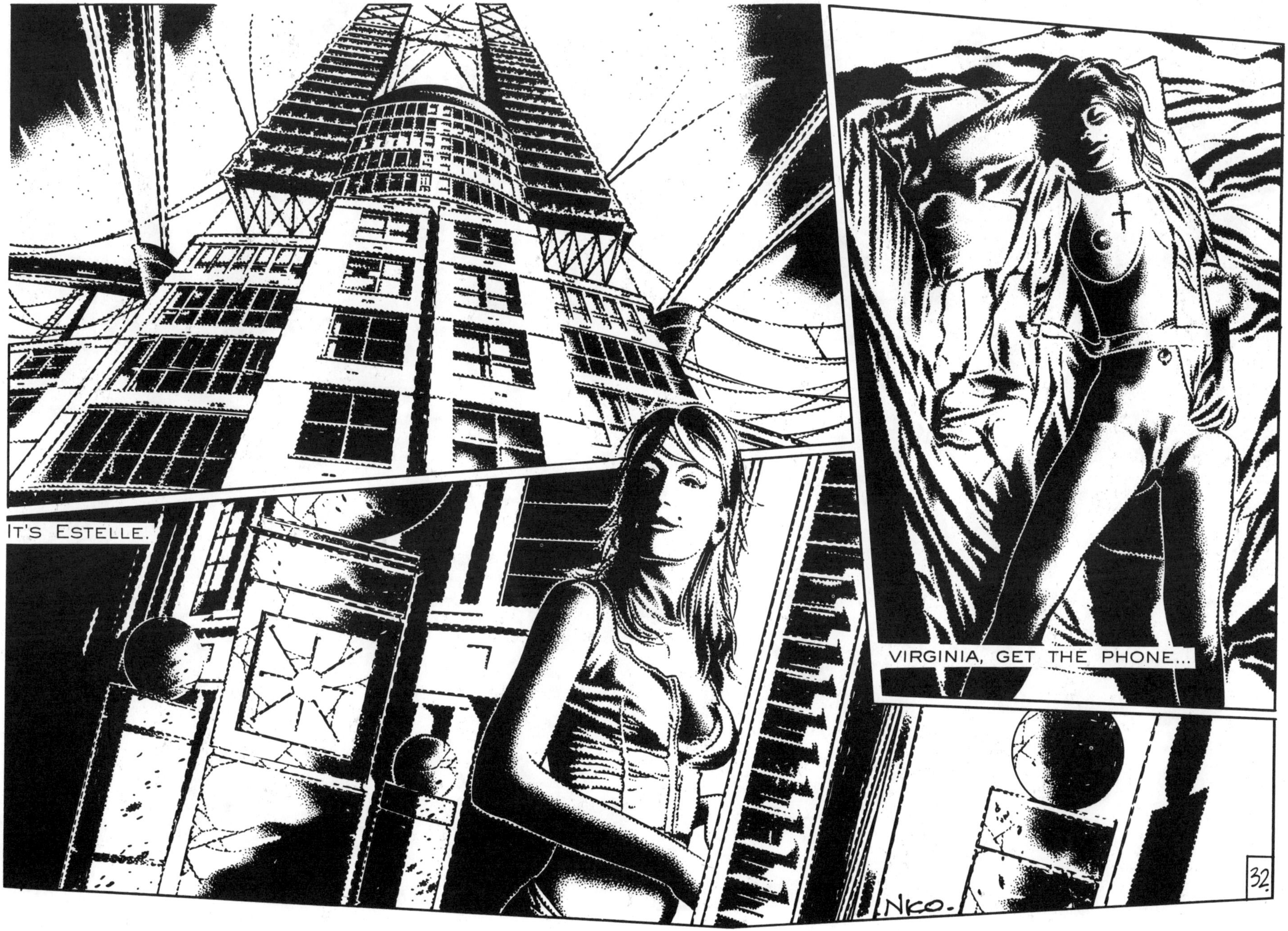
It's Estelle.
Virginia, get the phone...
Nko.

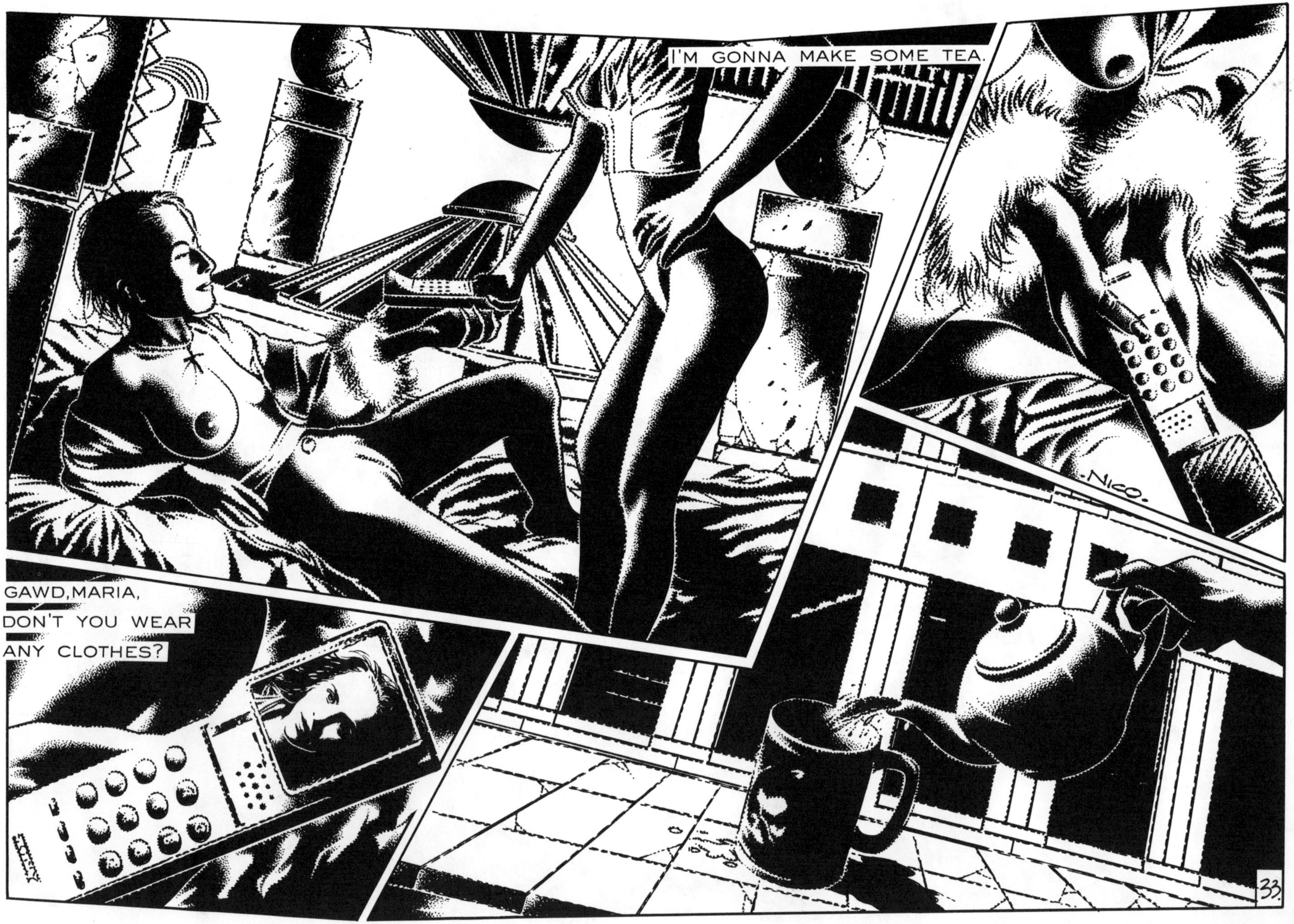
I'M GONNA MAKE SOME TEA.
GAWD,MARIA, DON'T YOU WEAR ANY CLOTHES?
NICO.

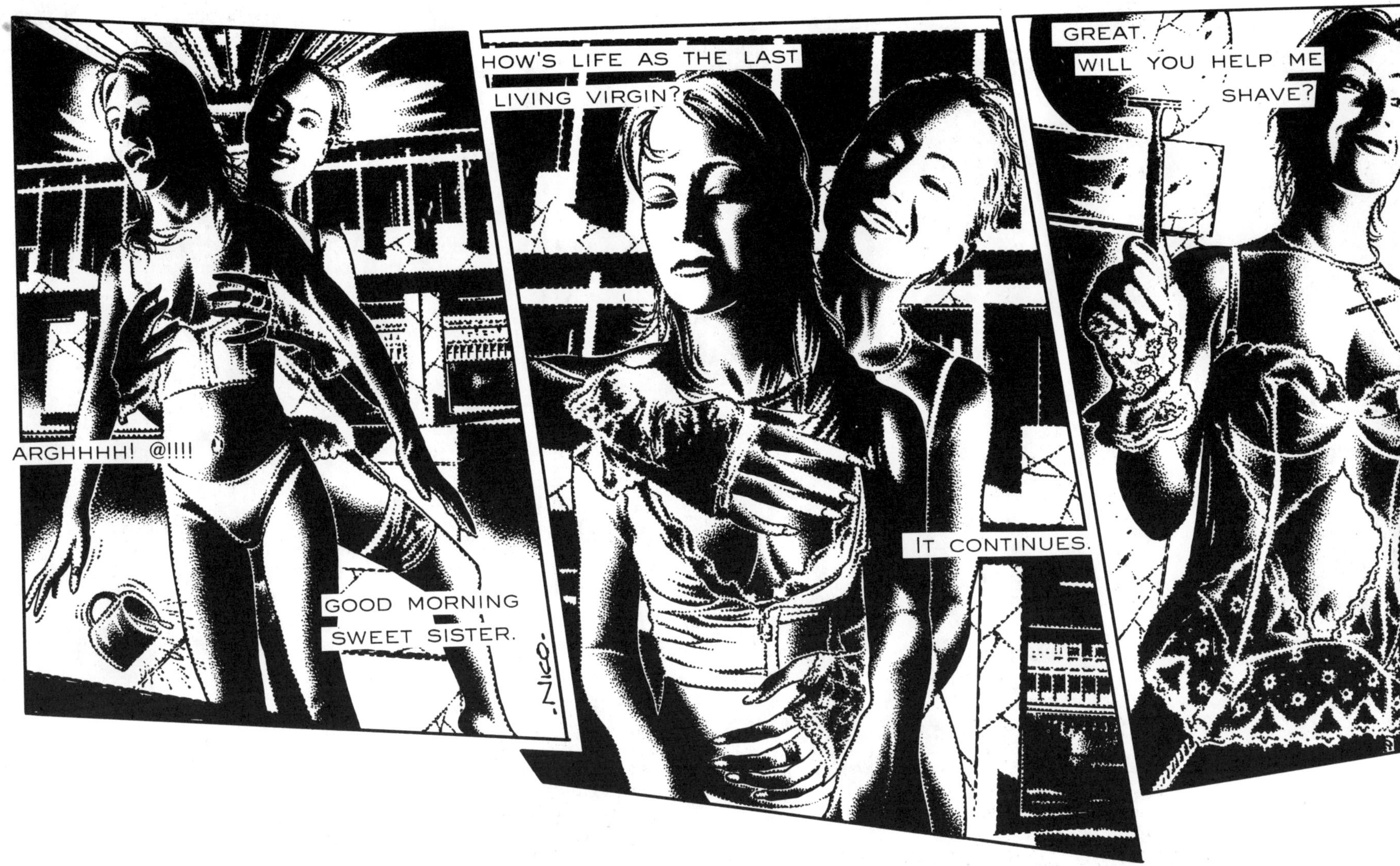
ARGHHHH! @!!!!
GOOD MORNING SWEET SISTER.
HOW'S LIFE AS THE LAST LIVING VIRGIN?
IT CONTINUES.
GREAT. WILL YOU HELP ME SHAVE?
NICO.
34

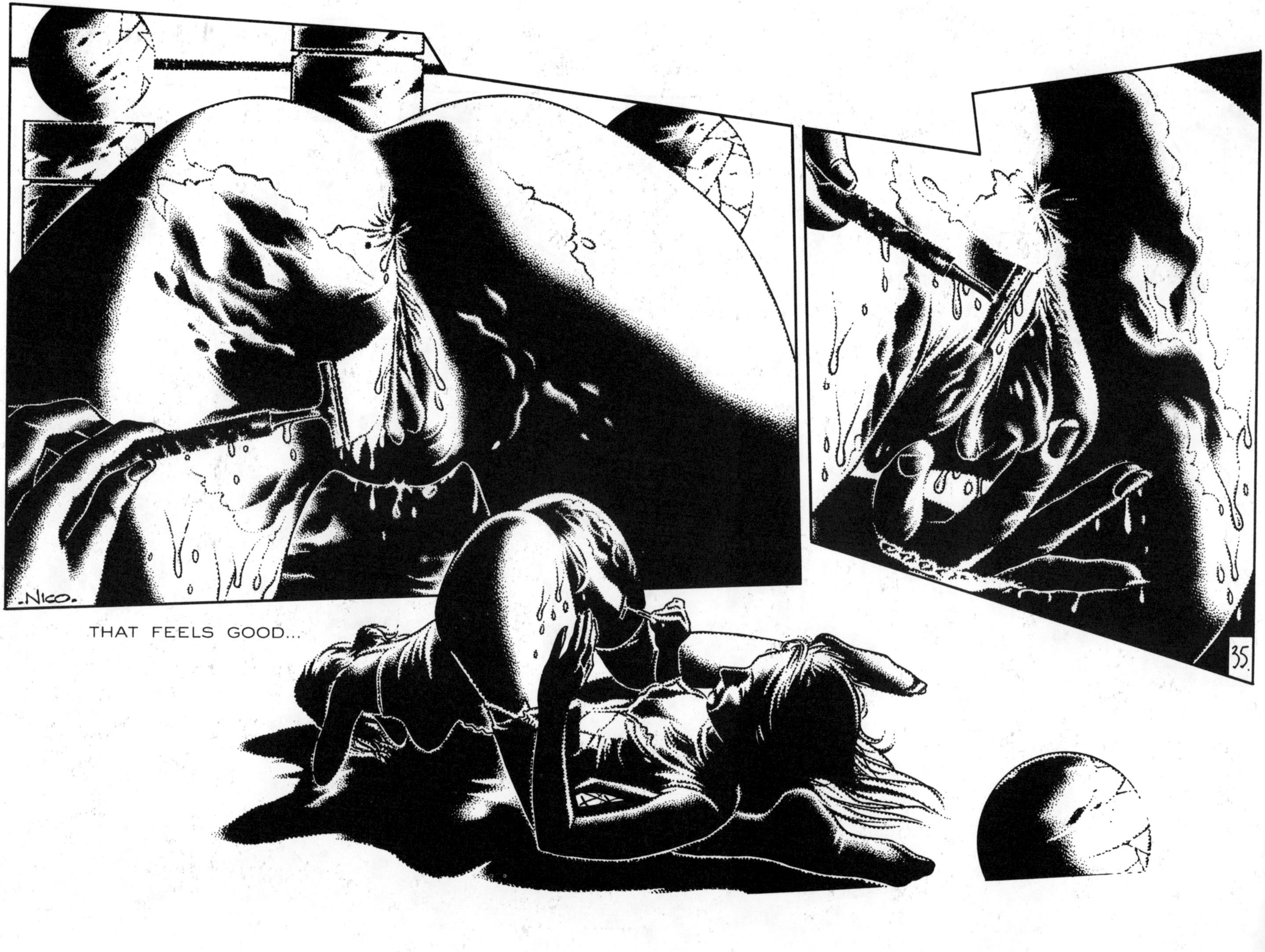
NICO
THAT FEELS GOOD...

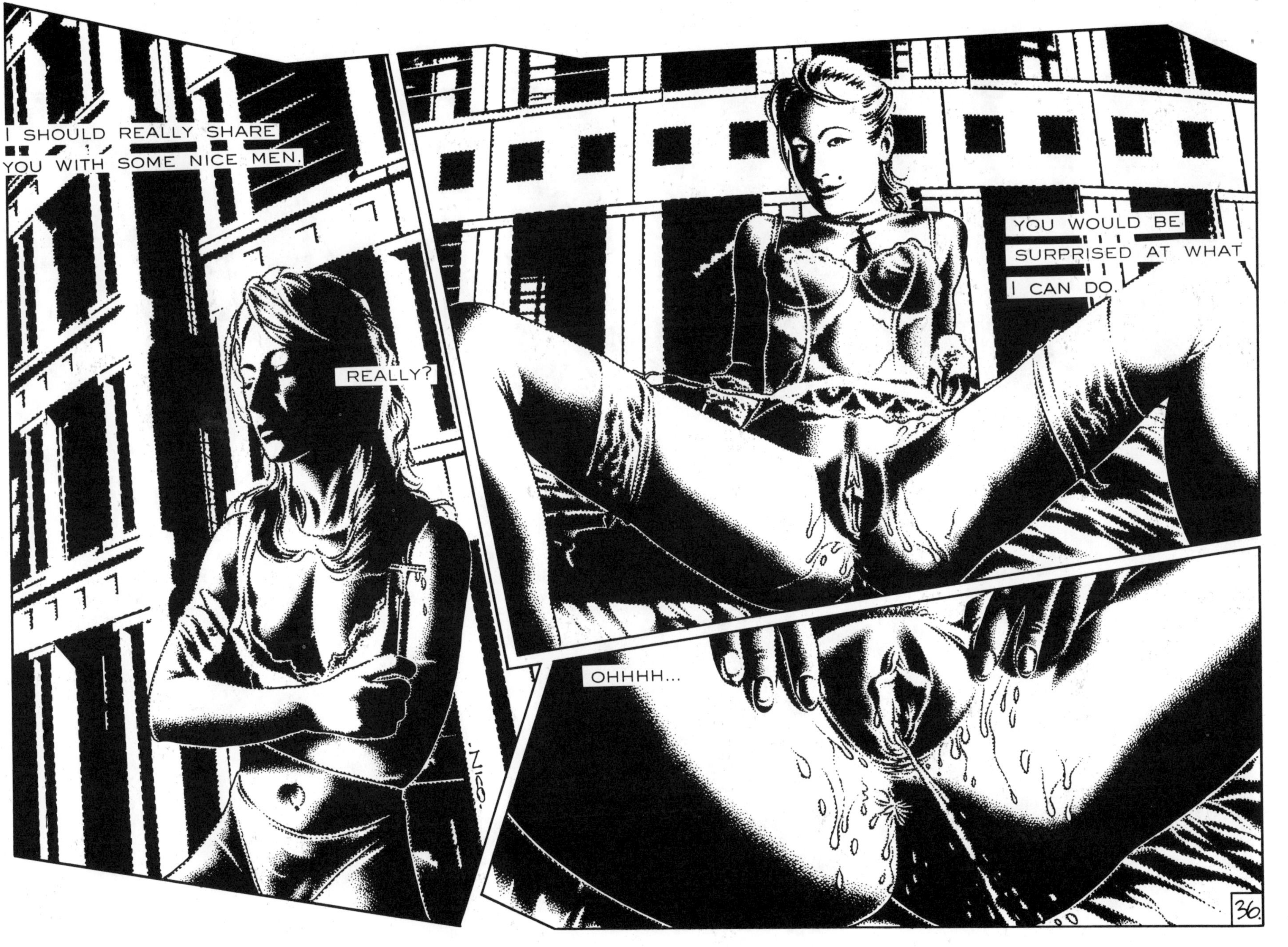
I SHOULD REALLY SHARE
YOU WITH SOME NICE MEN.
REALLY?
Nico.
YOU WOULD BE
SURPRISED AT WHAT
I CAN DO.
OHHHH...

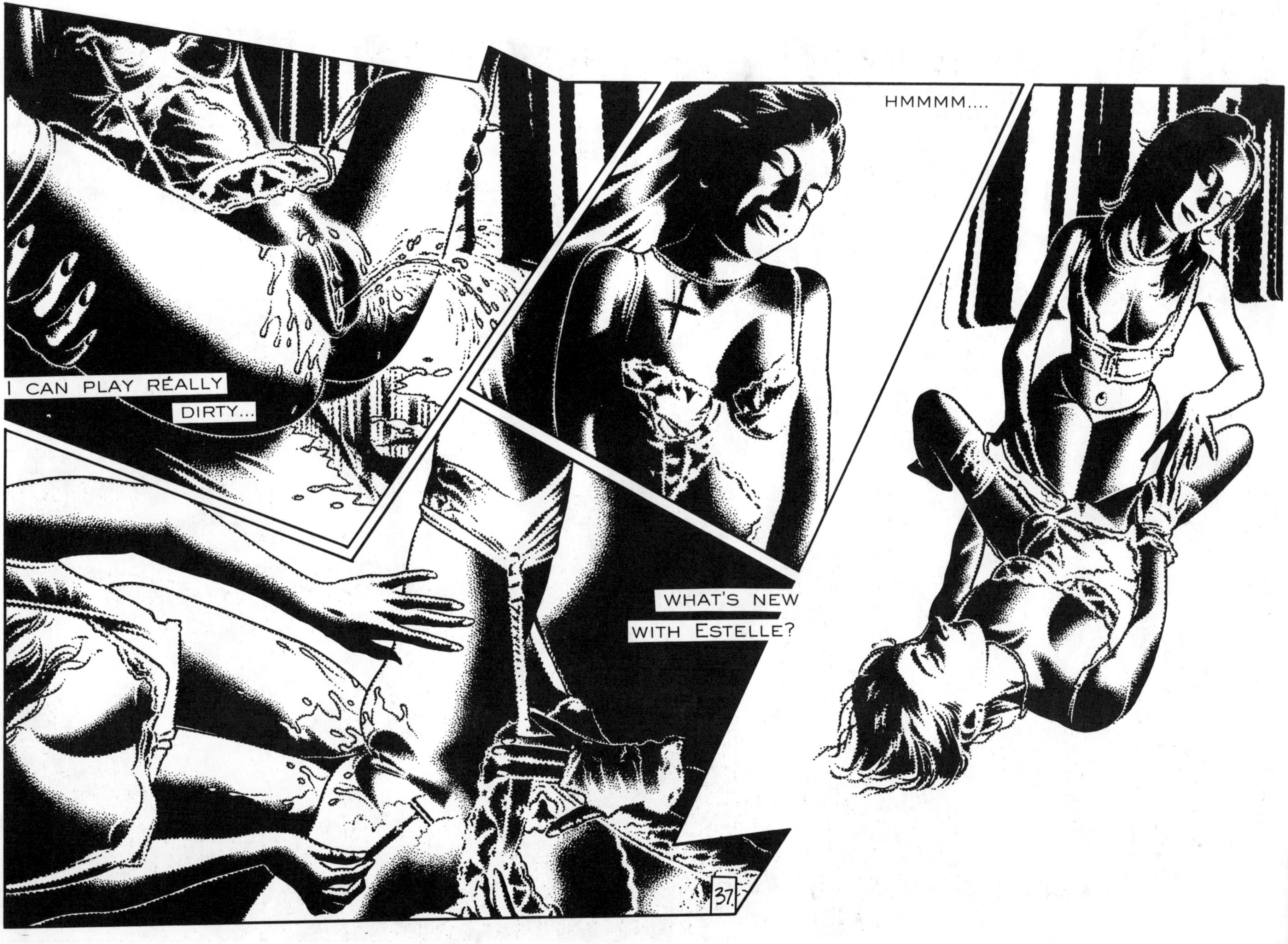
I CAN PLAY REALLY
DIRTY...
HMMMM....
WHAT'S NEW
WITH ESTELLE?

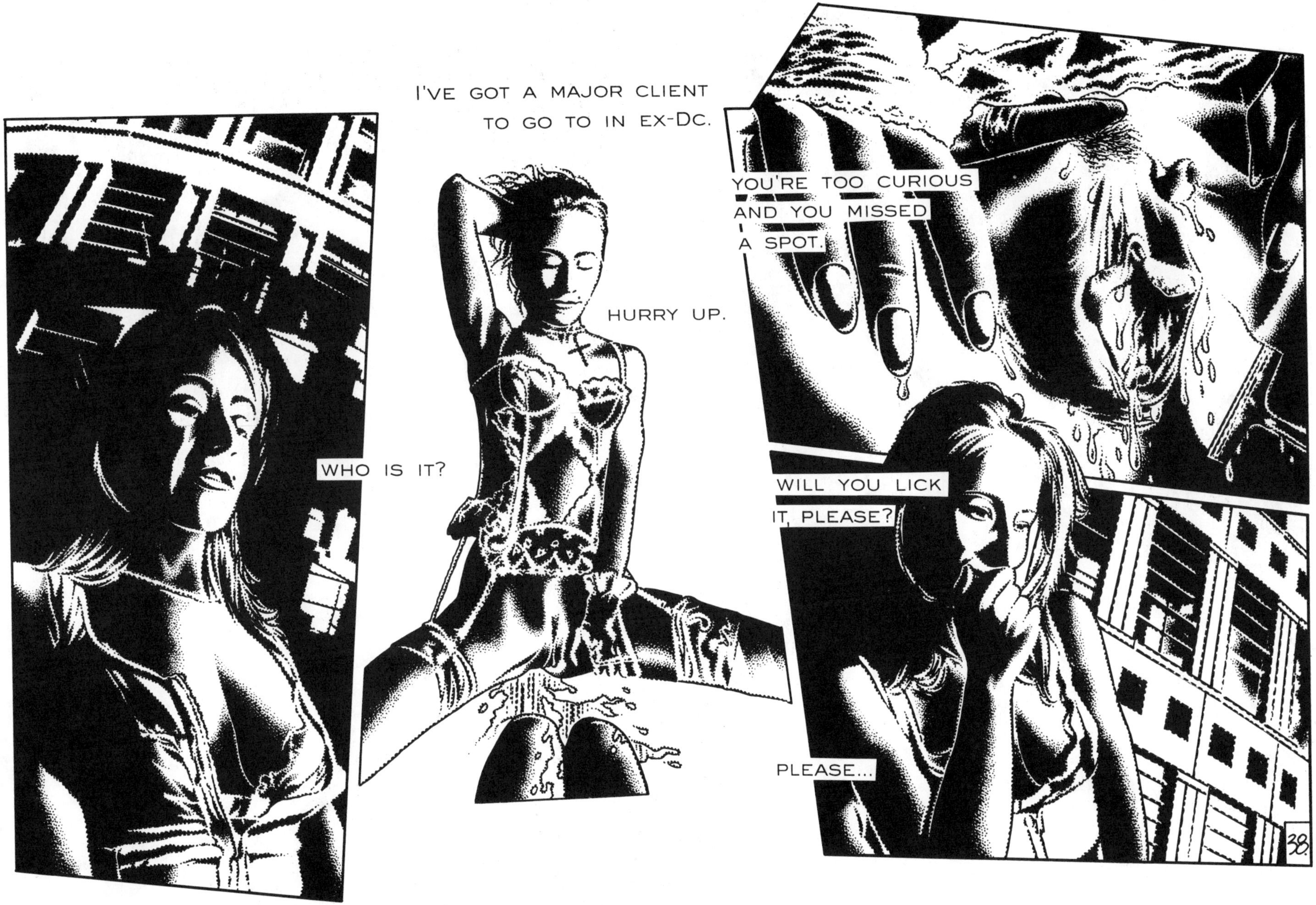
WHO IS IT?
I'VE GOT A MAJOR CLIENT TO GO TO IN EX-DC.
HURRY UP.
YOU'RE TOO CURIOUS AND YOU MISSED A SPOT.
WILL YOU LICK IT, PLEASE?
PLEASE...

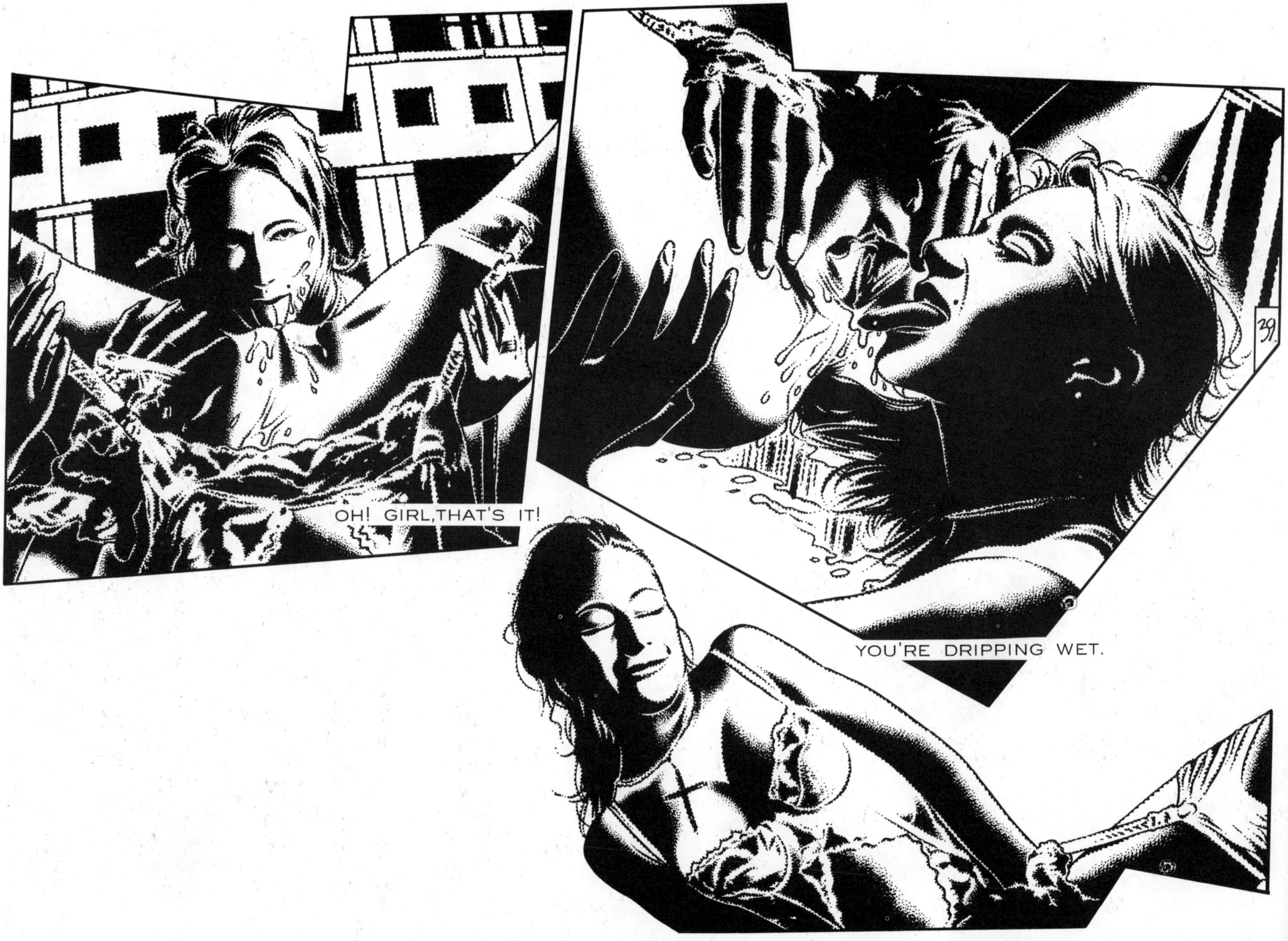
OH! GIRL,THAT'S IT!
YOU'RE DRIPPING WET.

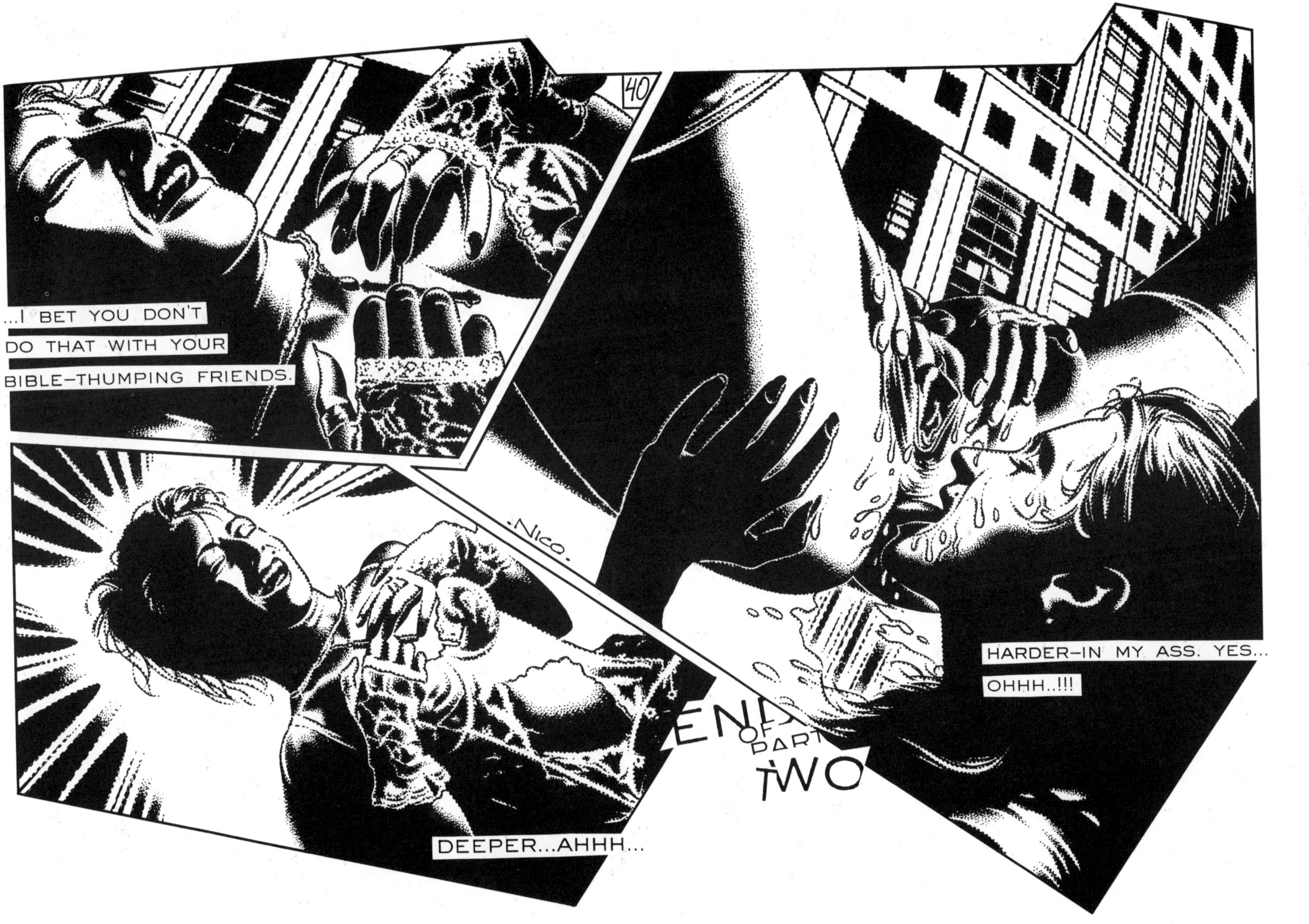
40
...I BET YOU DON'T DO THAT WITH YOUR BIBLE-THUMPING FRIENDS.
HARDER—IN MY ASS. YES... OHHH..!!!
DEEPER...AHHH...
.Nico.
END OF PART TWO

The fantasies may come individually as rewards for accomplished tasks, or as payments in the form of time blocks, to be used at will.

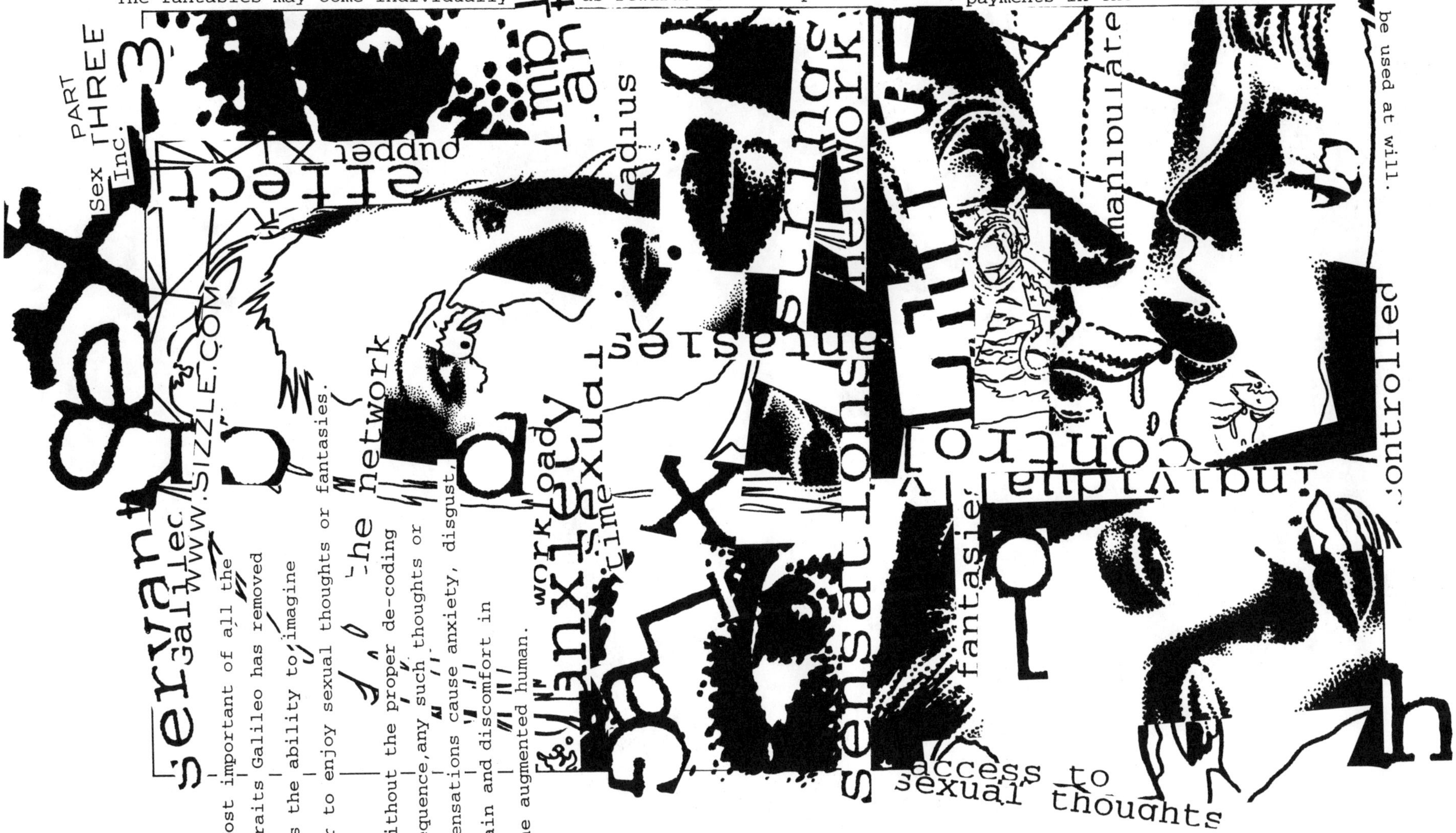

PART
Sex THREE
Inc.
3
puppet
affect
servant
Galileo
WWW.SIZZLE.COM
network
workload
anxiety
sexual
time
radius
fantasies
strings
network
sensations
control
individual
manipulate
controlled
fantasie
access to
sexual thoughts

Most important of all the traits Galileo has removed is the ability to imagine or to enjoy sexual thoughts or fantasies.

Without the proper de-coding sequence, any such thoughts or sensations cause anxiety, disgust, pain and discomfort in the augmented human.

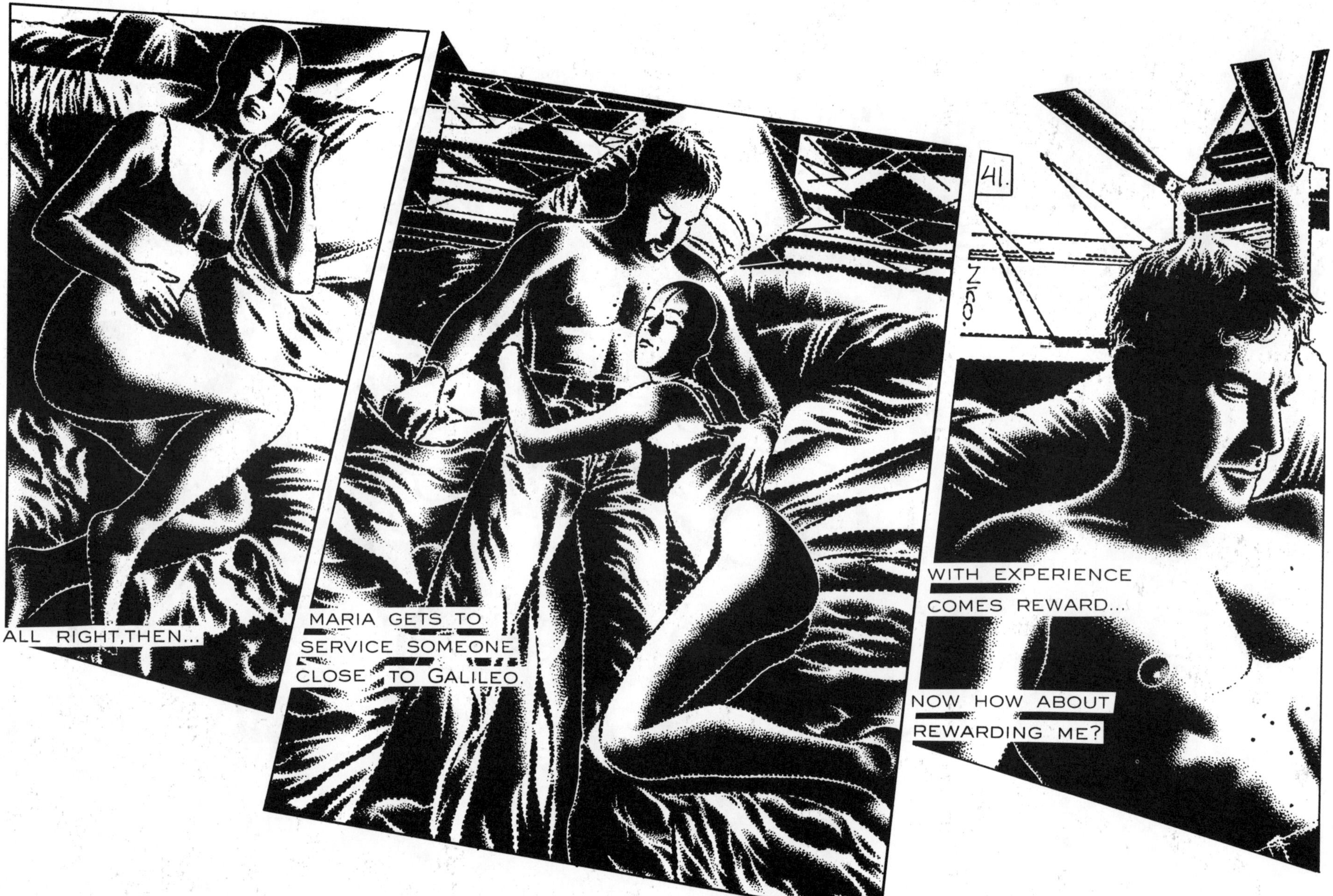
ALL RIGHT, THEN...
MARIA GETS TO SERVICE SOMEONE CLOSE TO GALILEO.
41.
NICO.
WITH EXPERIENCE COMES REWARD...
NOW HOW ABOUT REWARDING ME?

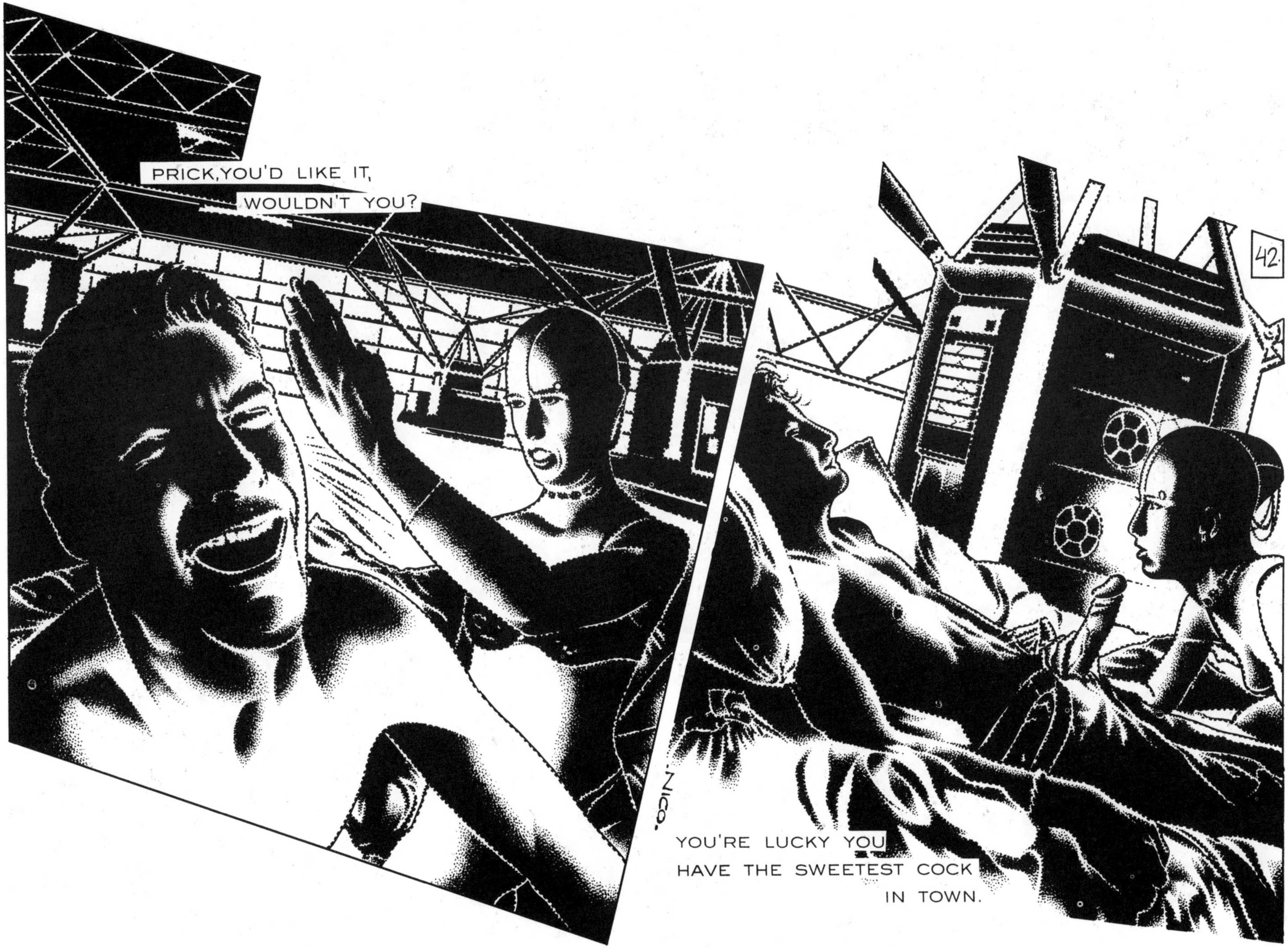
PRICK, YOU'D LIKE IT, WOULDN'T YOU?
YOU'RE LUCKY YOU HAVE THE SWEETEST COCK IN TOWN.
NICO.
42.

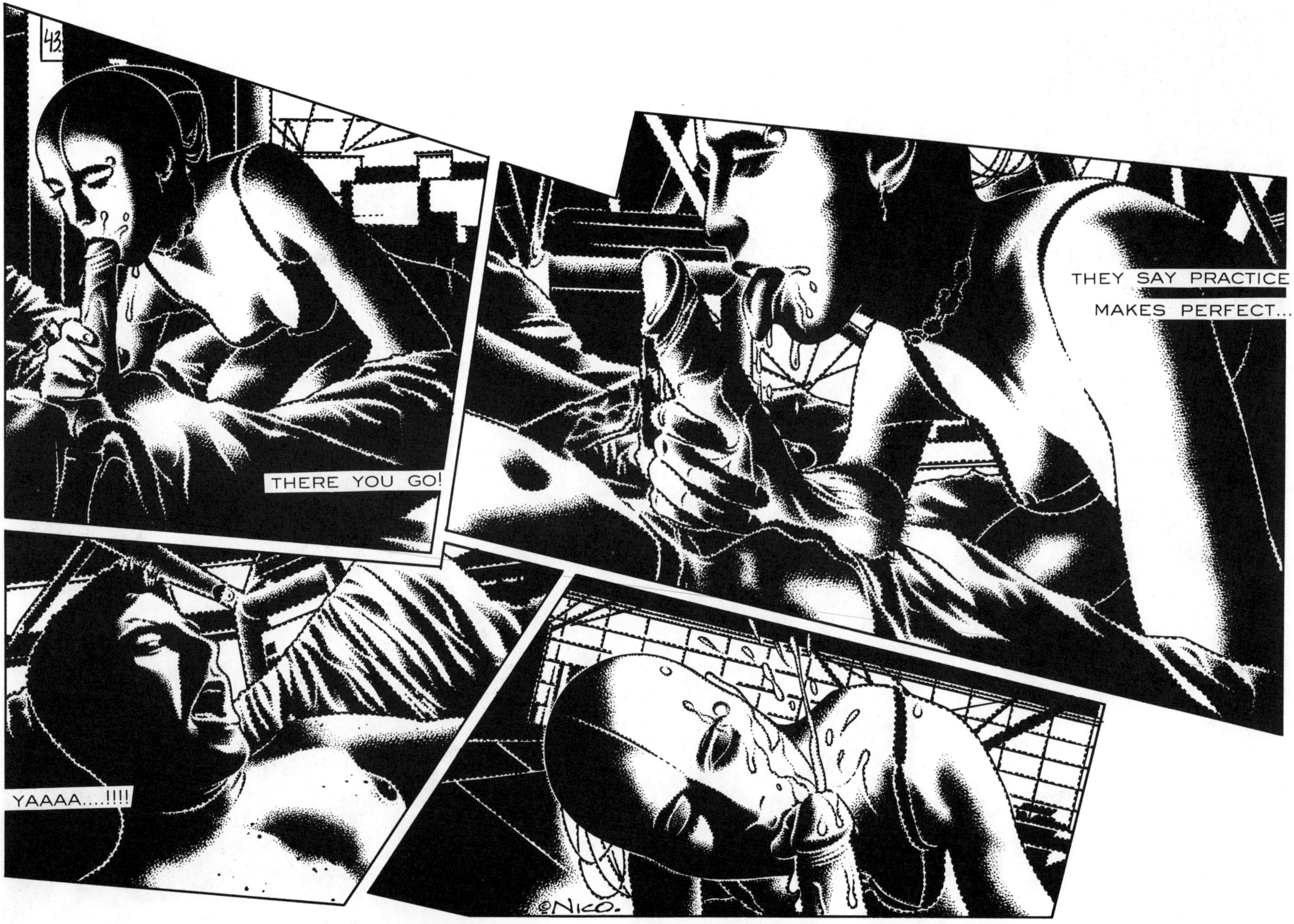
43
THERE YOU GO!
THEY SAY PRACTICE MAKES PERFECT...
YAAAA....!!!!
©NICO.

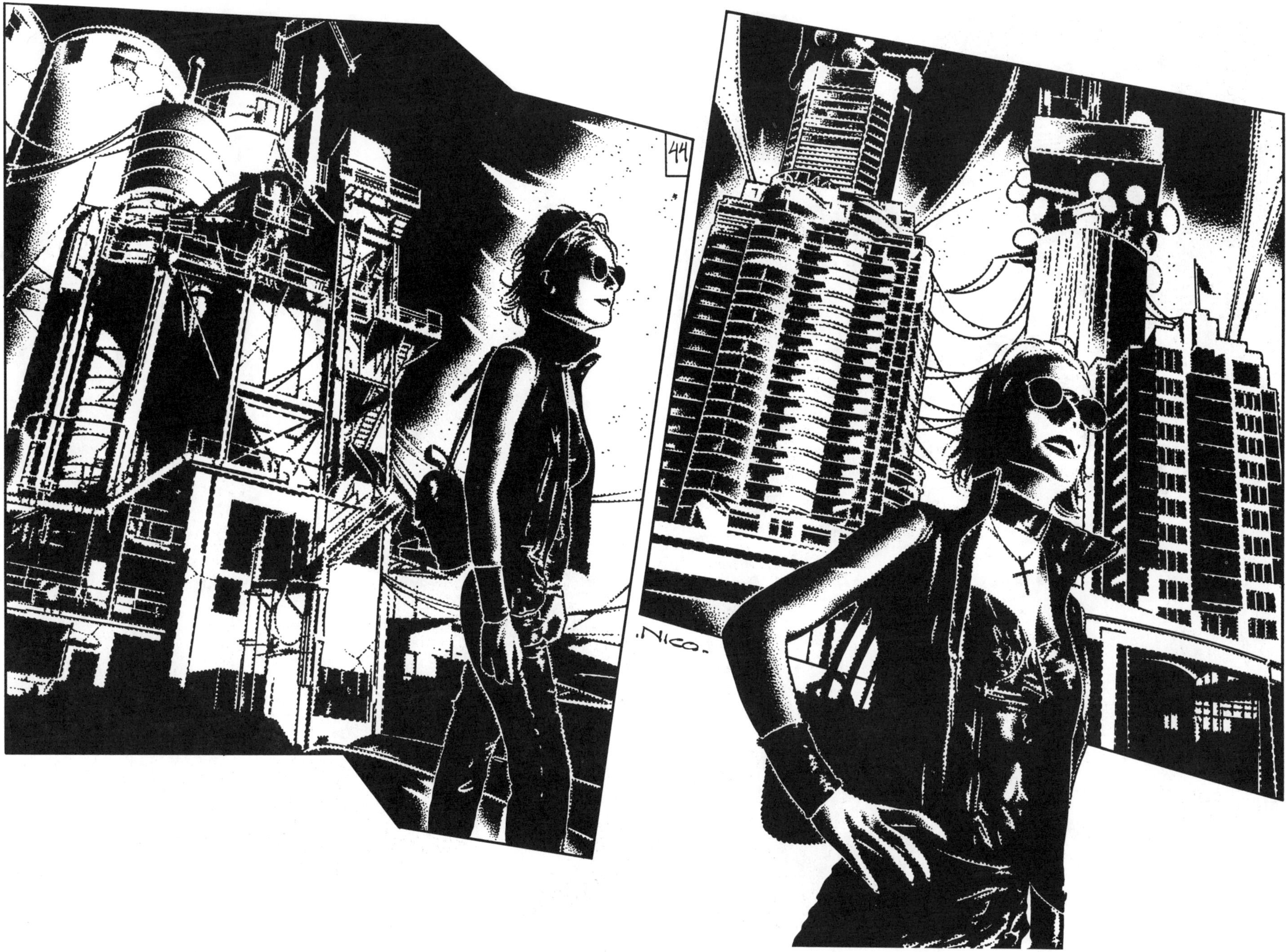
44
·NICO·

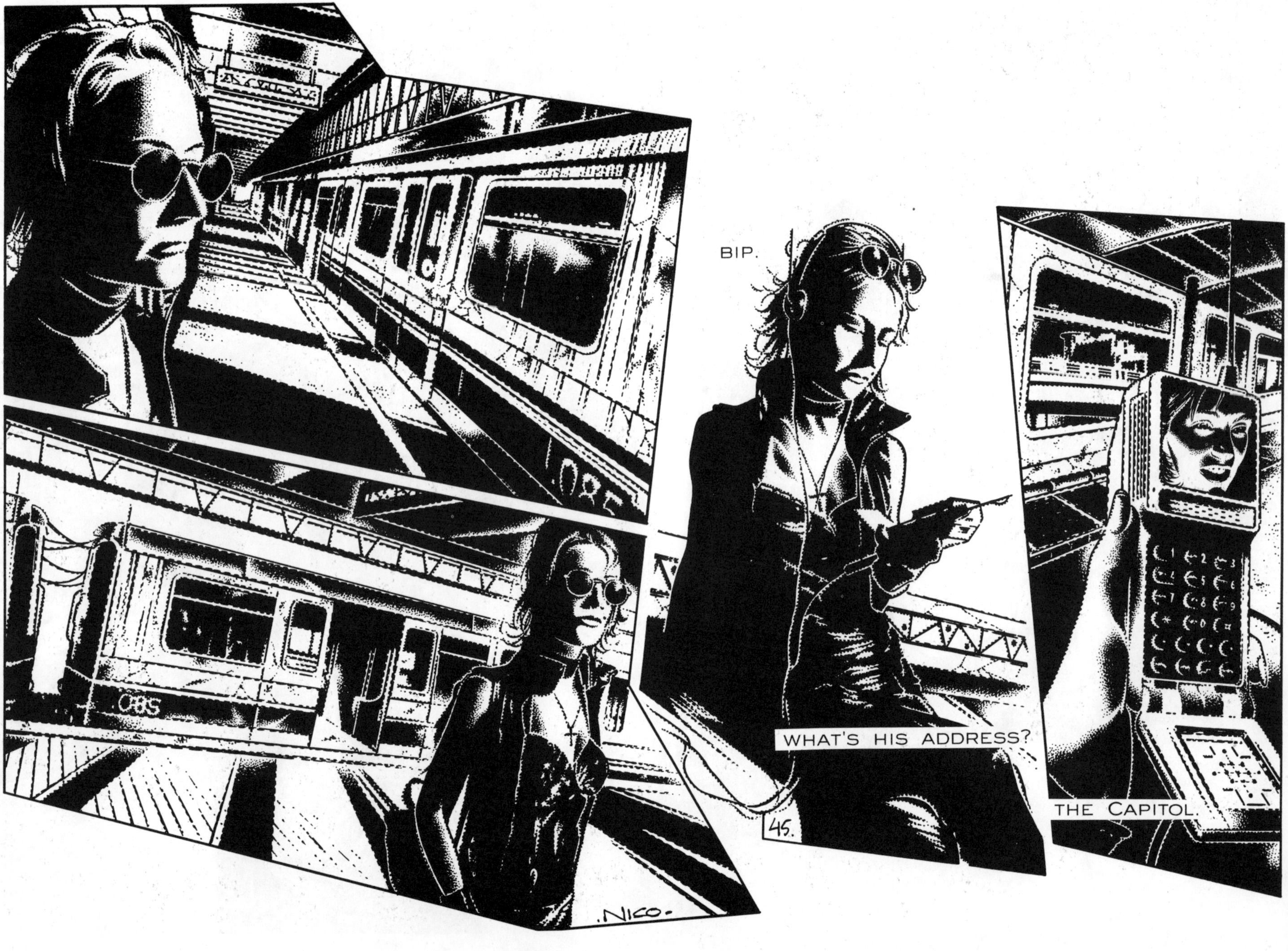
BIP.
WHAT'S HIS ADDRESS?
45.
THE CAPITOL.
NICO

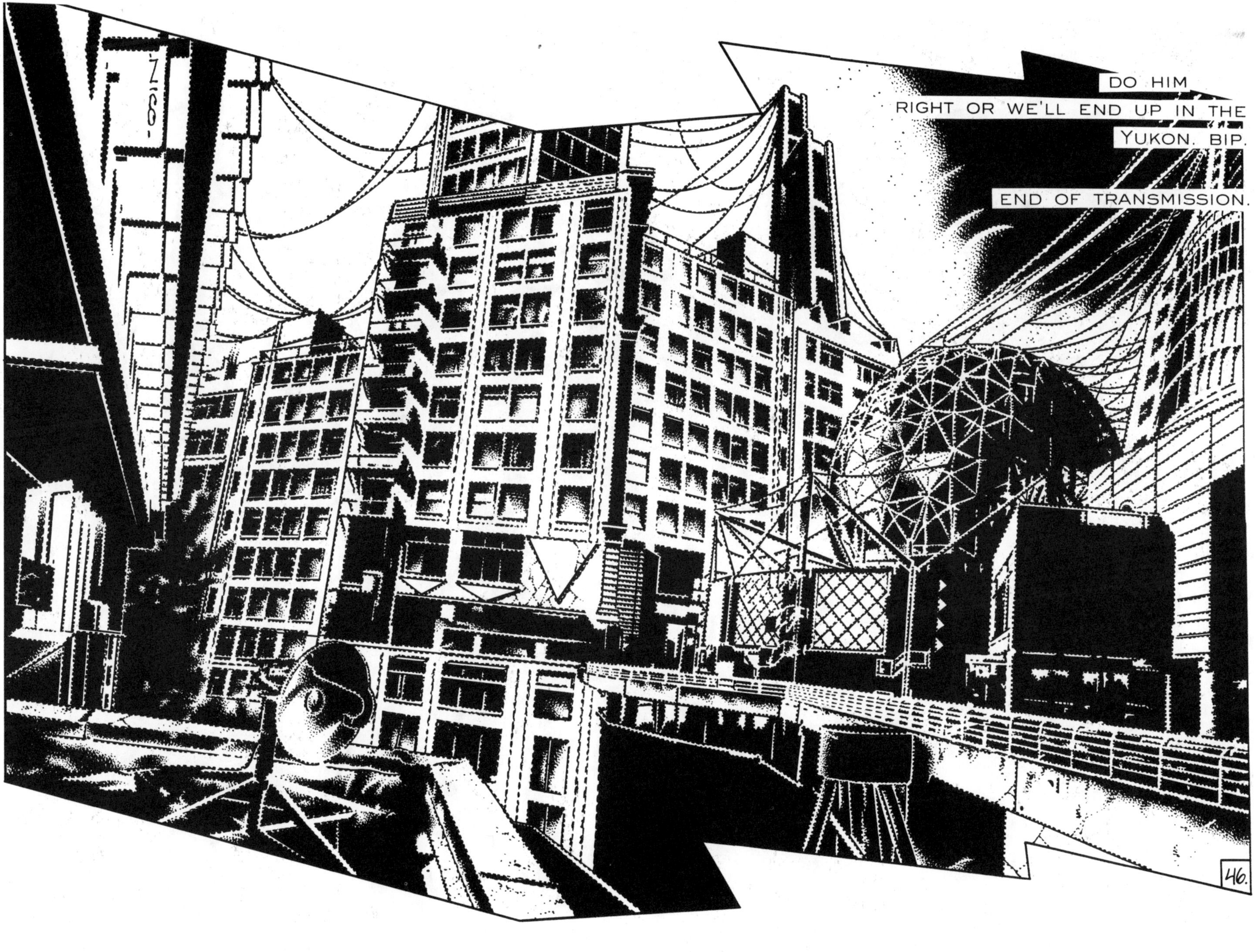
DO HIM
RIGHT OR WE'LL END UP IN THE
YUKON. BIP.
END OF TRANSMISSION.

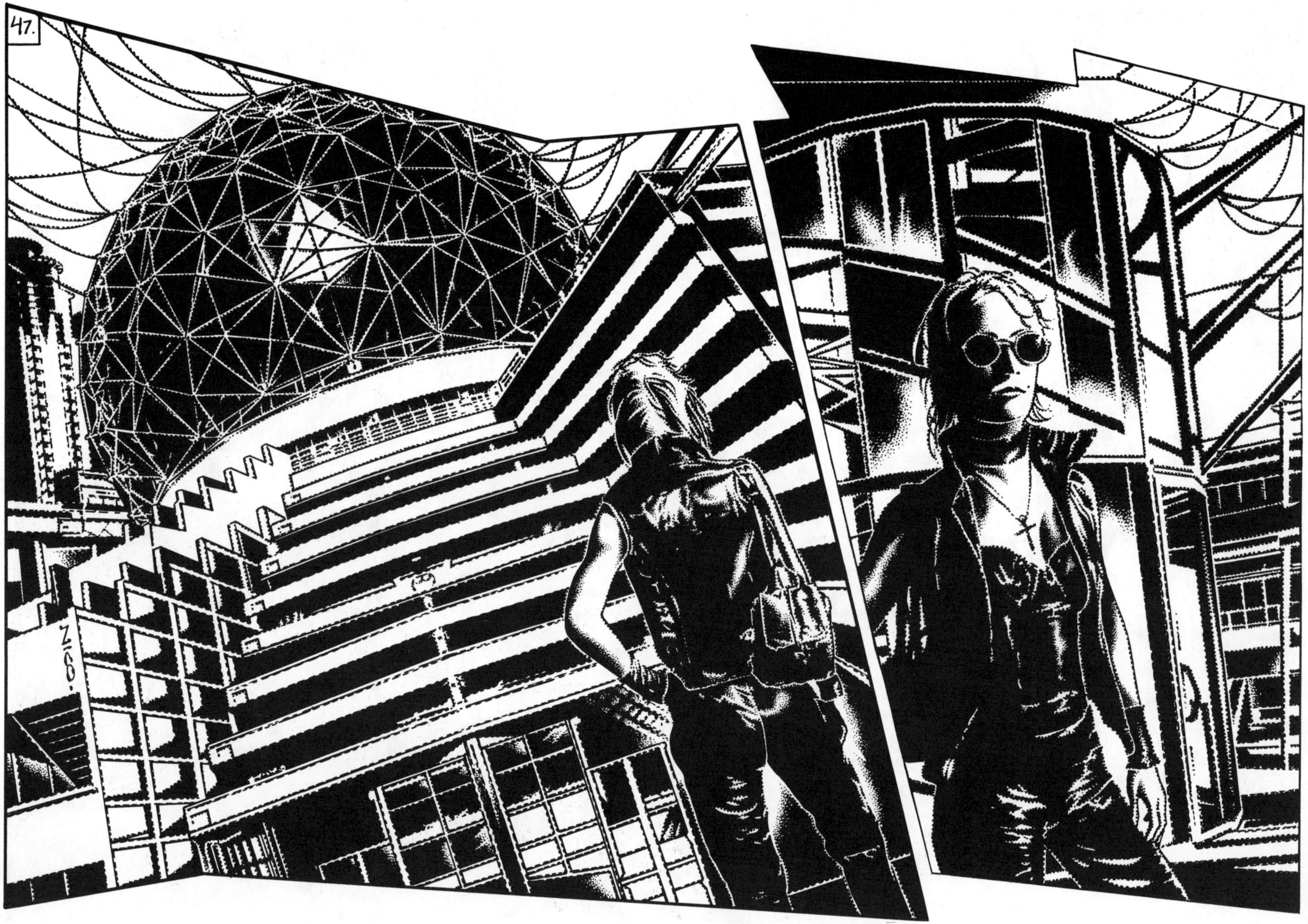

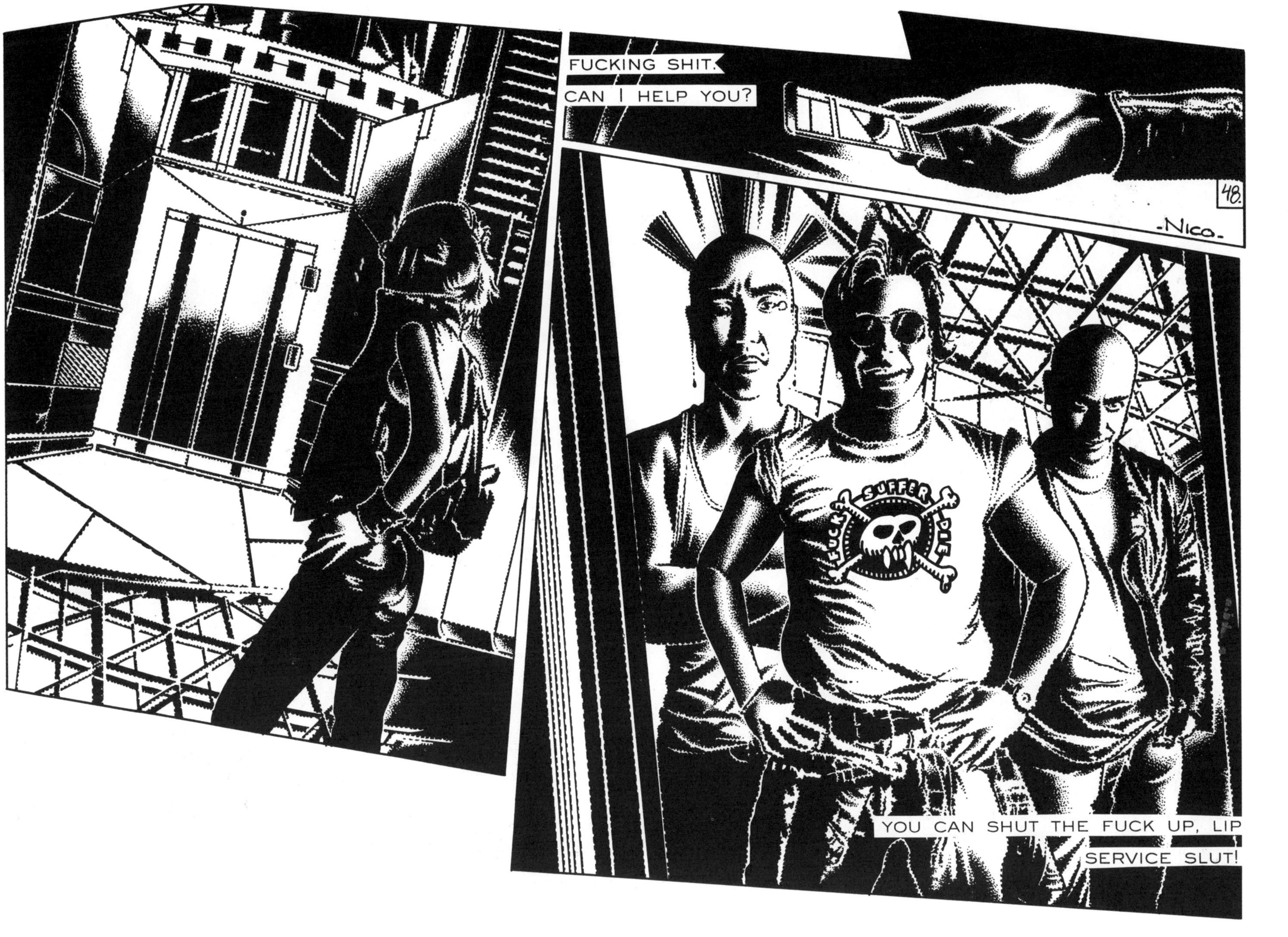
FUCKING SHIT.
CAN I HELP YOU?
48.
-Nico-
FUCK SUFFER DIE
YOU CAN SHUT THE FUCK UP, LIP
SERVICE SLUT!

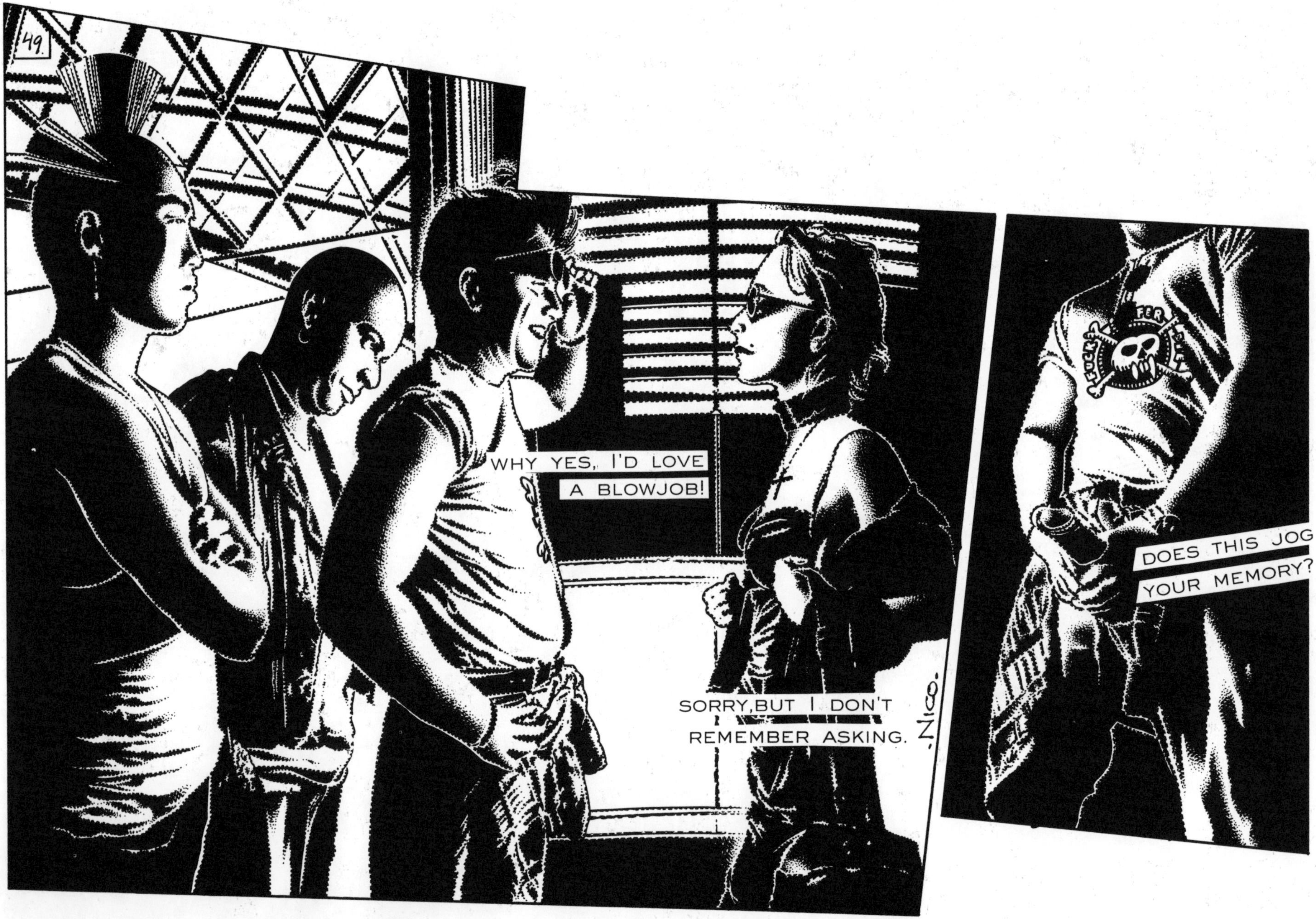
49.
WHY YES, I'D LOVE A BLOWJOB!
SORRY, BUT I DON'T REMEMBER ASKING.
DOES THIS JOG YOUR MEMORY?

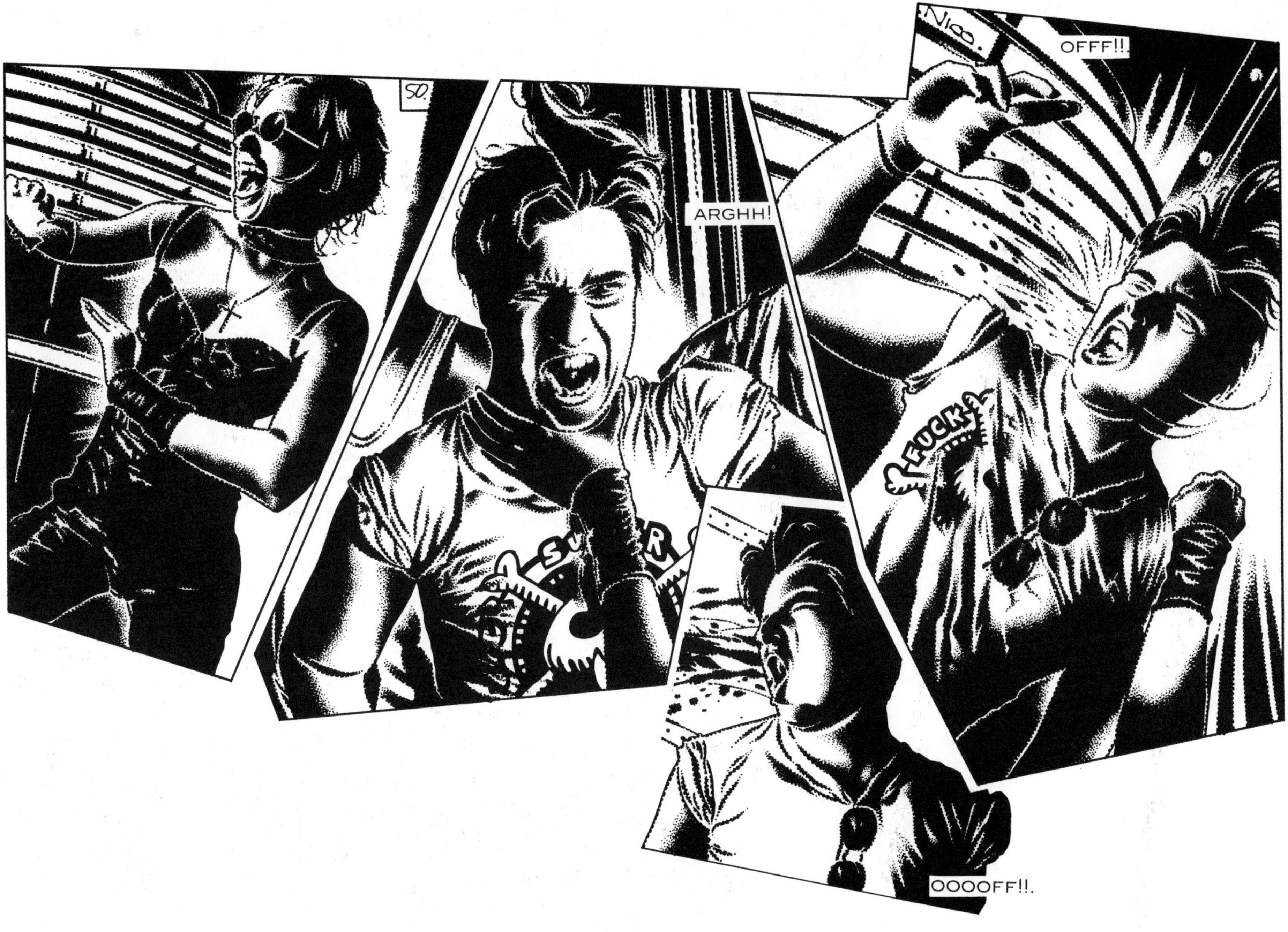
SO.
ARGHH!
NICO.
OFFF!!.
FUCK
OOOOFF!!.

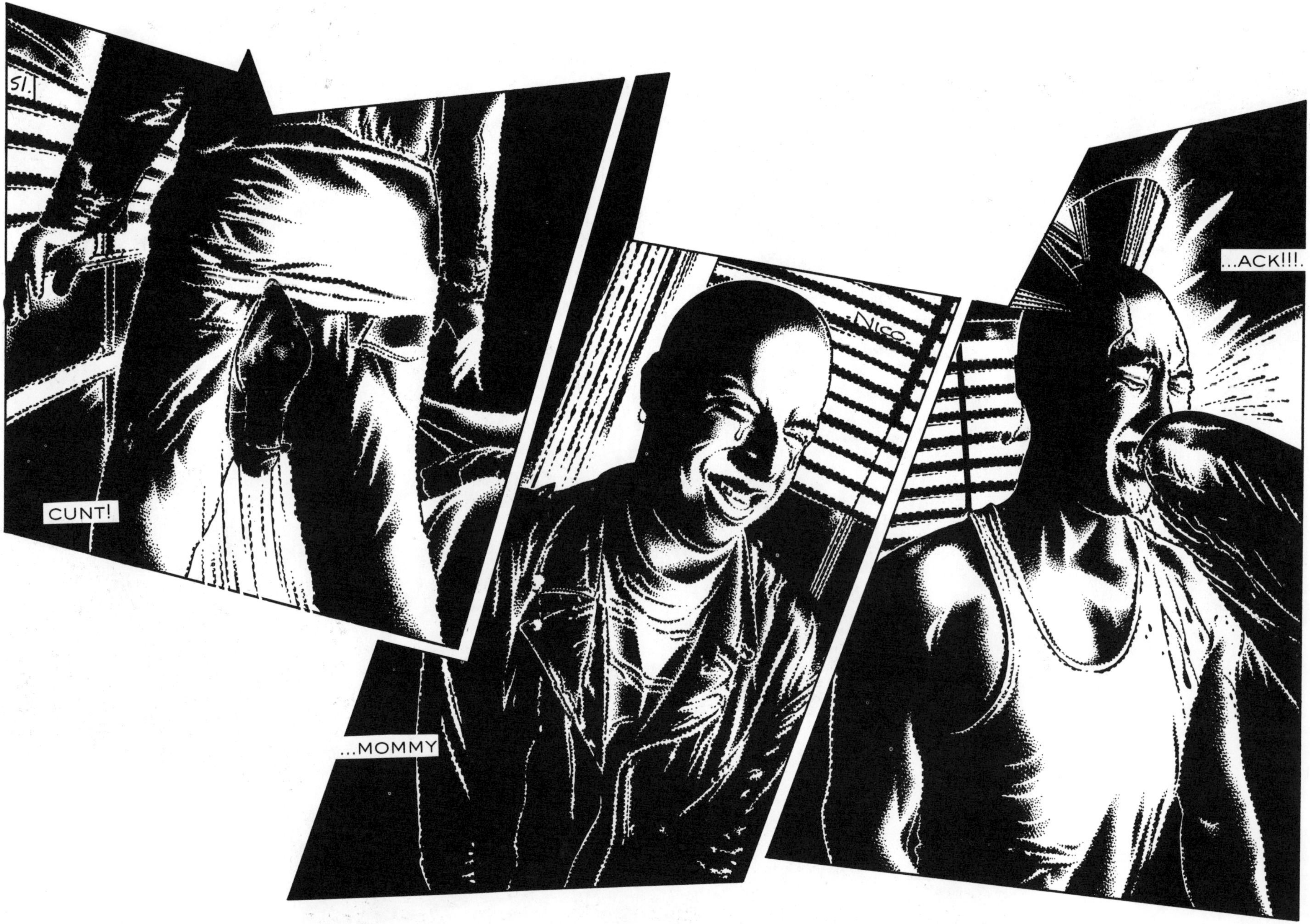
51.
CUNT!
...MOMMY
Nico
...ACK!!!

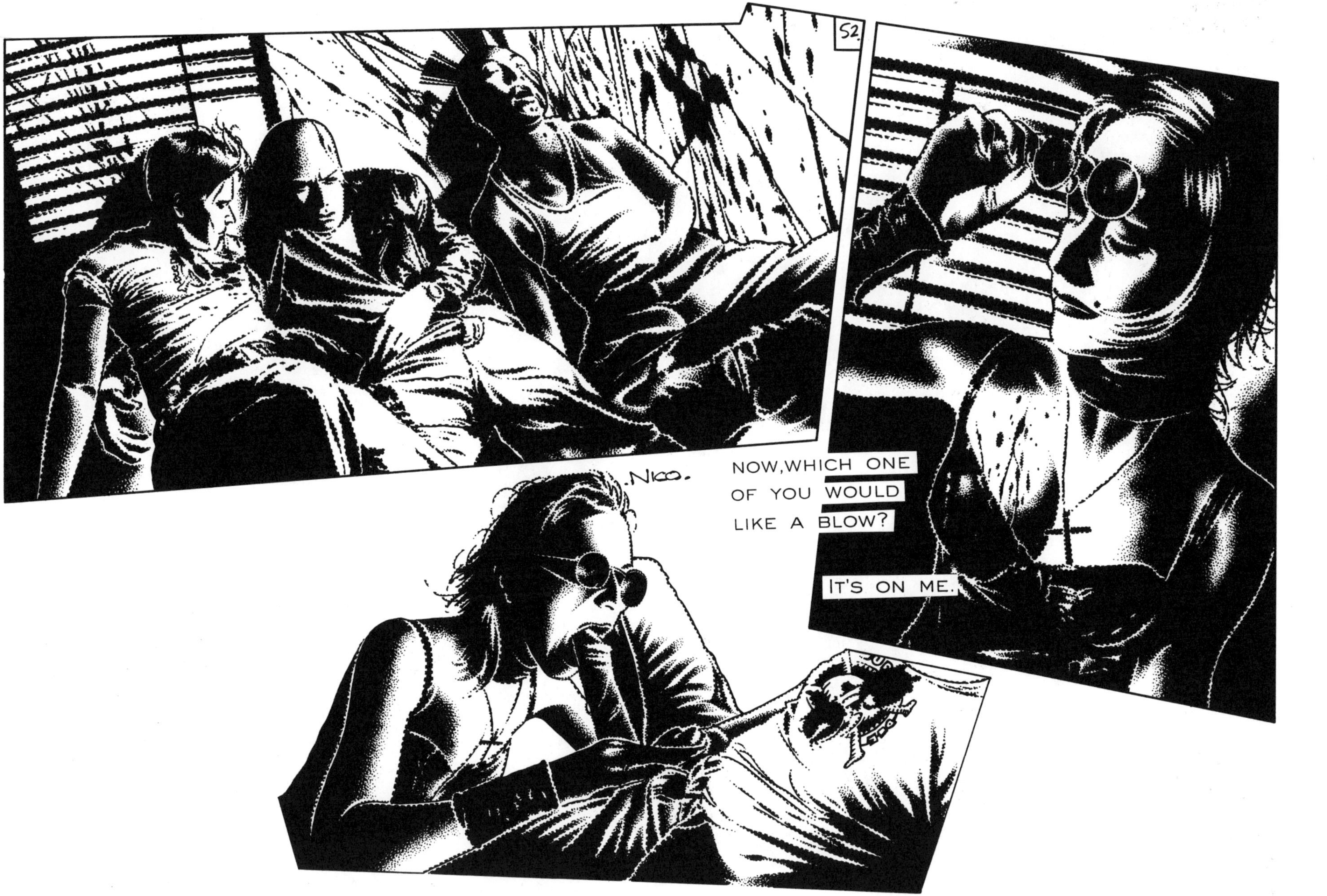
52
NOW, WHICH ONE OF YOU WOULD LIKE A BLOW?
IT'S ON ME.

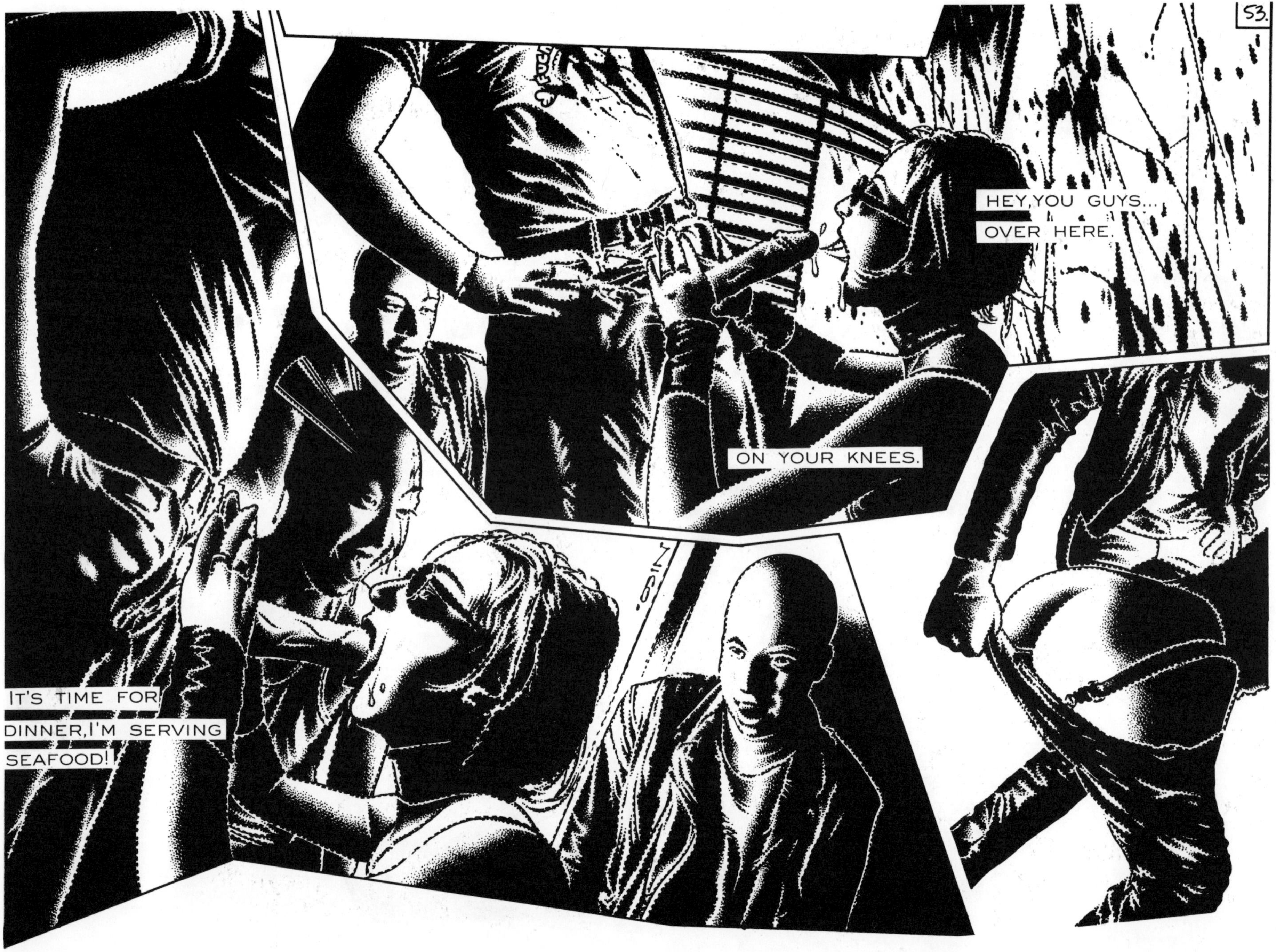
HEY, YOU GUYS...
OVER HERE.
ON YOUR KNEES.
IT'S TIME FOR DINNER, I'M SERVING SEAFOOD!

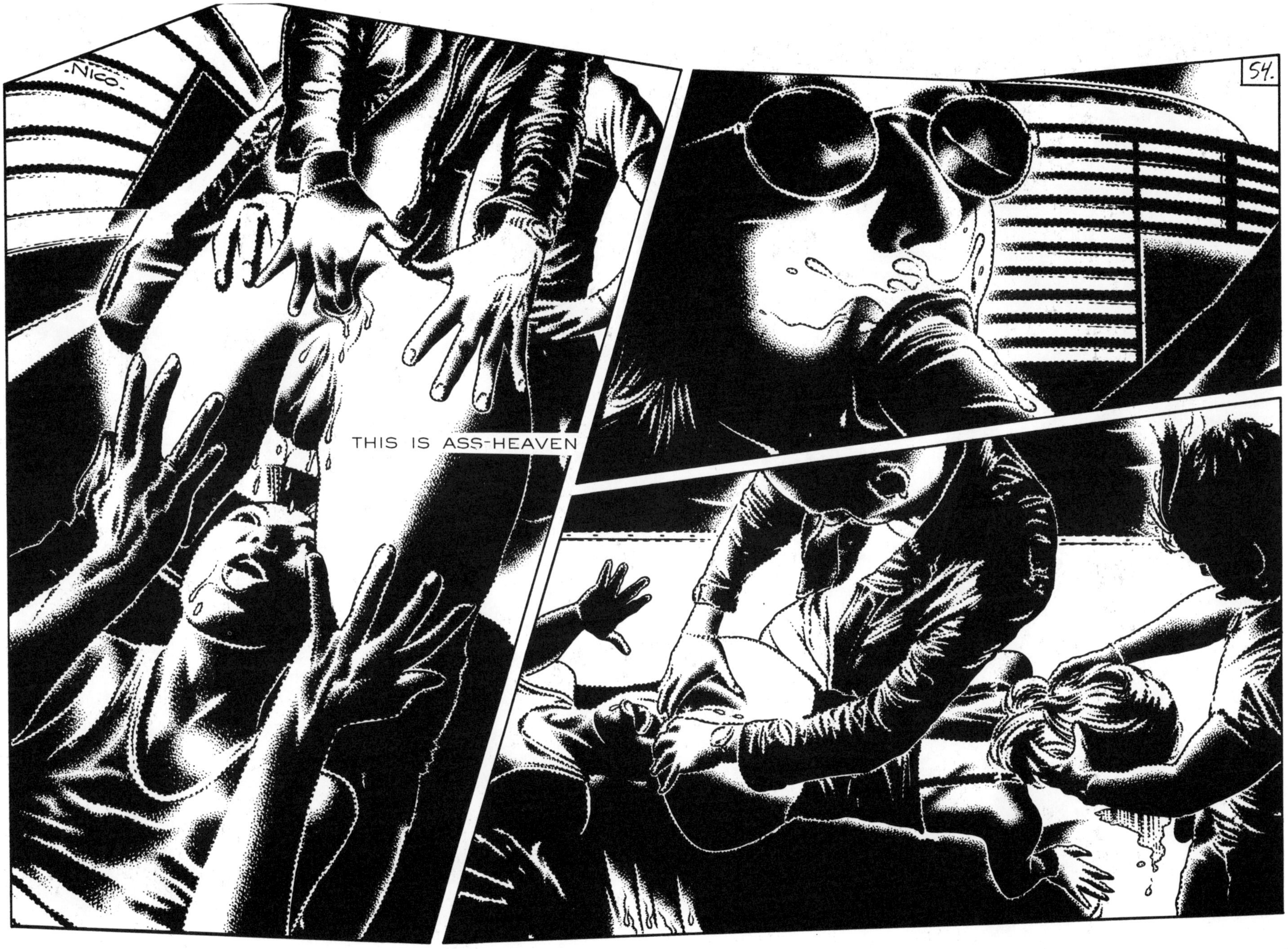
THIS IS ASS-HEAVEN

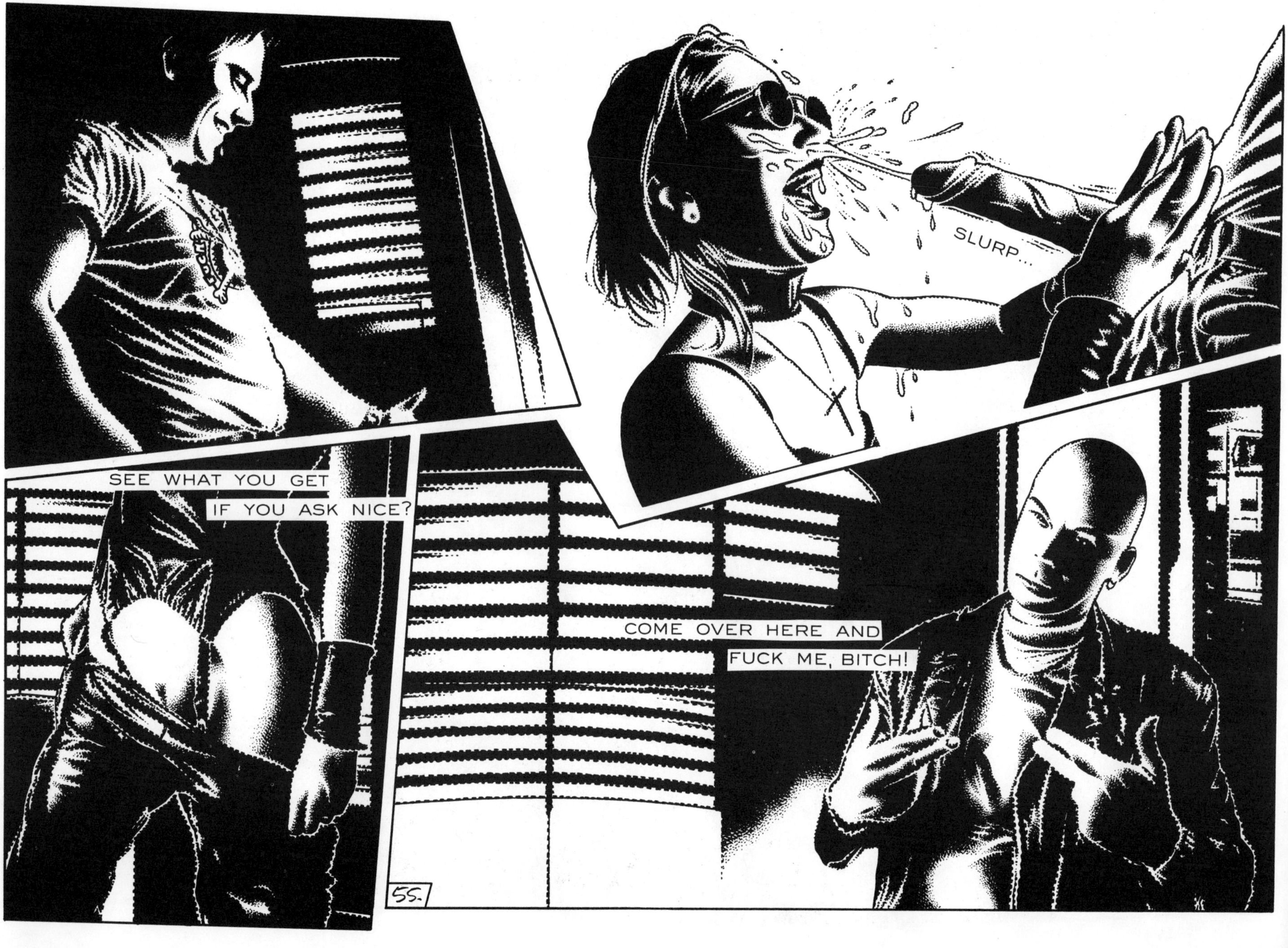
SLURP...
SEE WHAT YOU GET
IF YOU ASK NICE?
COME OVER HERE AND
FUCK ME, BITCH!

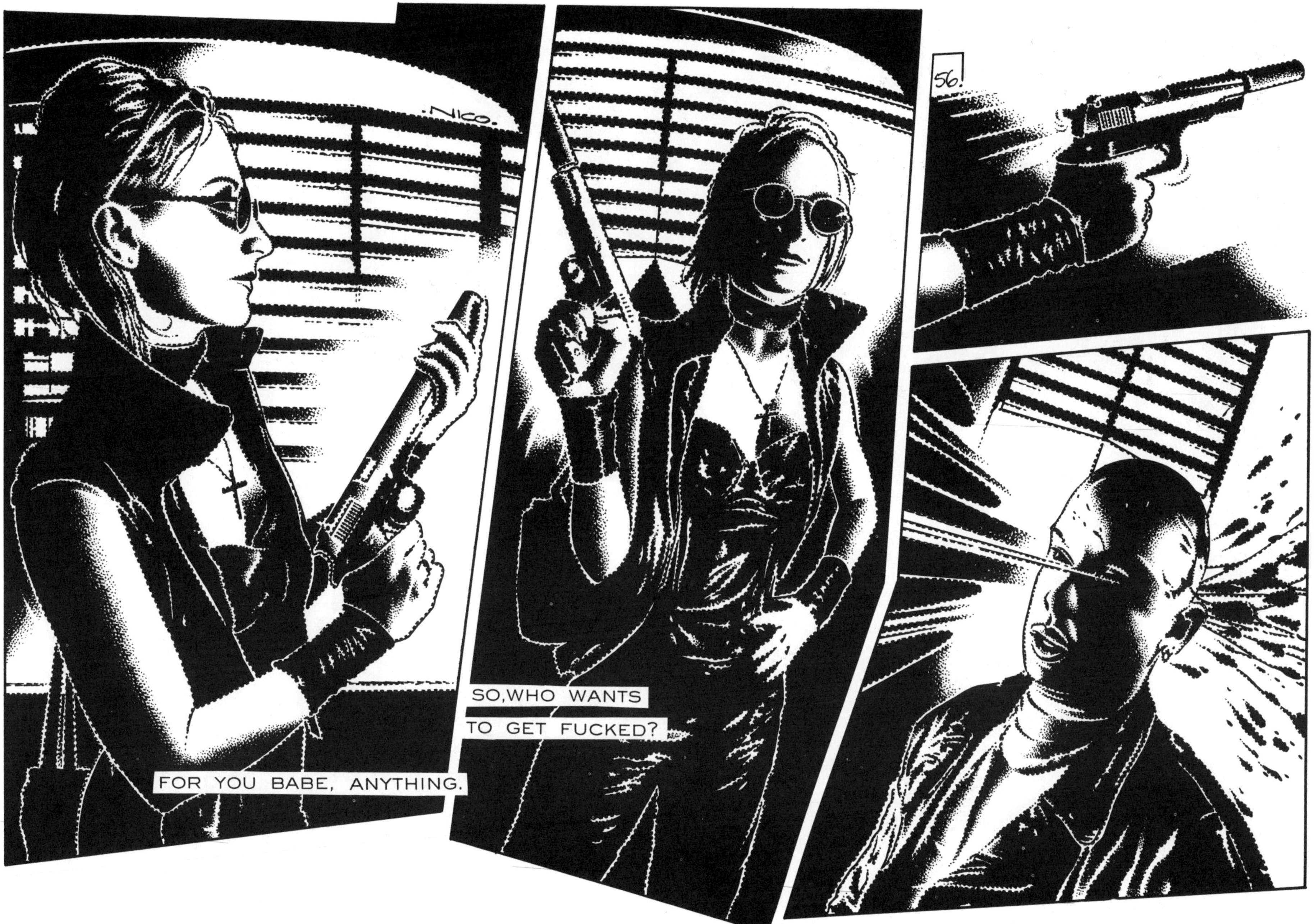
.NICO.
FOR YOU BABE, ANYTHING.
SO,WHO WANTS
TO GET FUCKED?

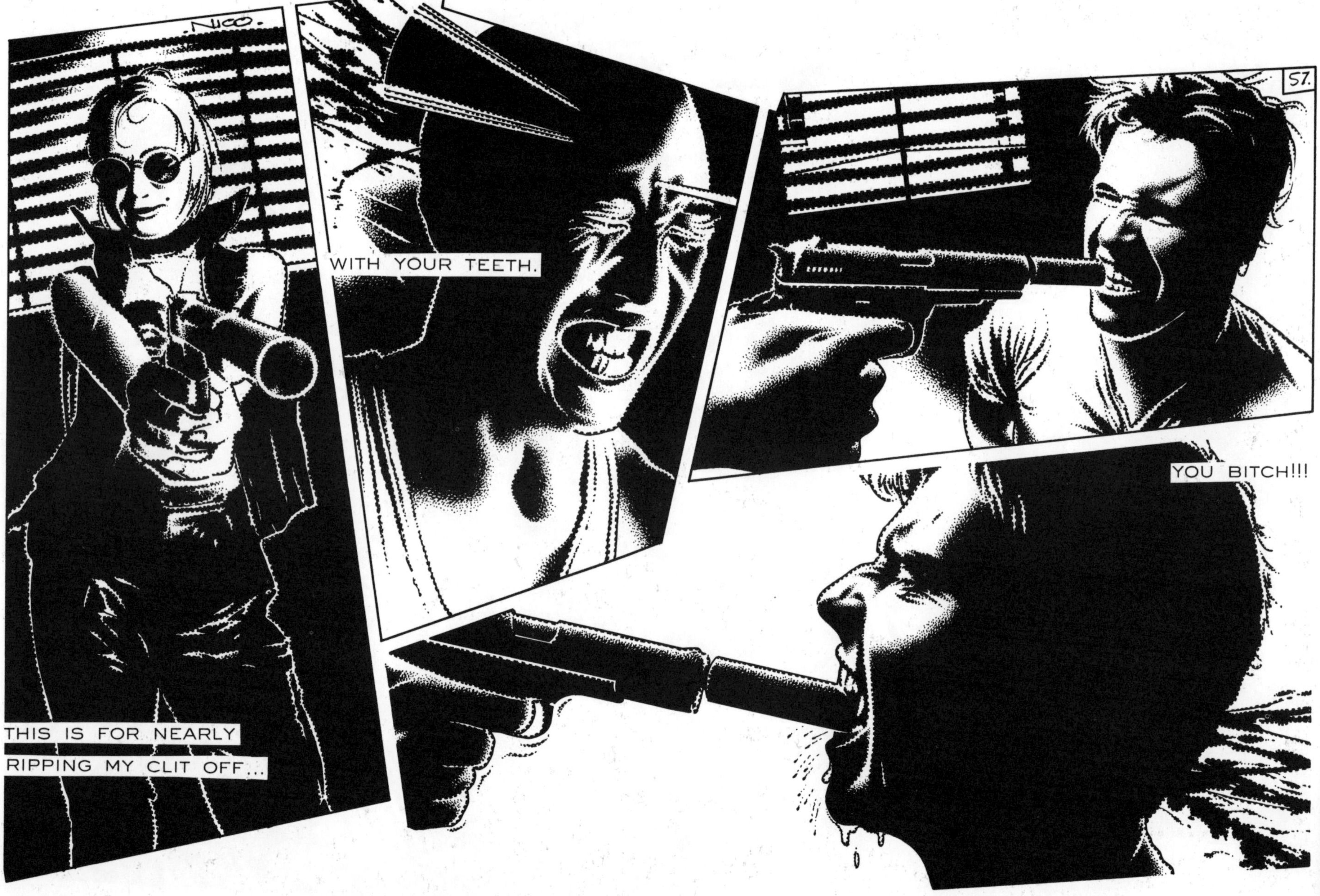

NICO.
57.
THIS IS FOR NEARLY
RIPPING MY CLIT OFF...
WITH YOUR TEETH.
YOU BITCH!!!

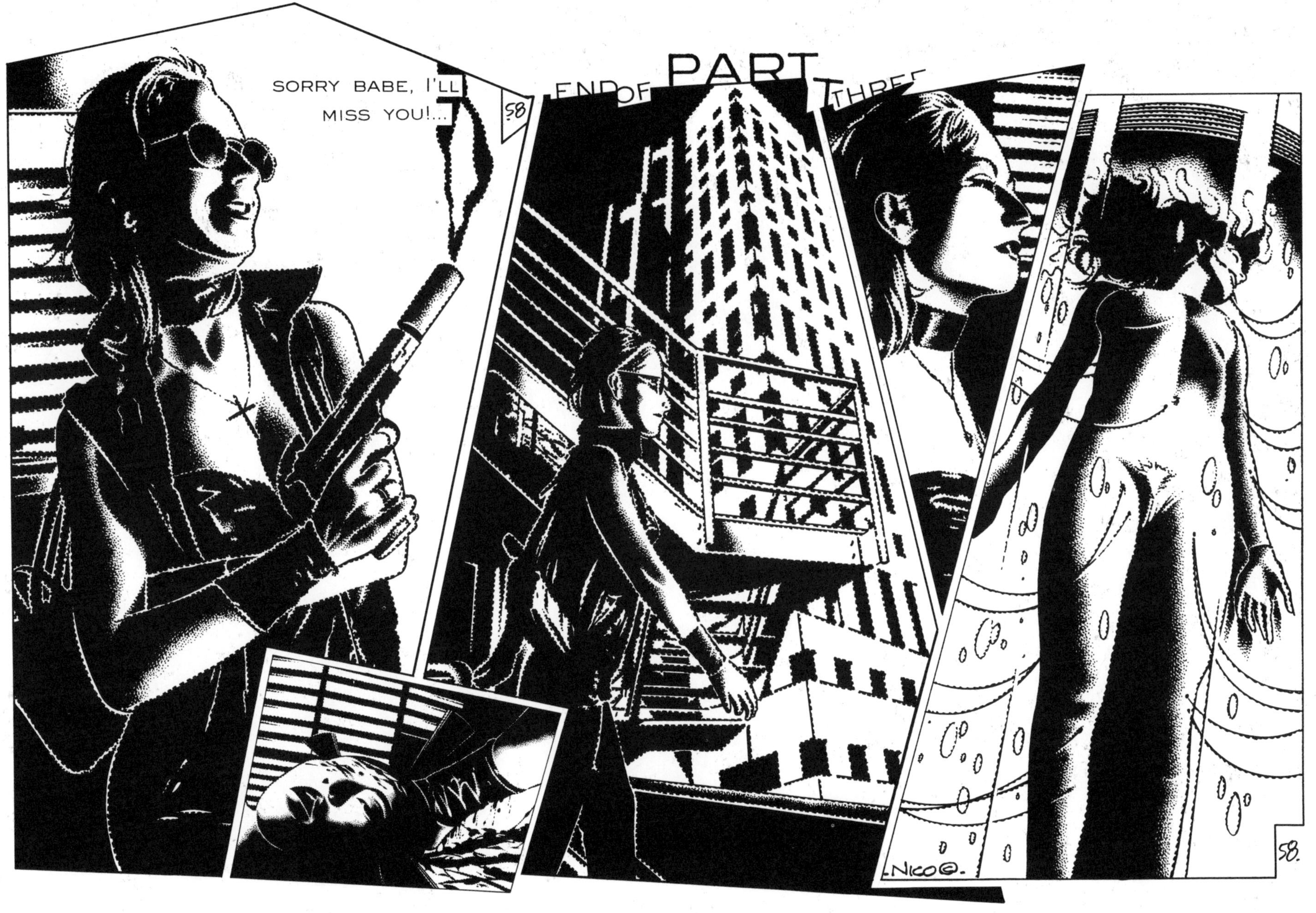
SORRY BABE, I'LL MISS YOU!...
58
END OF PART THREE
NICO©.
58.

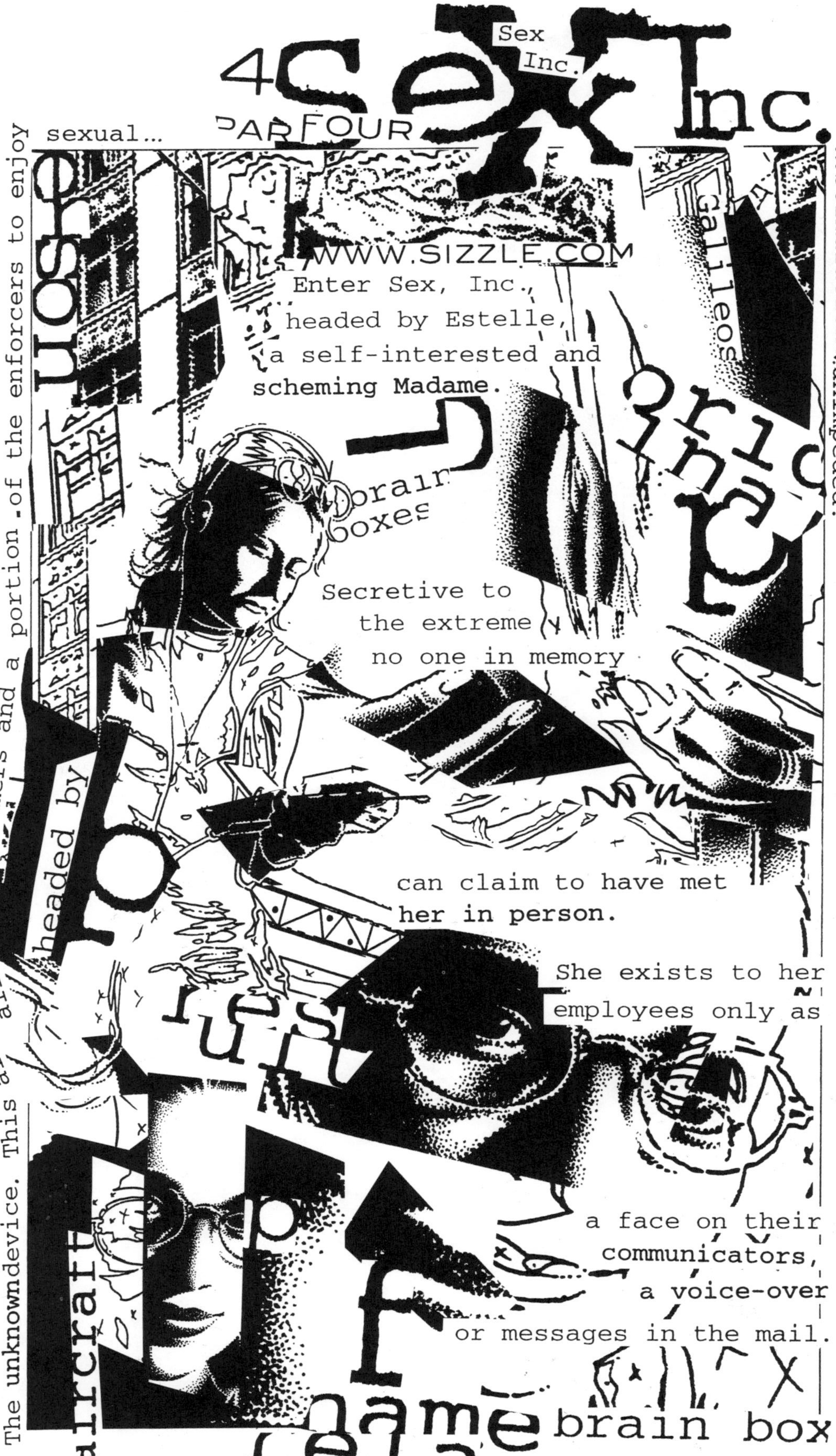
4 Sex Inc.
Sex
Inc.
PART FOUR
sexual...
...stimulation...unimpeded.
WWW.SIZZLE.COM
Enter Sex, Inc.,
headed by Estelle,
a self-interested and
scheming Madame.
Galileos
brain
boxes
Secretive to
the extreme
no one in memory
can claim to have met
her in person.
She exists to her
employees only as
a face on their
communicators,
a voice-over
or messages in the mail.
brain box
headed by
aircraft
The unknowndevice. This allows all of programmers and a portion of the enforcers to enjoy

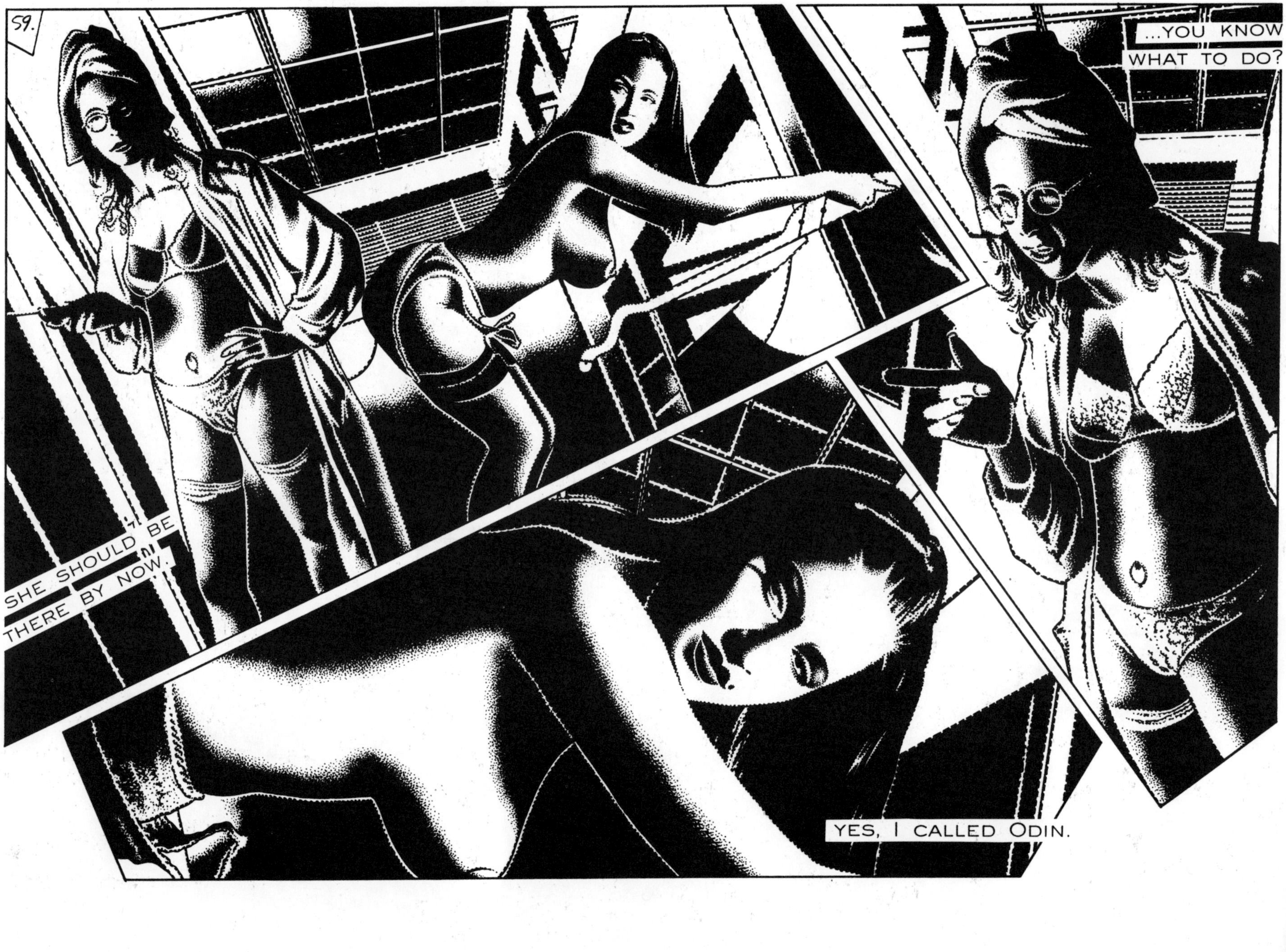
SHE SHOULD BE
THERE BY NOW.
...YOU KNOW
WHAT TO DO?
YES, I CALLED ODIN.

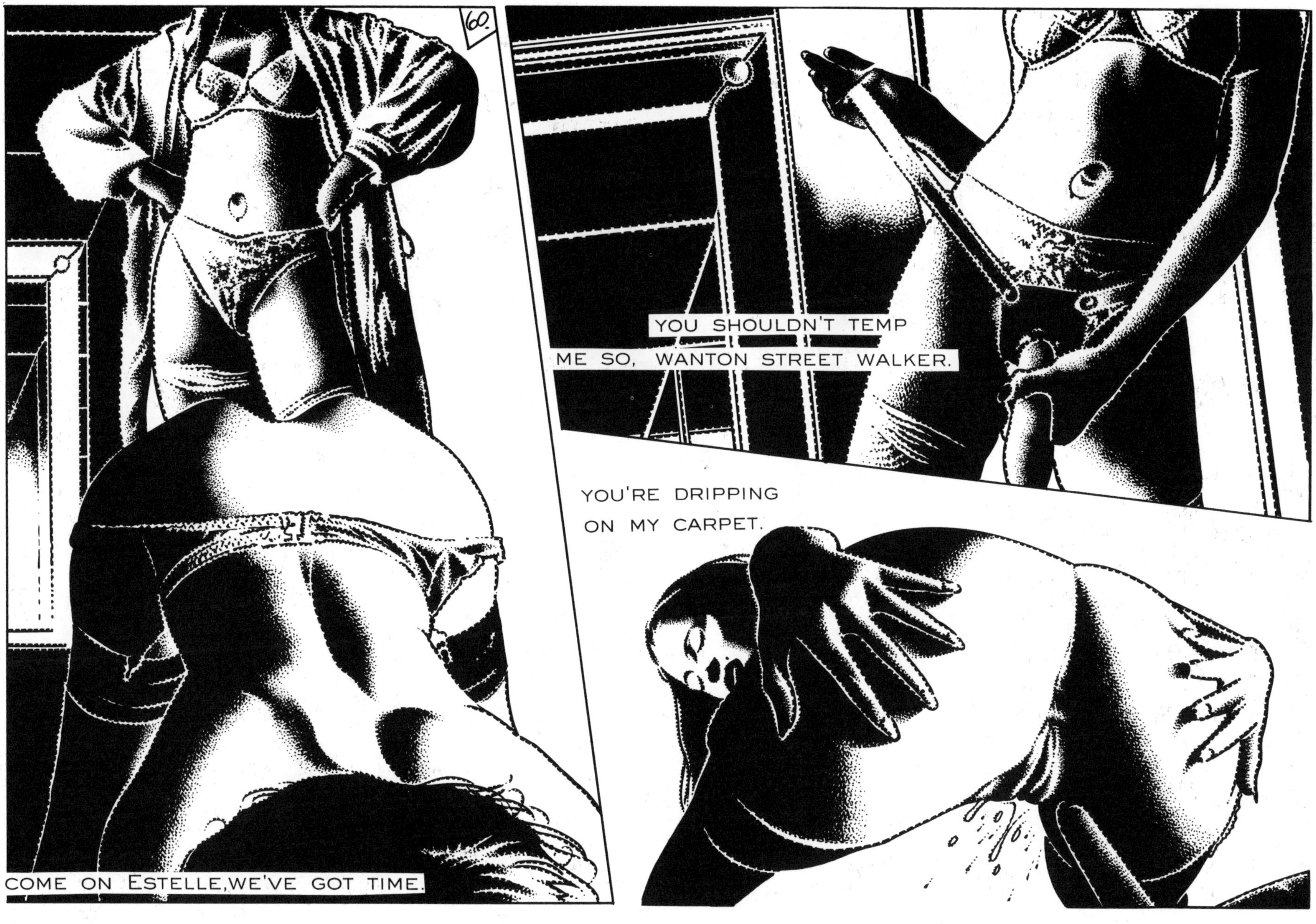
COME ON ESTELLE, WE'VE GOT TIME.
YOU SHOULDN'T TEMP ME SO, WANTON STREET WALKER.
YOU'RE DRIPPING ON MY CARPET.

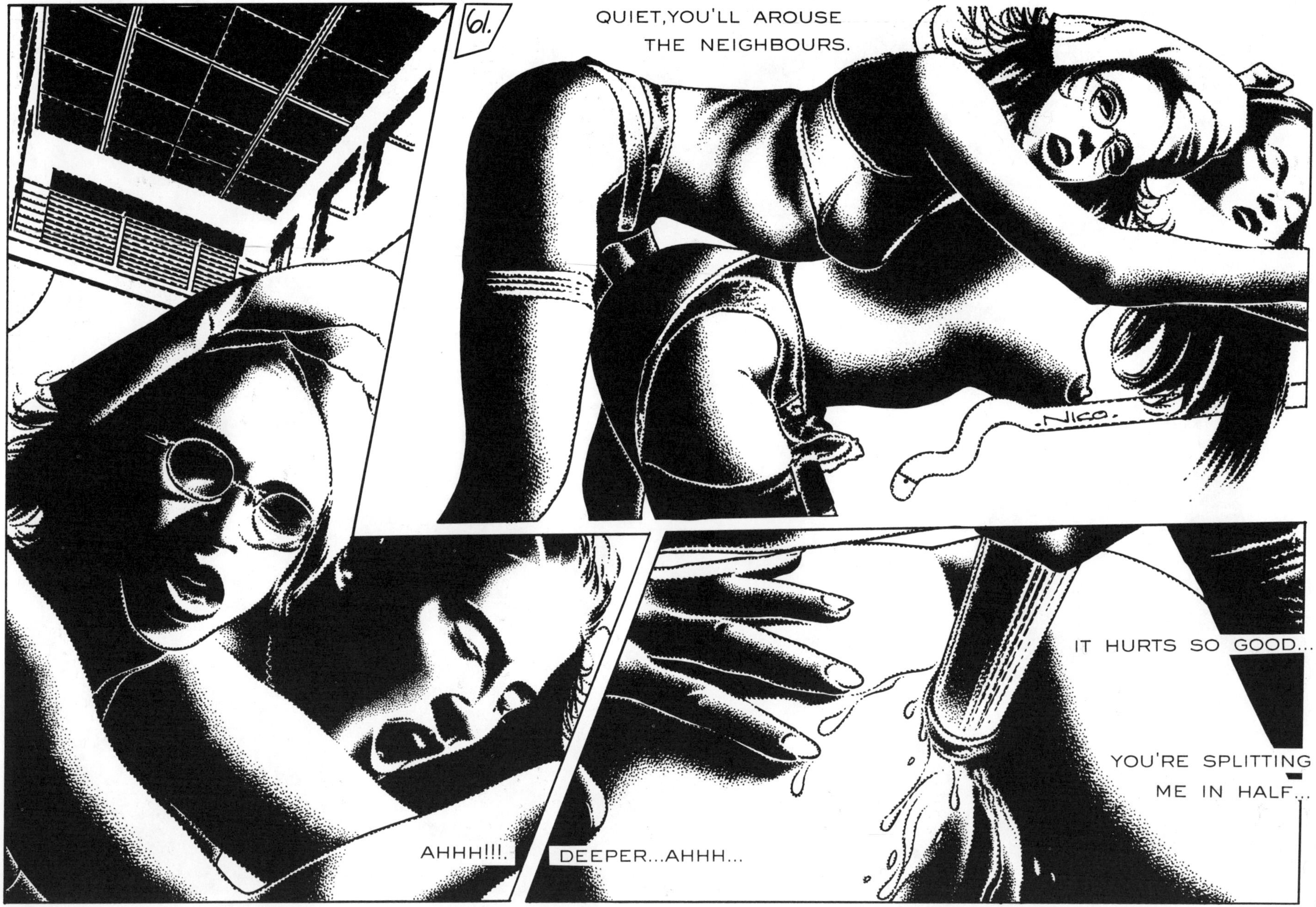
61.
QUIET, YOU'LL AROUSE THE NEIGHBOURS.
.Nico.
AHHH!!!.
DEEPER...AHHH...
IT HURTS SO GOOD...
YOU'RE SPLITTING ME IN HALF...

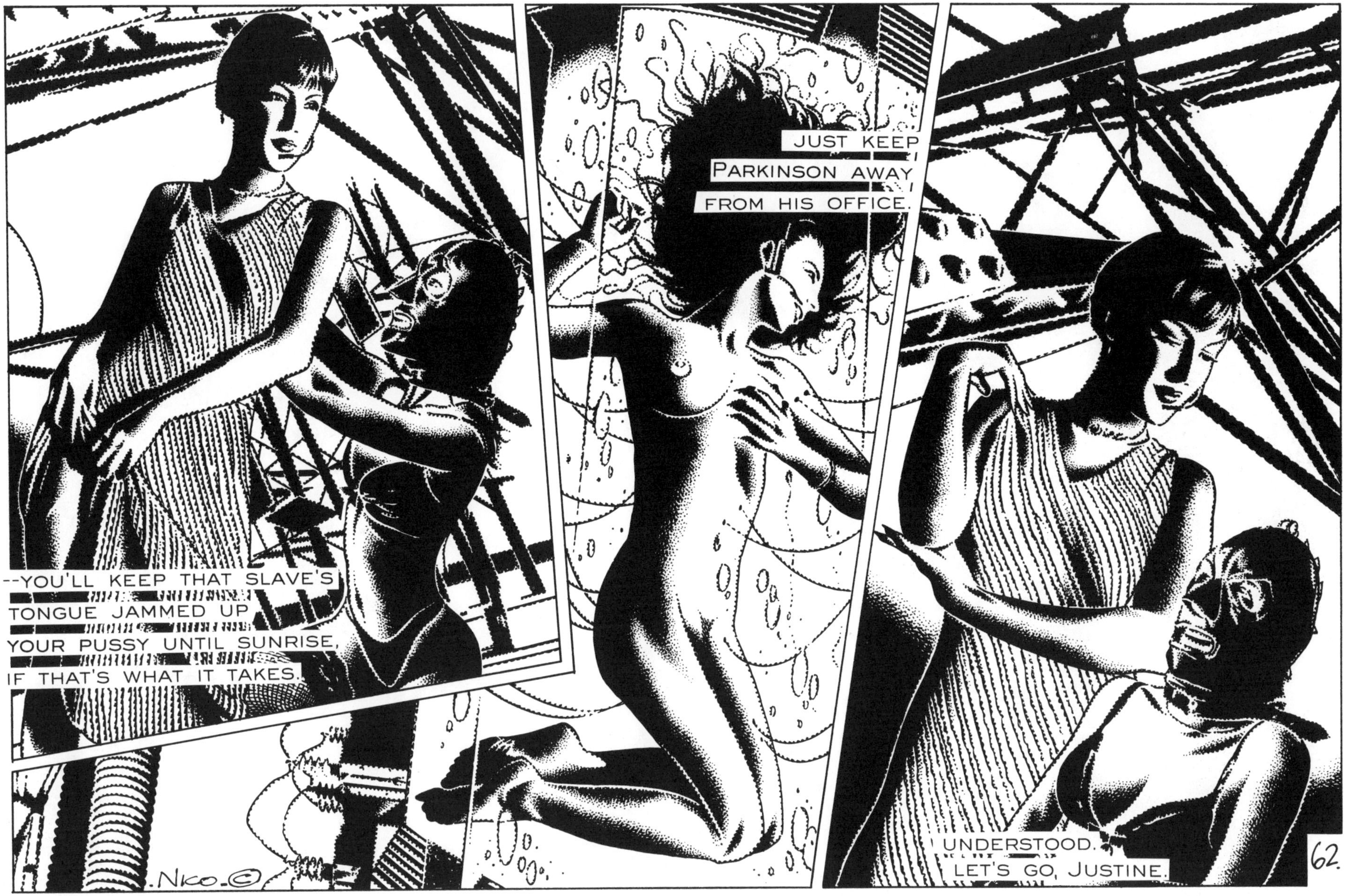
--YOU'LL KEEP THAT SLAVE'S
TONGUE JAMMED UP
YOUR PUSSY UNTIL SUNRISE,
IF THAT'S WHAT IT TAKES.
.NKO.©
JUST KEEP
PARKINSON AWAY
FROM HIS OFFICE.
UNDERSTOOD.
LET'S GO, JUSTINE.

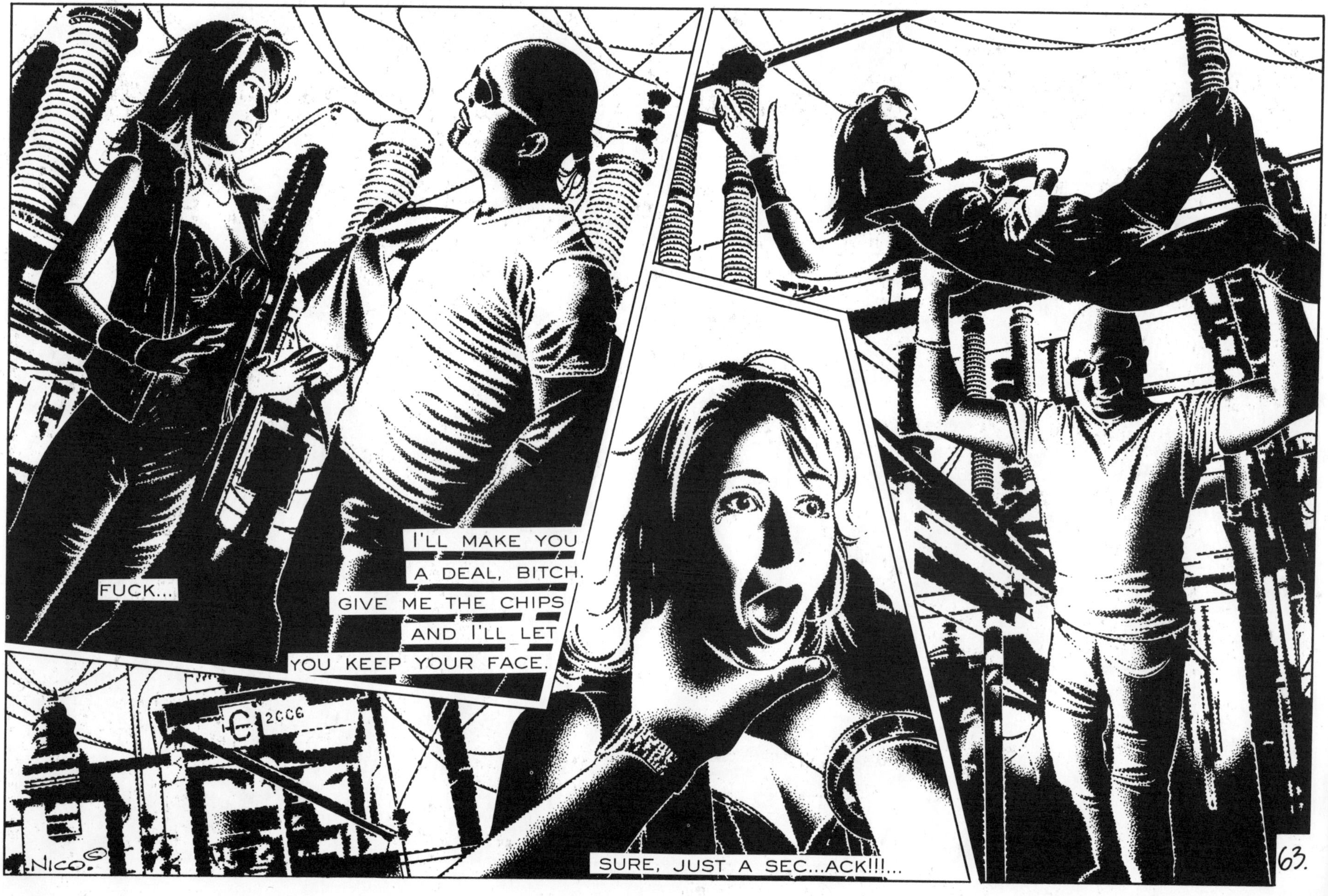
FUCK...
I'LL MAKE YOU A DEAL, BITCH. GIVE ME THE CHIPS AND I'LL LET YOU KEEP YOUR FACE.
SURE, JUST A SEC...ACK!!!...
NICO ©
© 2006

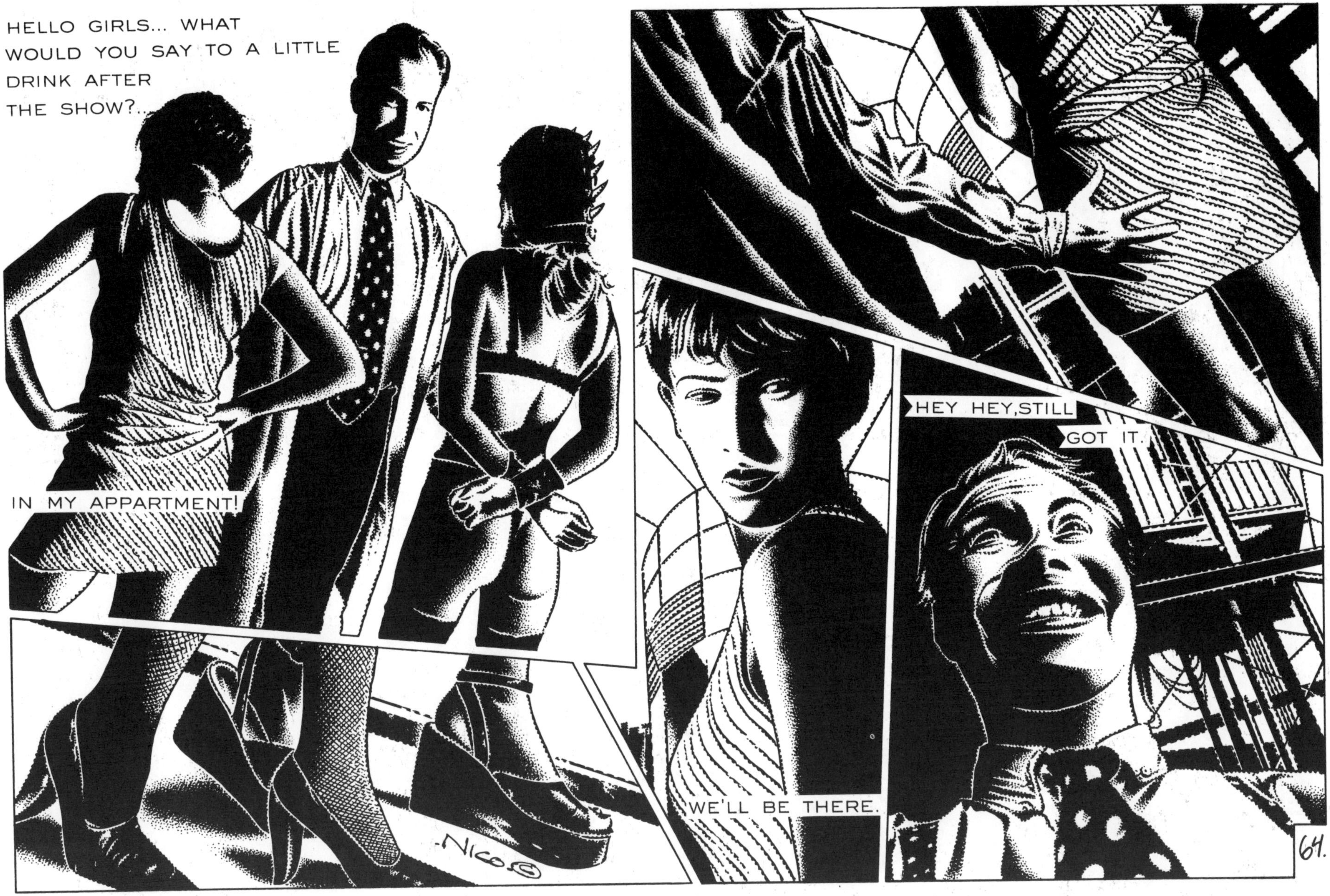
HELLO GIRLS... WHAT WOULD YOU SAY TO A LITTLE DRINK AFTER THE SHOW?...
IN MY APPARTMENT!
WE'LL BE THERE.
HEY HEY, STILL
GOT IT.
NICO©
64.

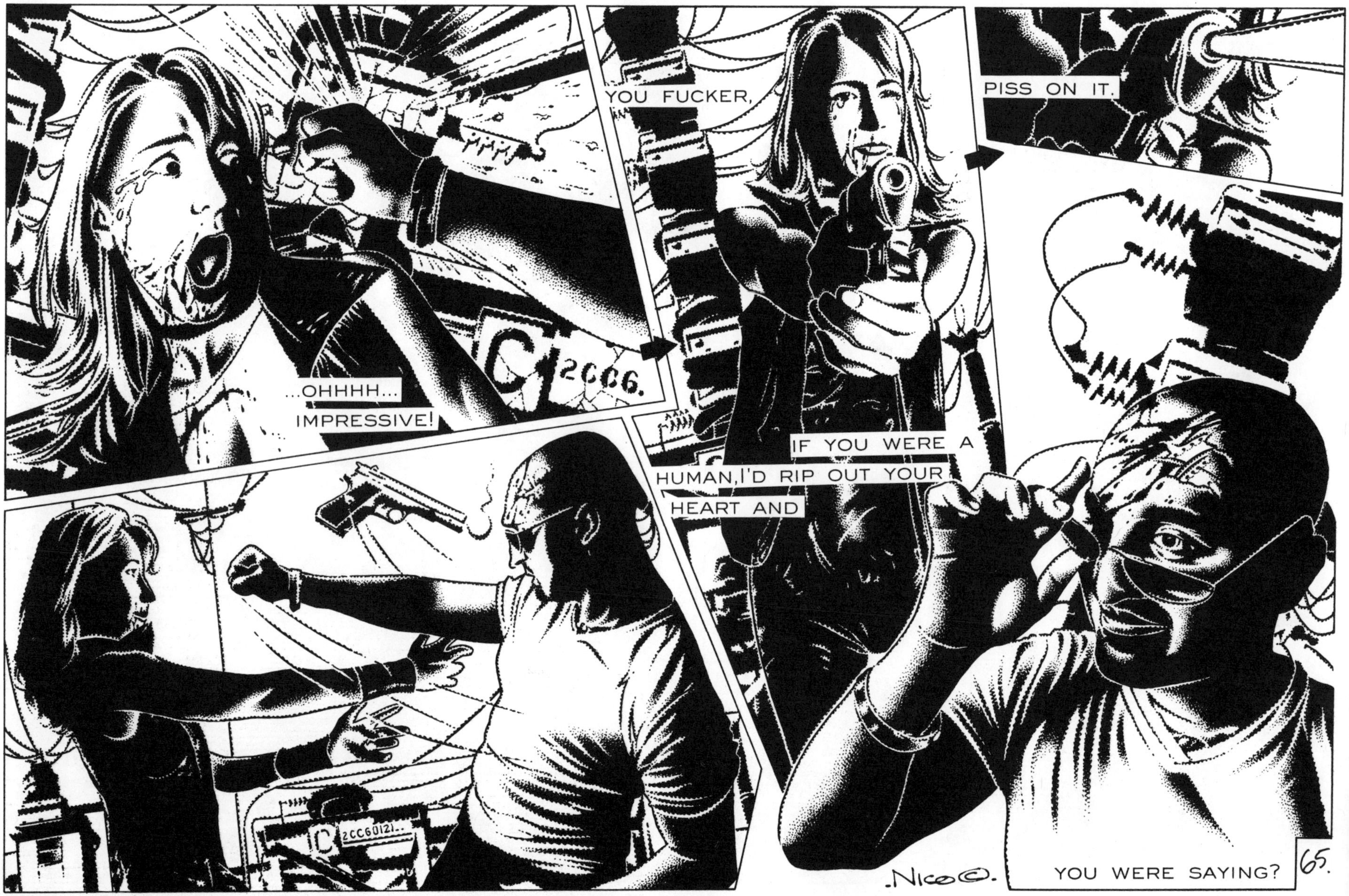
...OHHHH...
IMPRESSIVE!
C 2CC6.
YOU FUCKER,
IF YOU WERE A
HUMAN, I'D RIP OUT YOUR
HEART AND
PISS ON IT.
YOU WERE SAYING?
.NICO©.

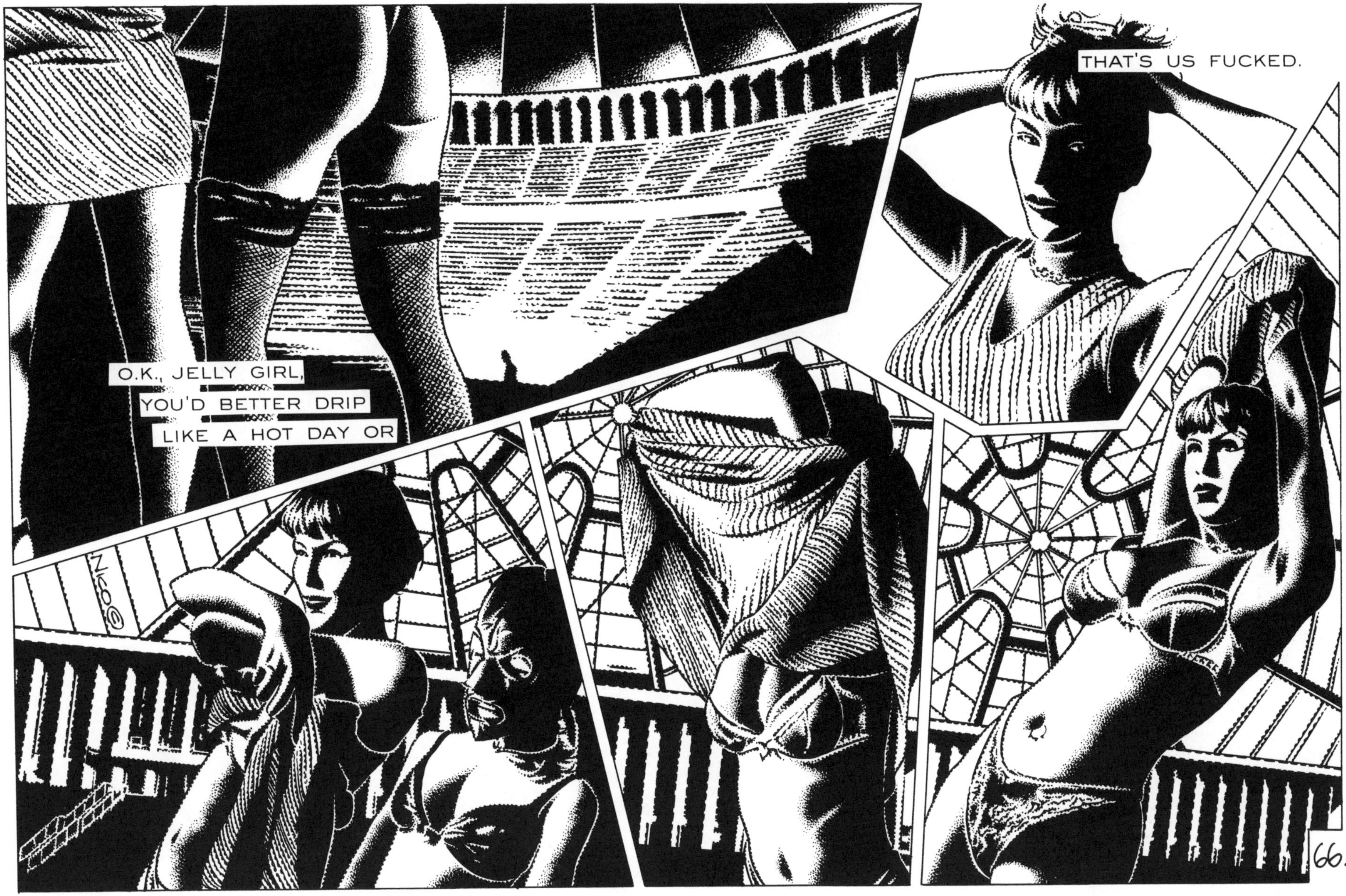
O.K., JELLY GIRL,
YOU'D BETTER DRIP
LIKE A HOT DAY OR
THAT'S US FUCKED.
66.

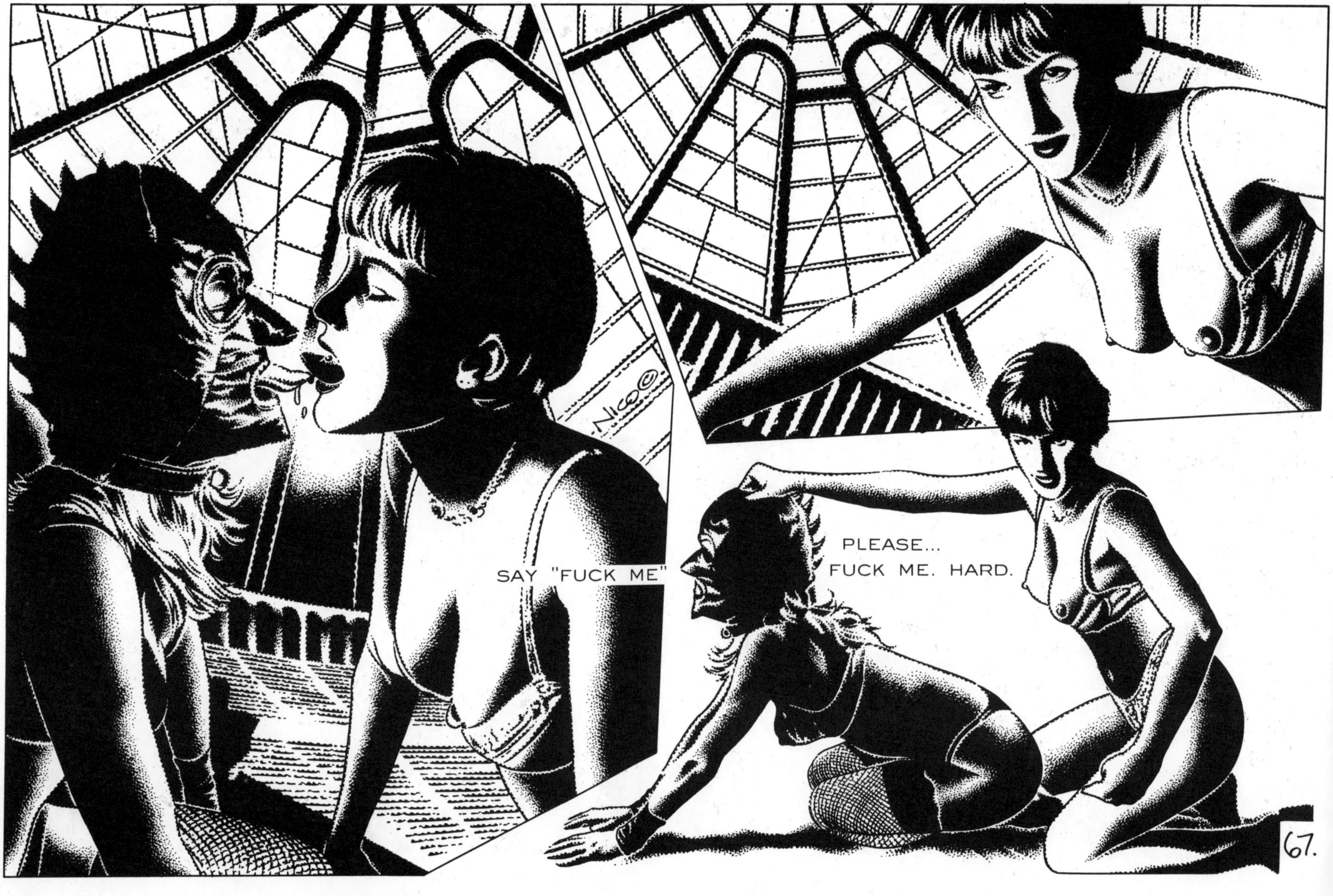
SAY "FUCK ME"
PLEASE...
FUCK ME. HARD.

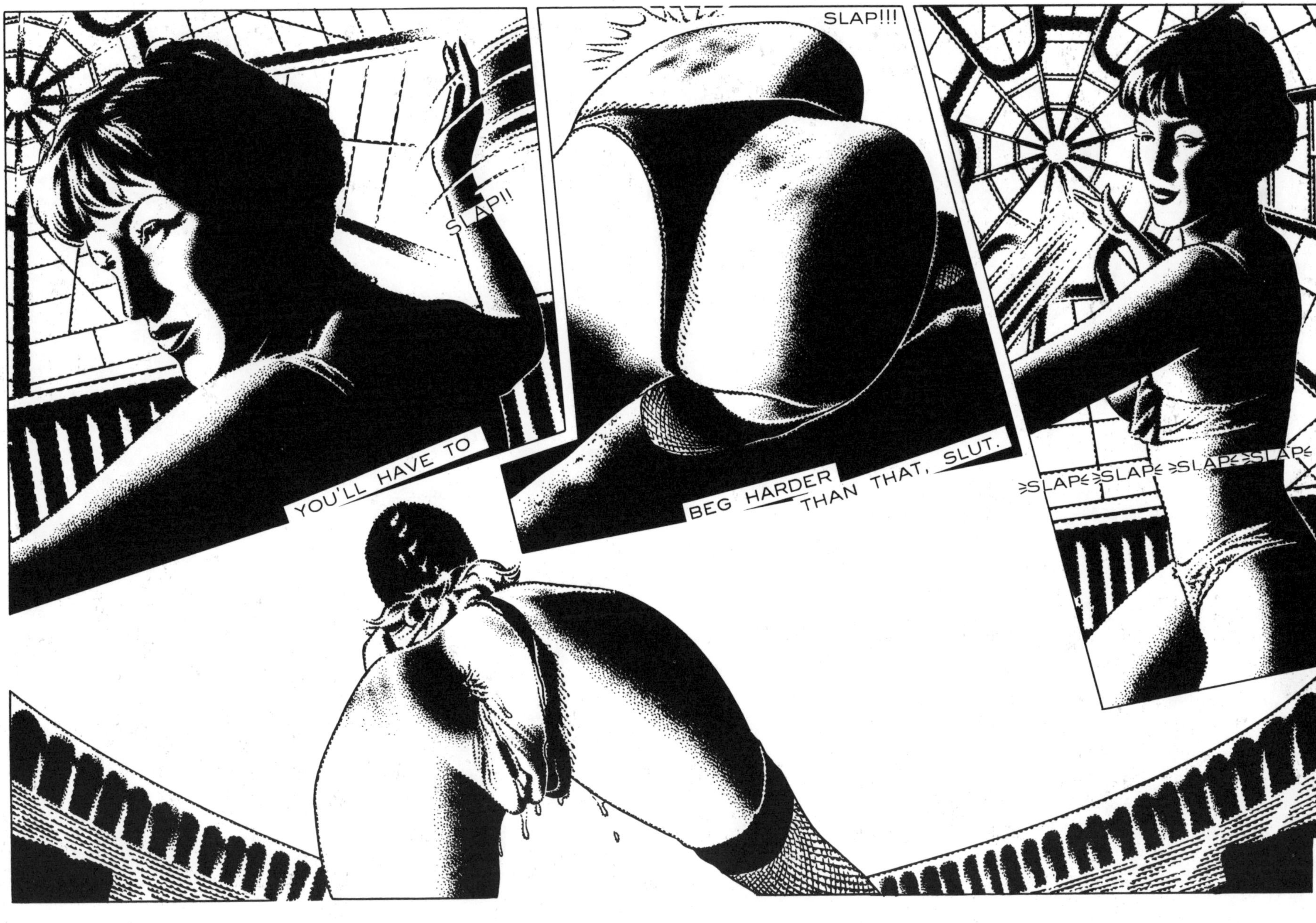
SLAP!!
YOU'LL HAVE TO
SLAP!!!
BEG HARDER THAN THAT, SLUT.
SLAP SLAP SLAP SLAP

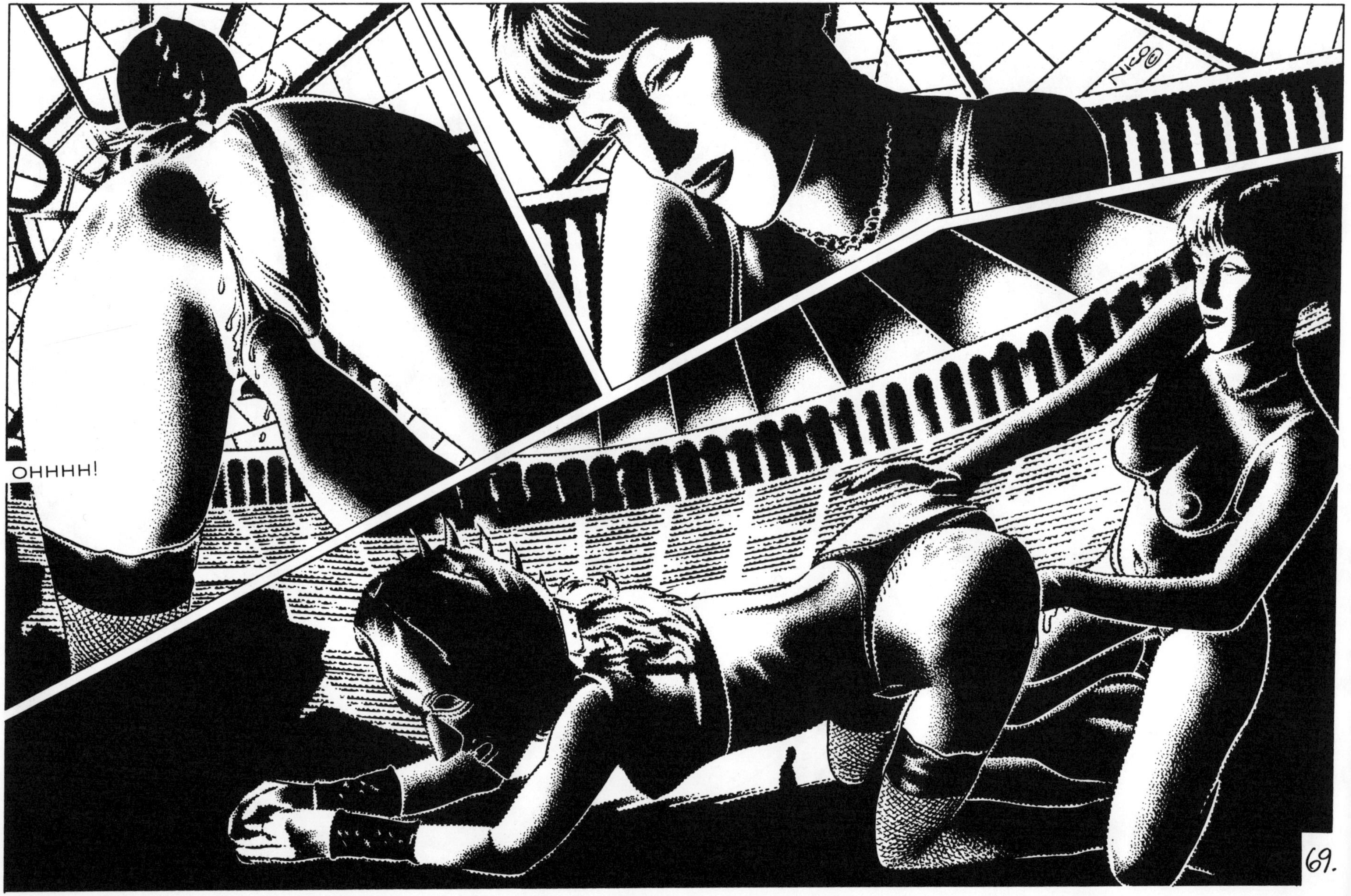
OHHHH!

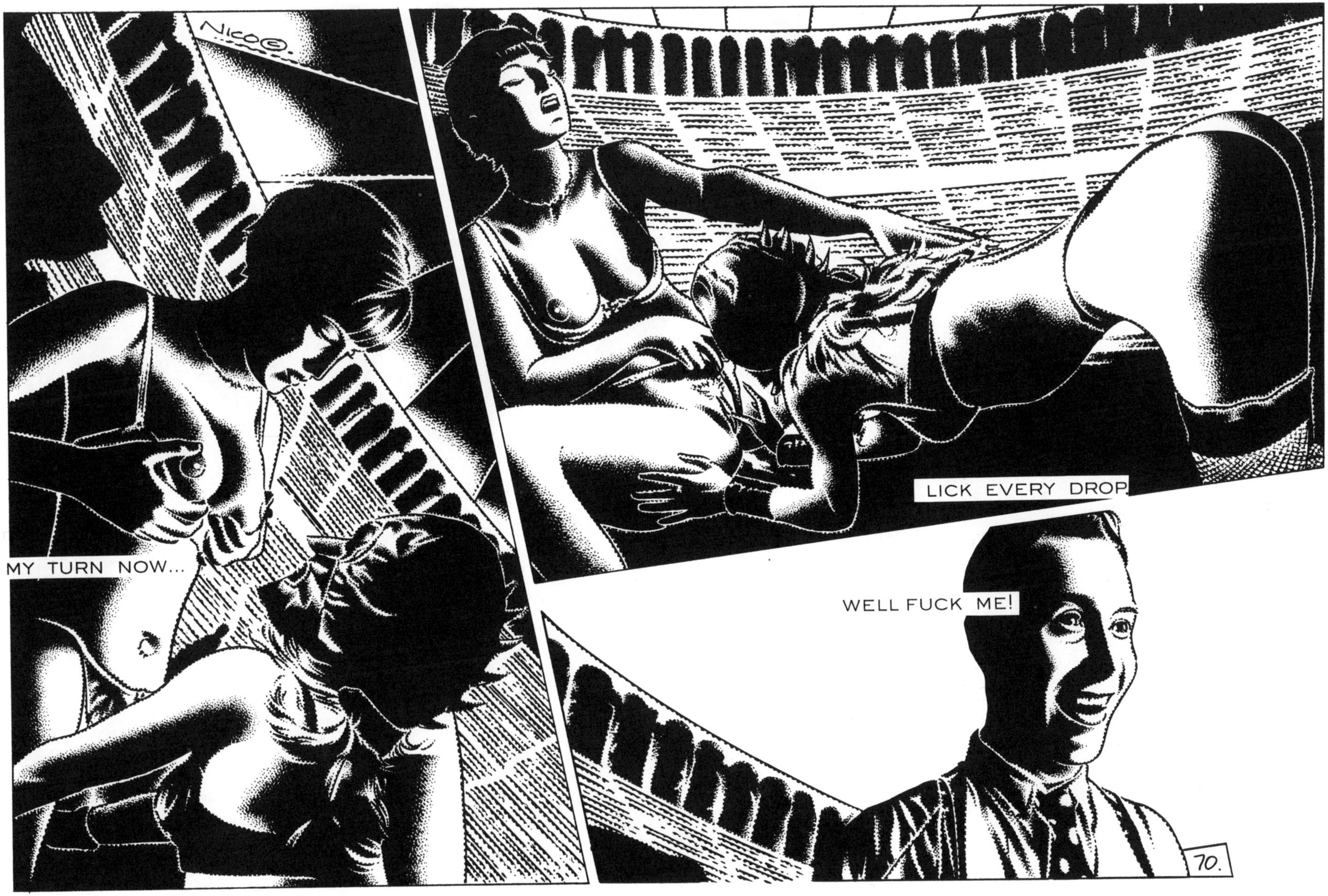
MY TURN NOW...
LICK EVERY DROP
WELL FUCK ME!

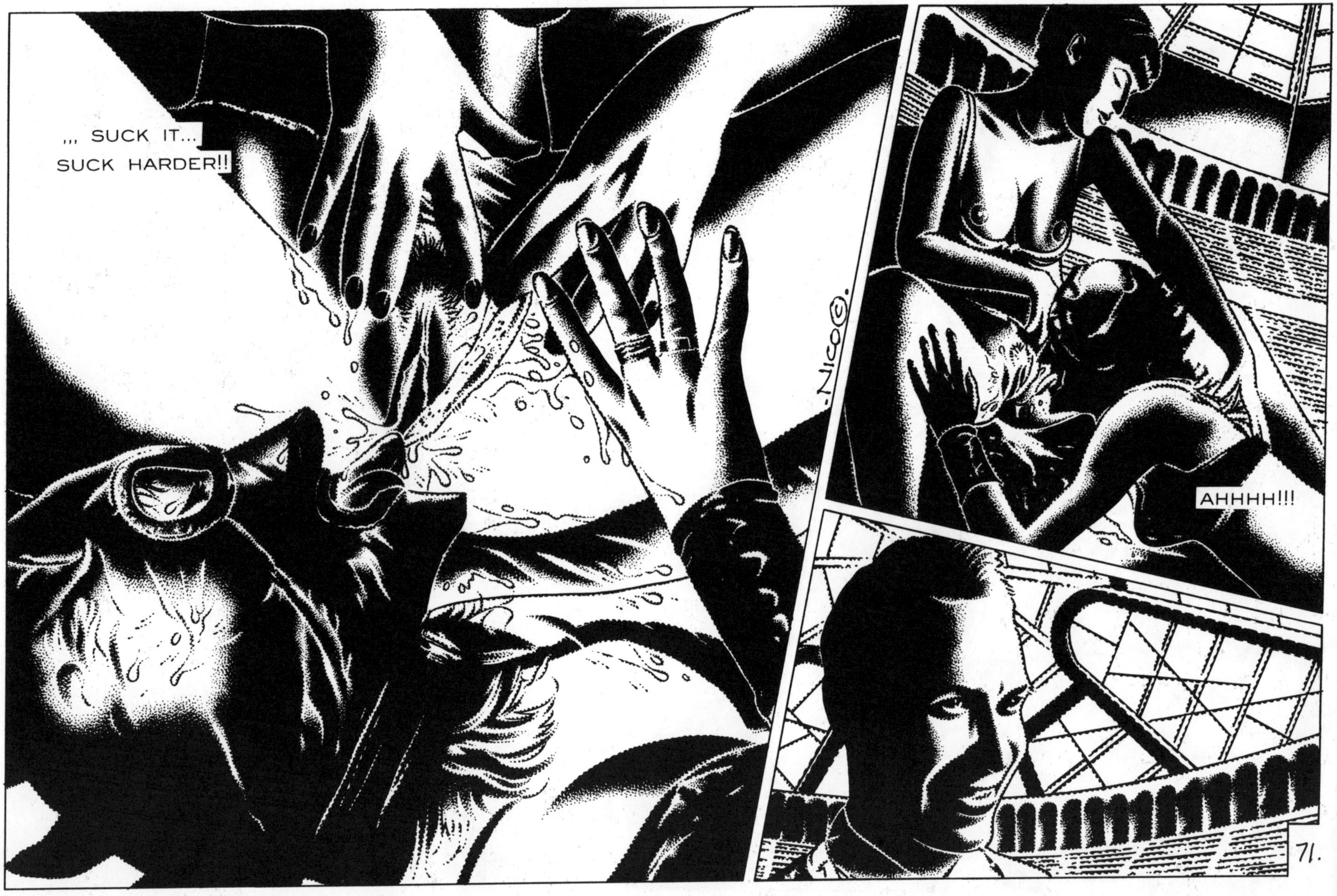
,,, SUCK IT...
SUCK HARDER!!
AHHHH!!!

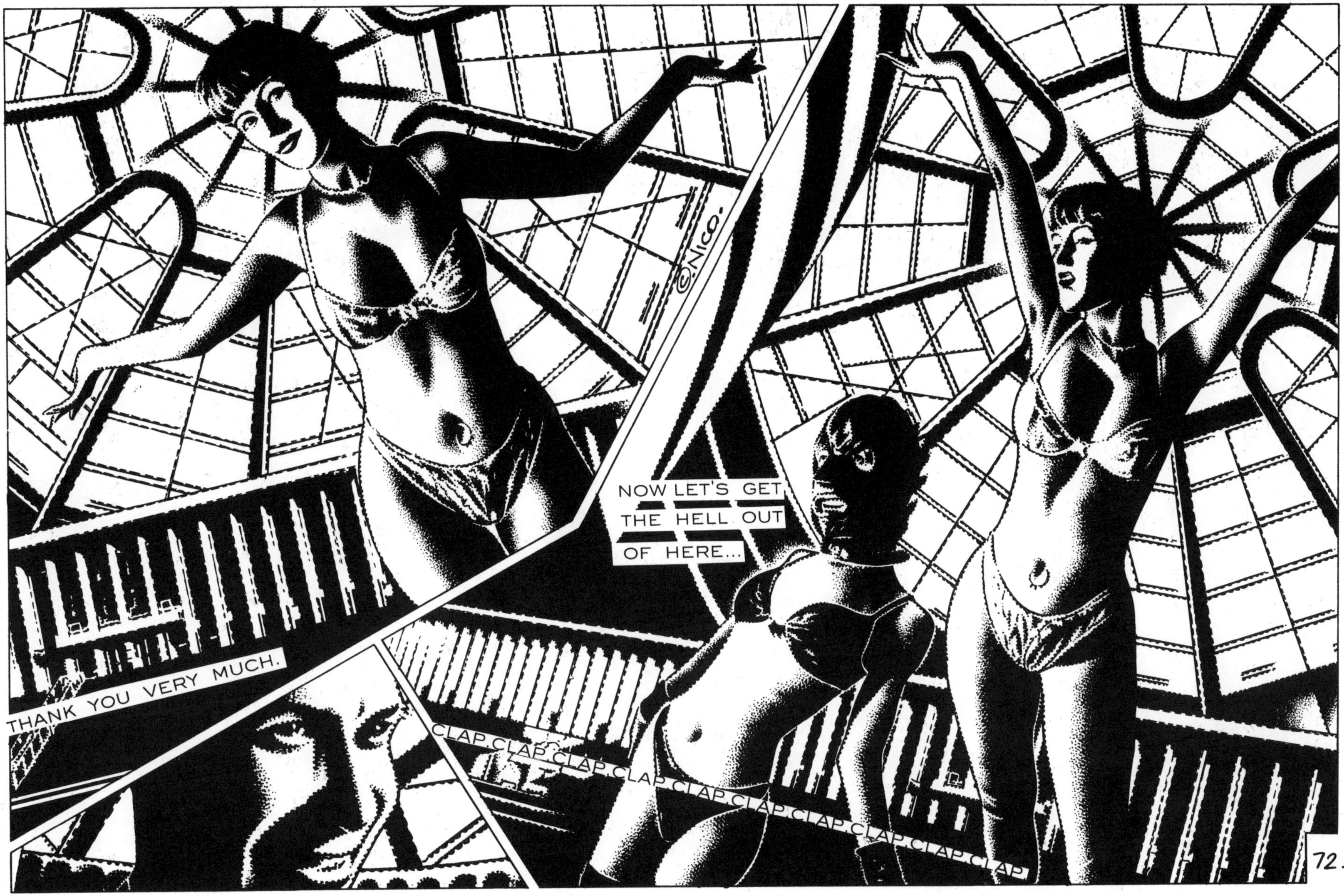
©Nico.
THANK YOU VERY MUCH.
NOW LET'S GET THE HELL OUT OF HERE...
CLAP.CLAP.CLAP.CLAP.CLAP.CLAP.CLAP.CLAP.CLAP.CLAP.CLAP

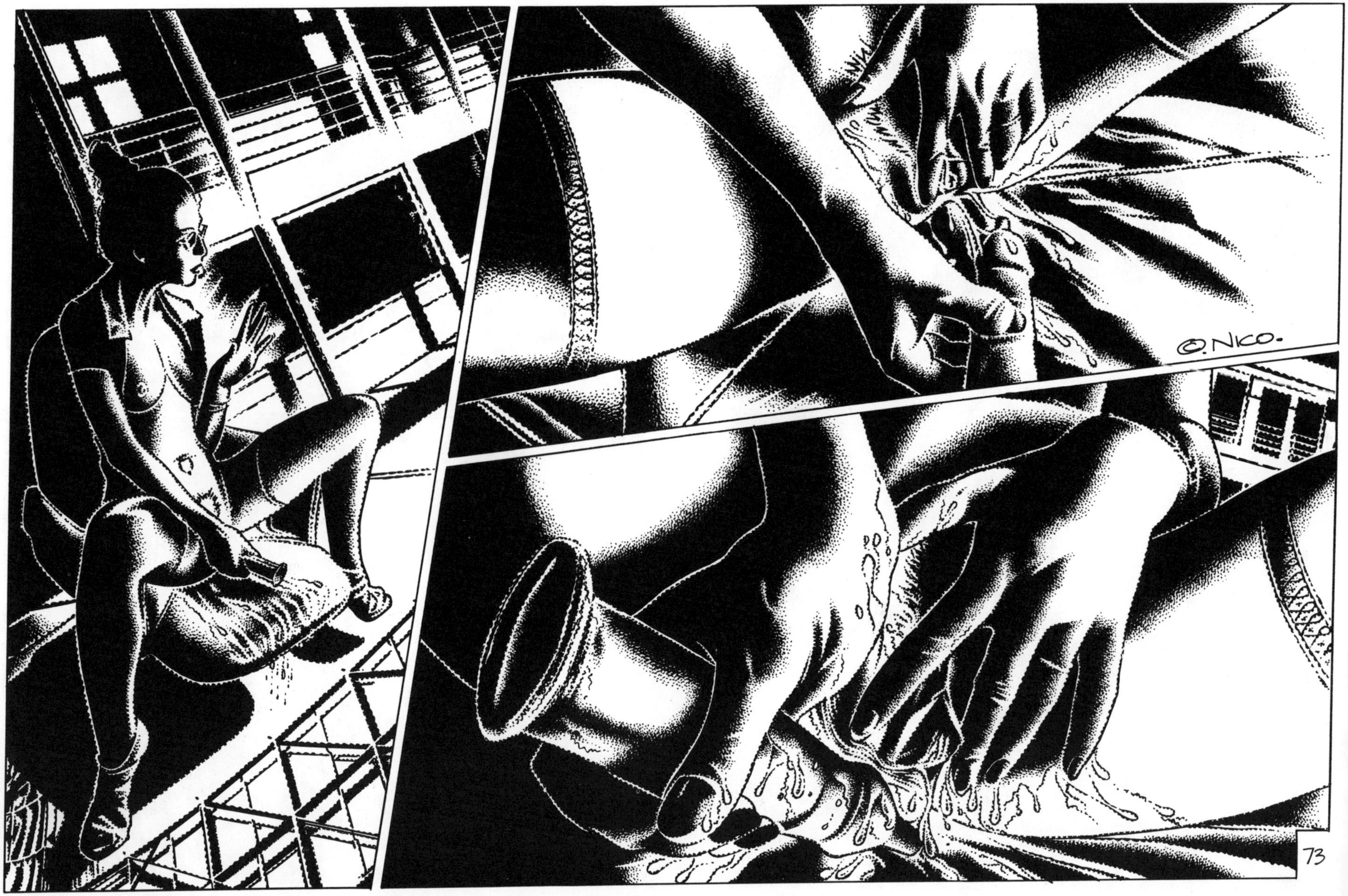
©.NKO.

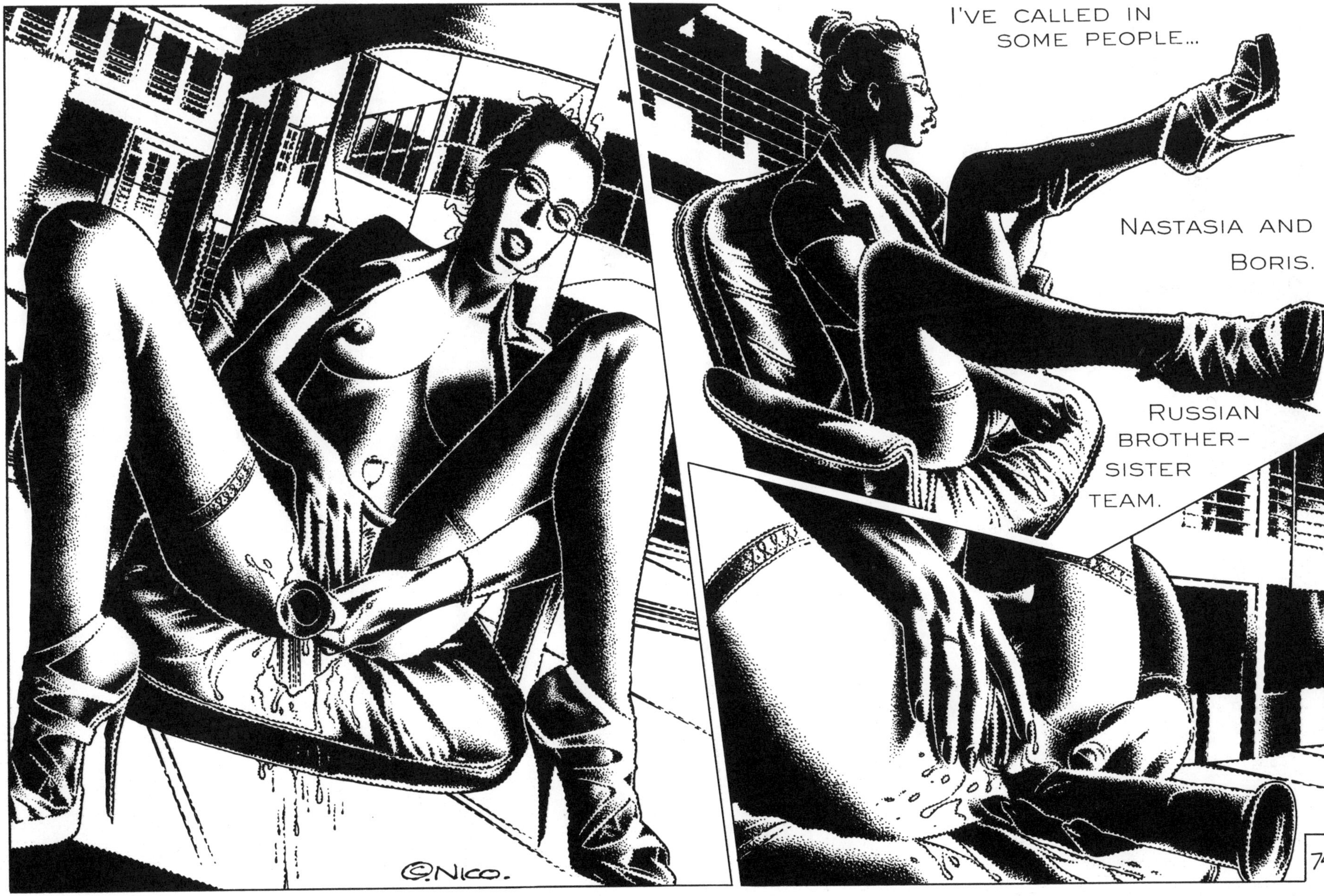
I'VE CALLED IN SOME PEOPLE...
NASTASIA AND BORIS.
RUSSIAN BROTHER-SISTER TEAM.
©NICO.

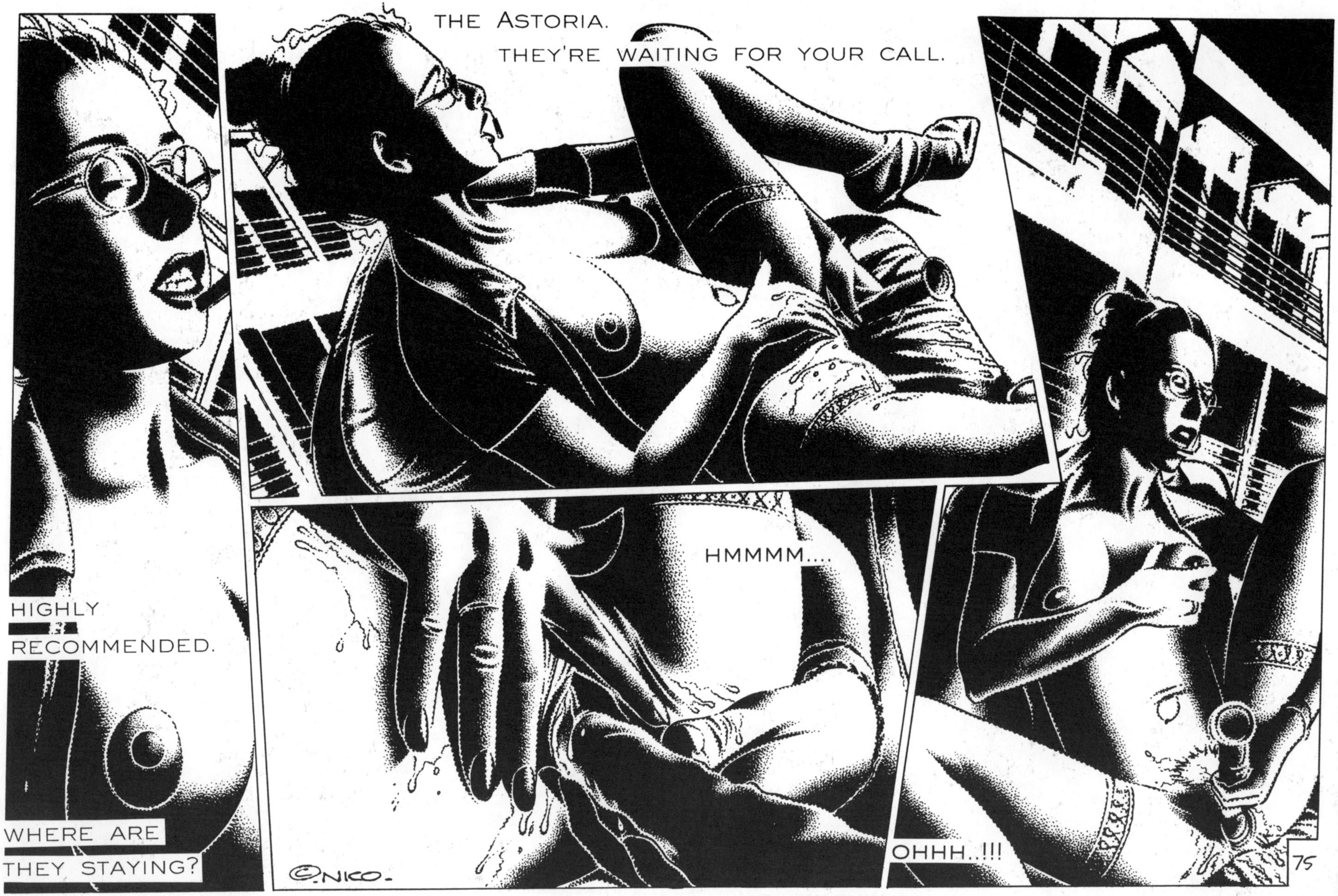
HIGHLY
RECOMMENDED.
WHERE ARE
THEY STAYING?
THE ASTORIA.
THEY'RE WAITING FOR YOUR CALL.
HMMMM....
OHHH..!!!
©NICO

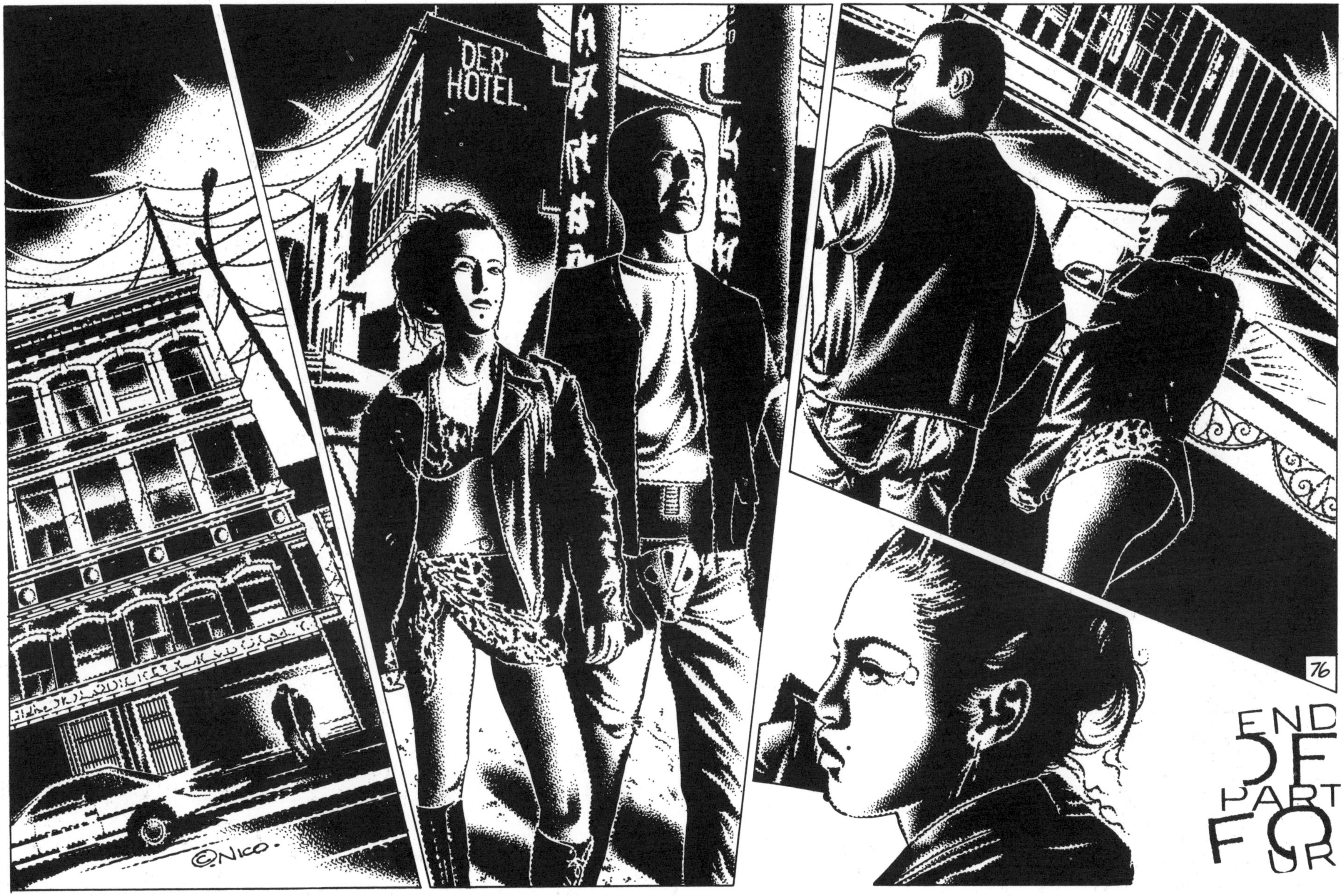
DER' HOTEL
©NICO
76
END OF PART FOUR

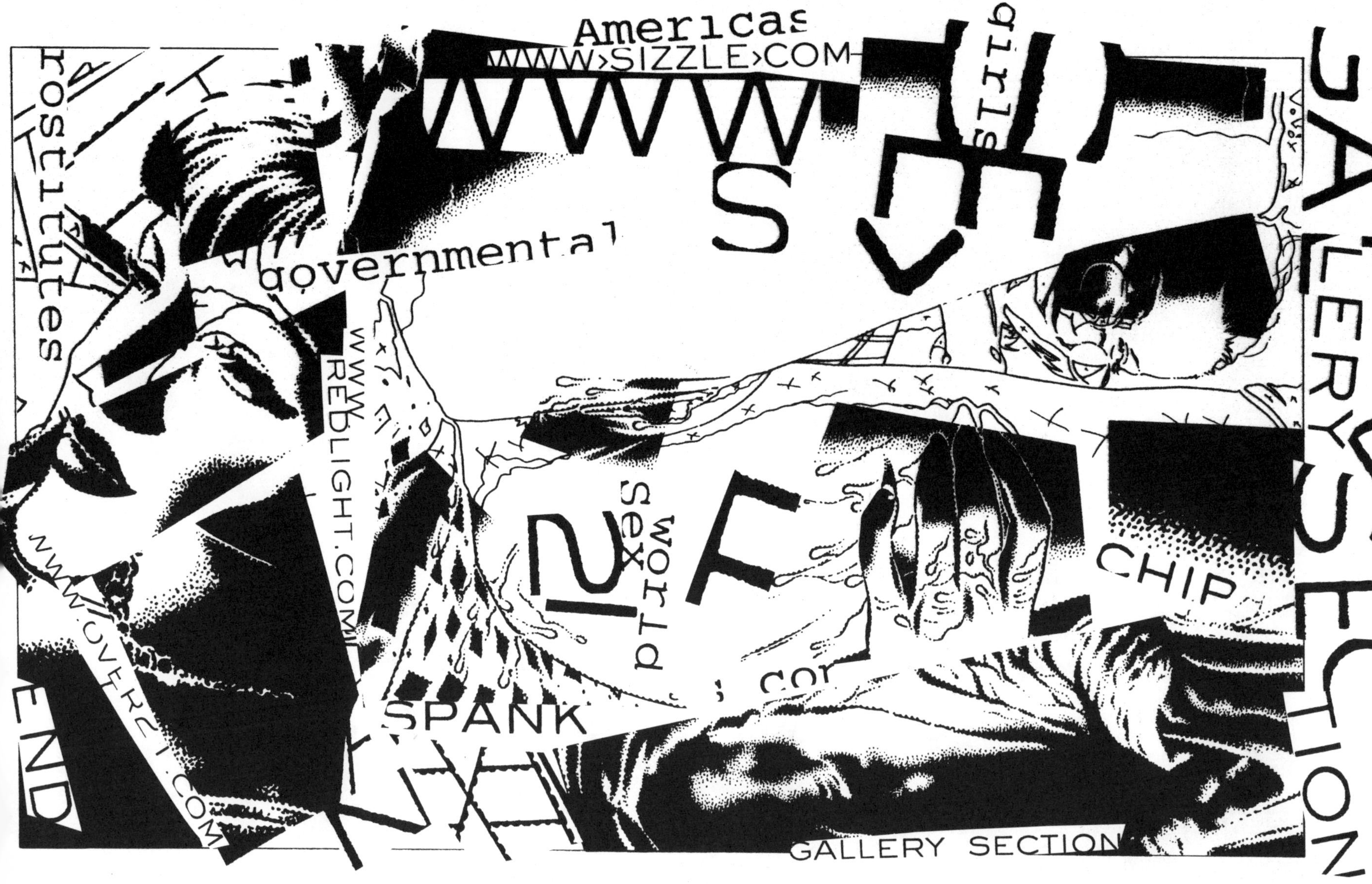
Americas
WWW›SIZZLE›COM
girls
GALLERY SECTION
governmental
rostitutes
WWW
REDLIGHT.COM
world
sex
CHIP
SPANK
WWW.OVER21.COM
END
GALLERY SECTION

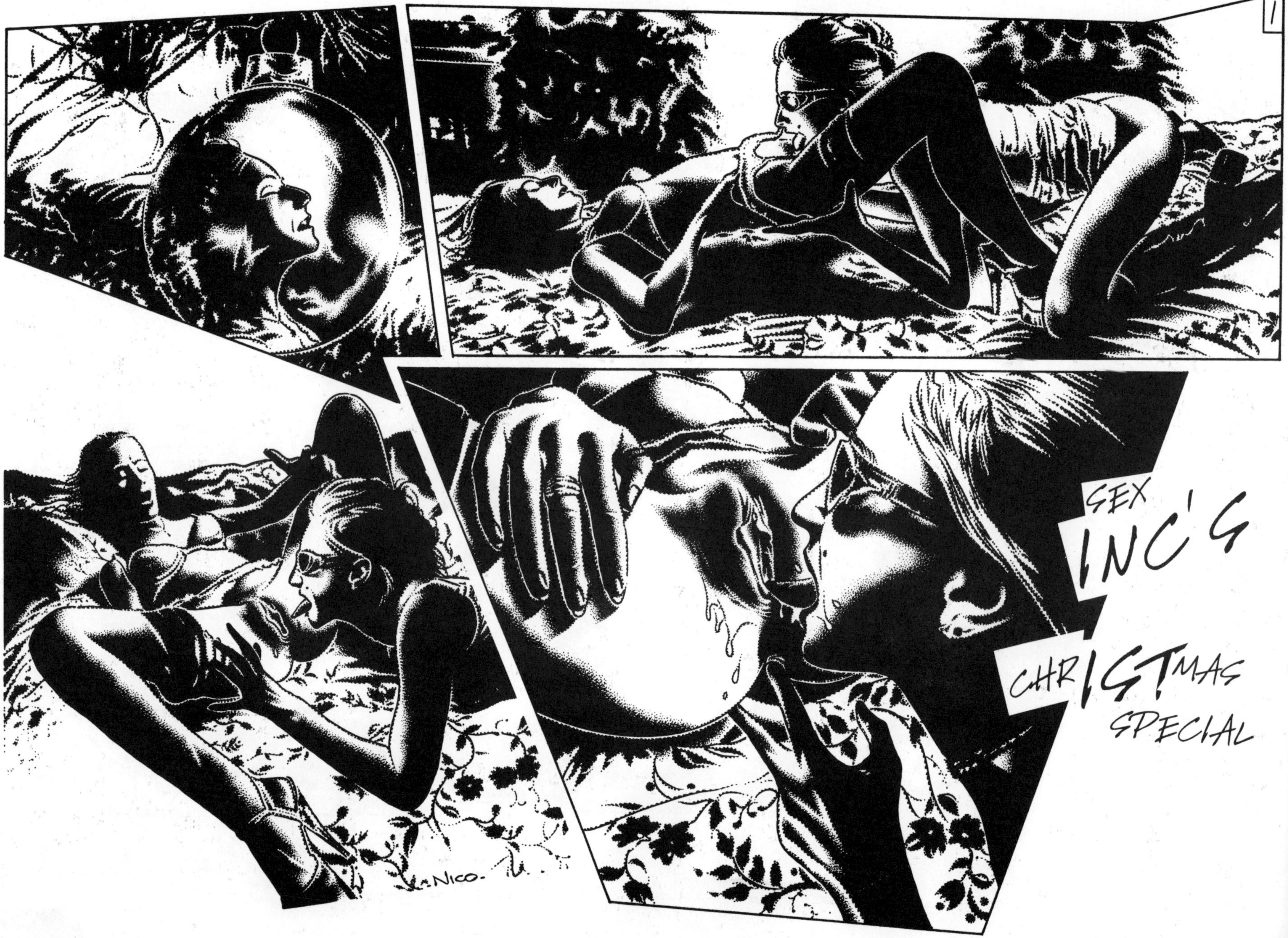
1
SEX
INC'S
CHRISTMAS
SPECIAL
NICO

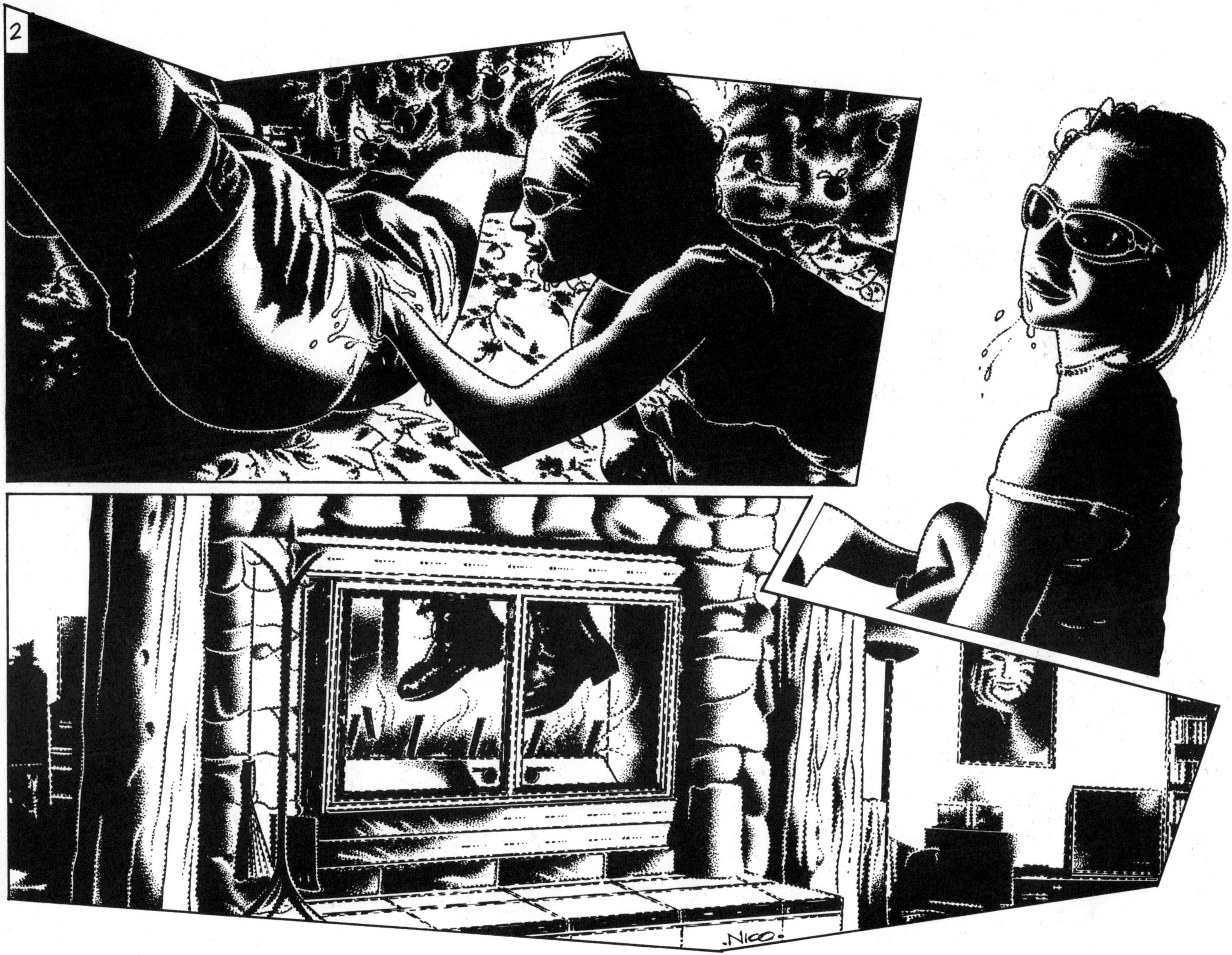
2
NICO

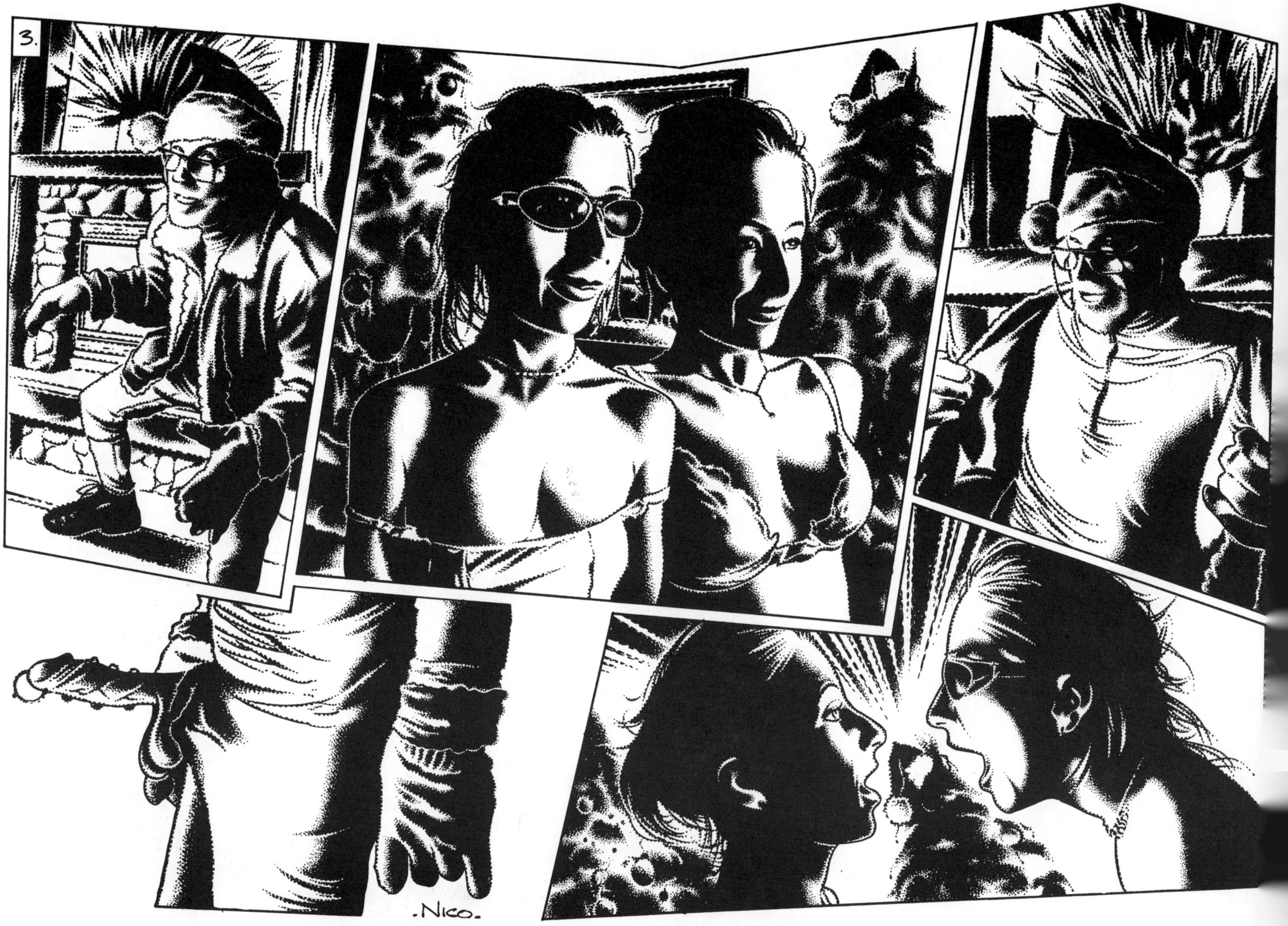
3.
·NICO·

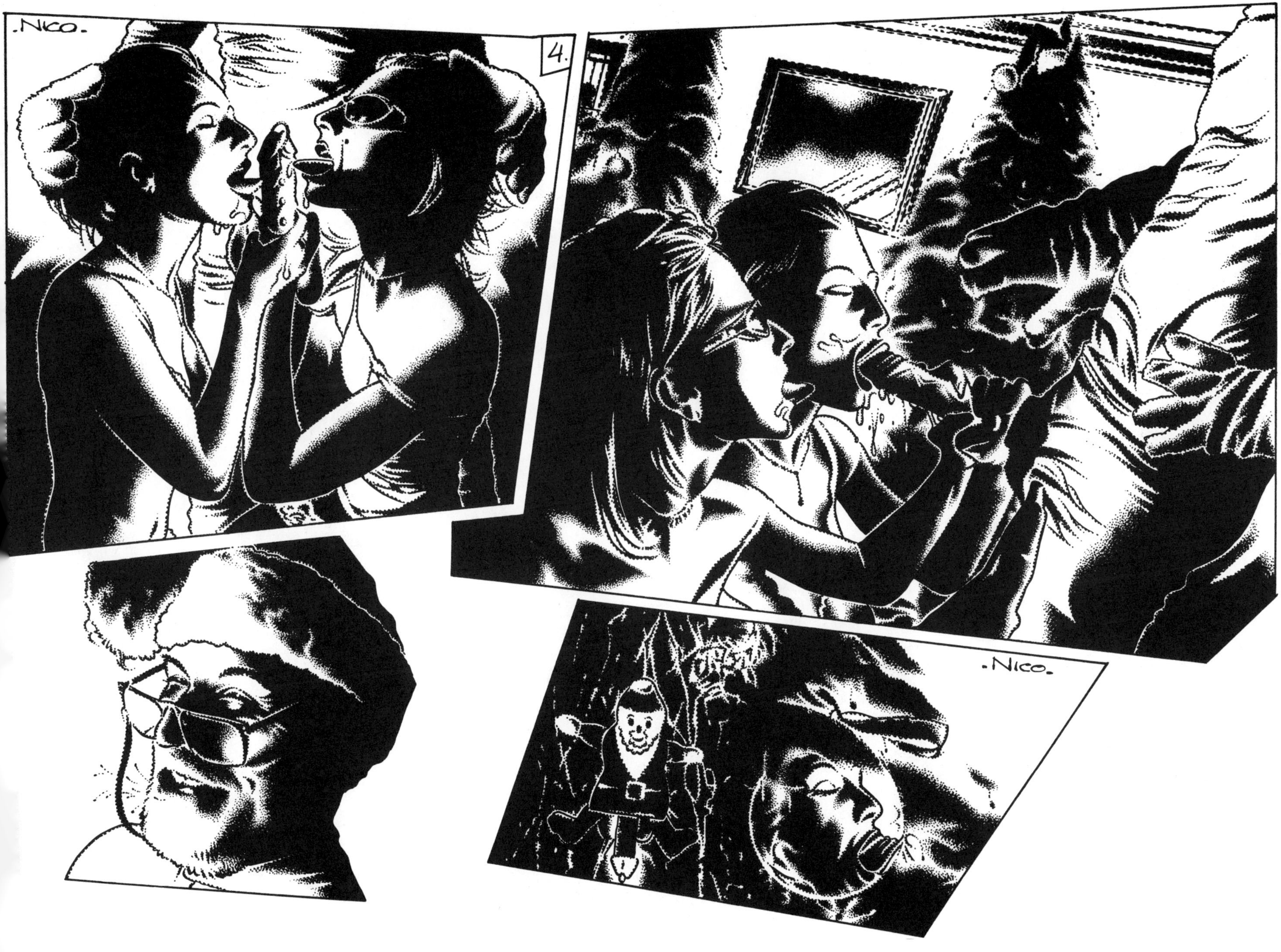
.NICO.
4.
.Nico.

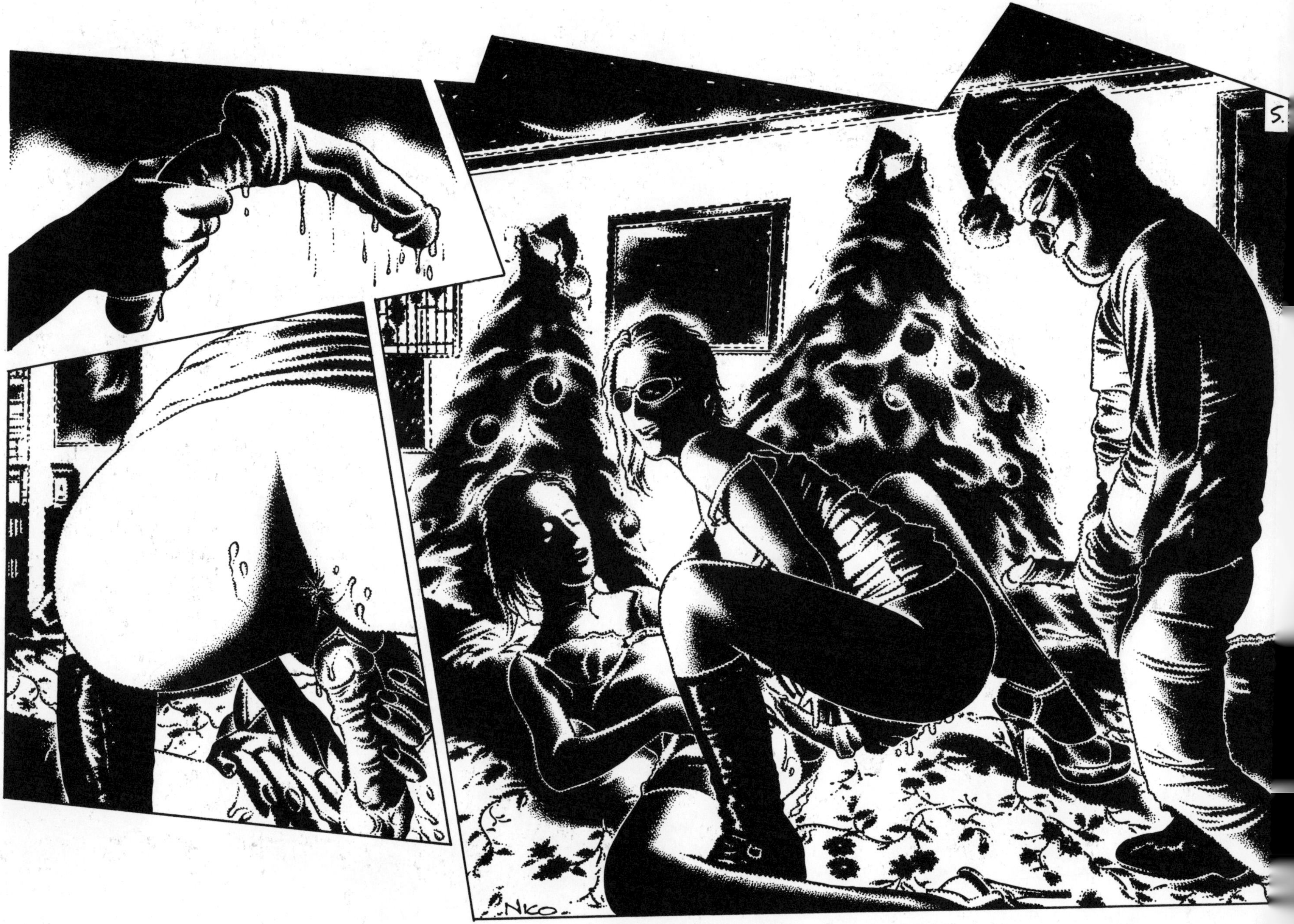
5.
NKO

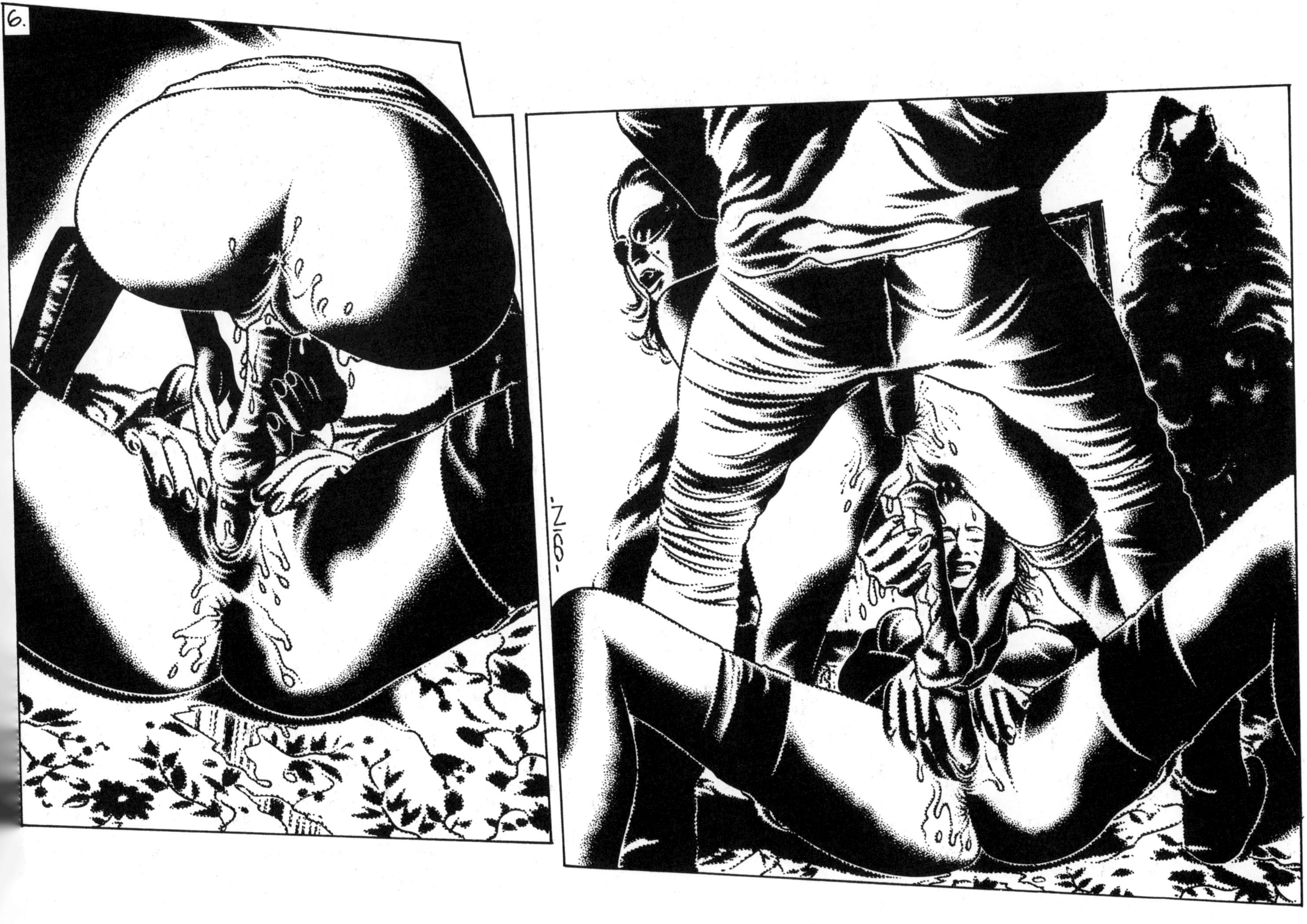
6.

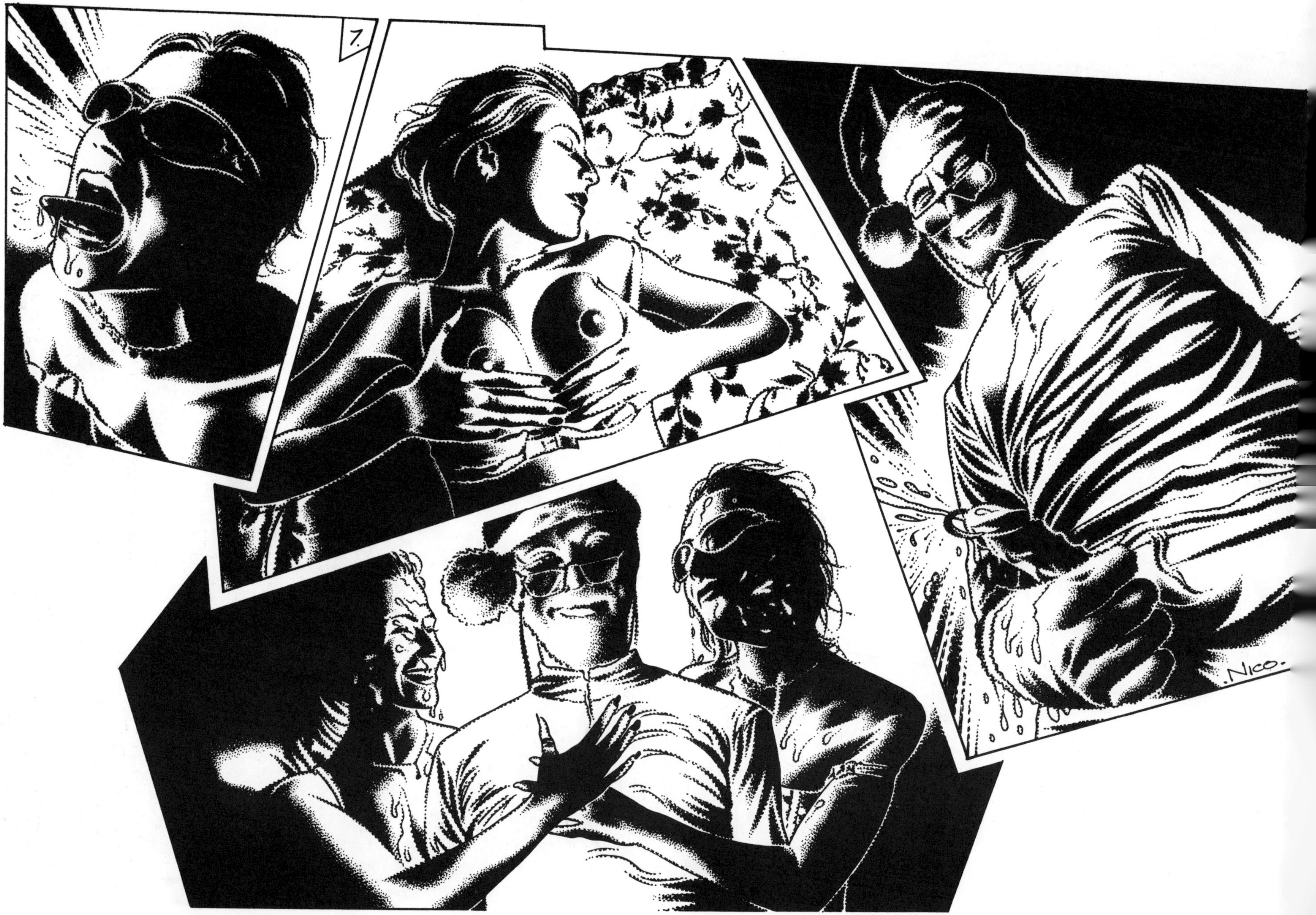
7.
NICO.

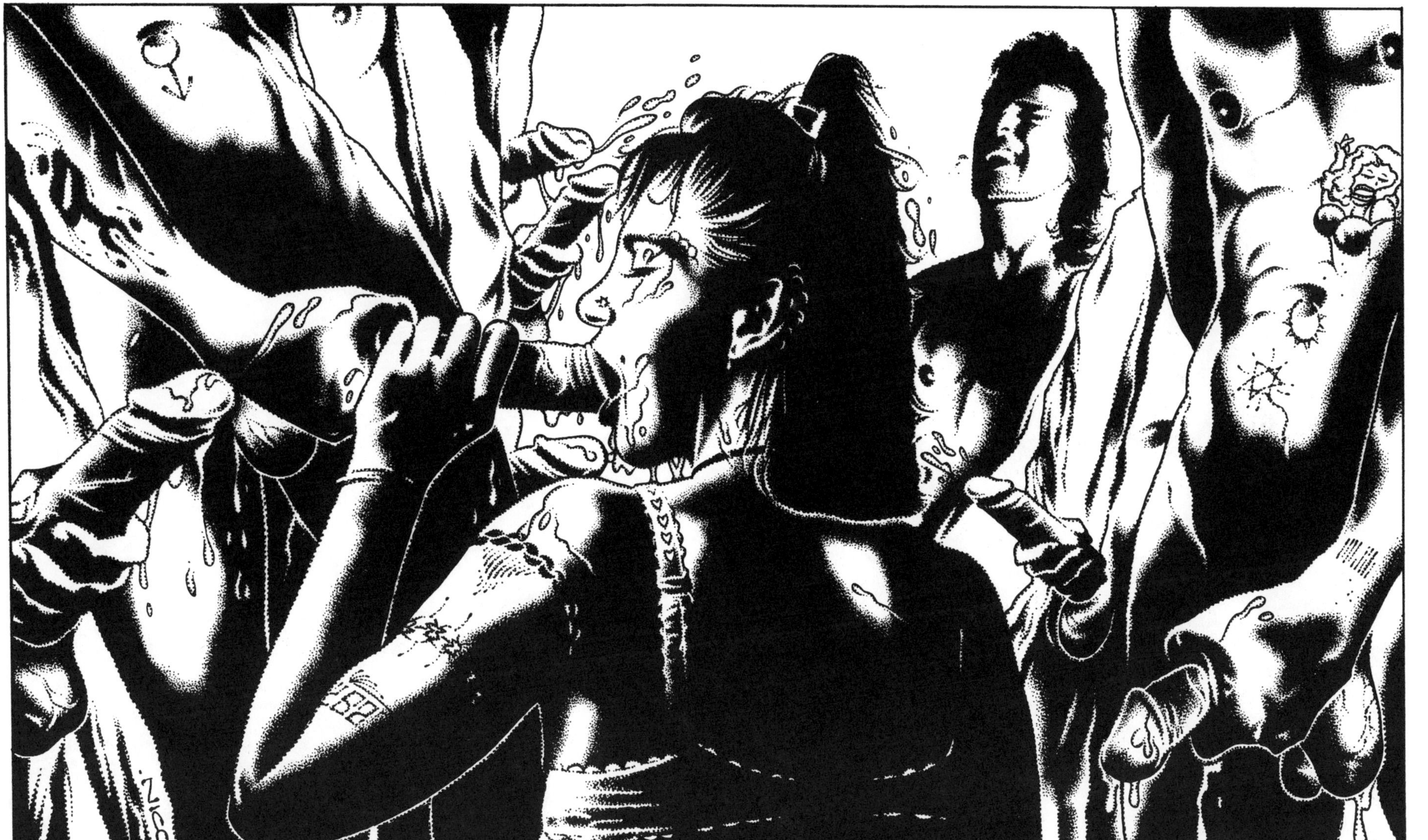
NICO

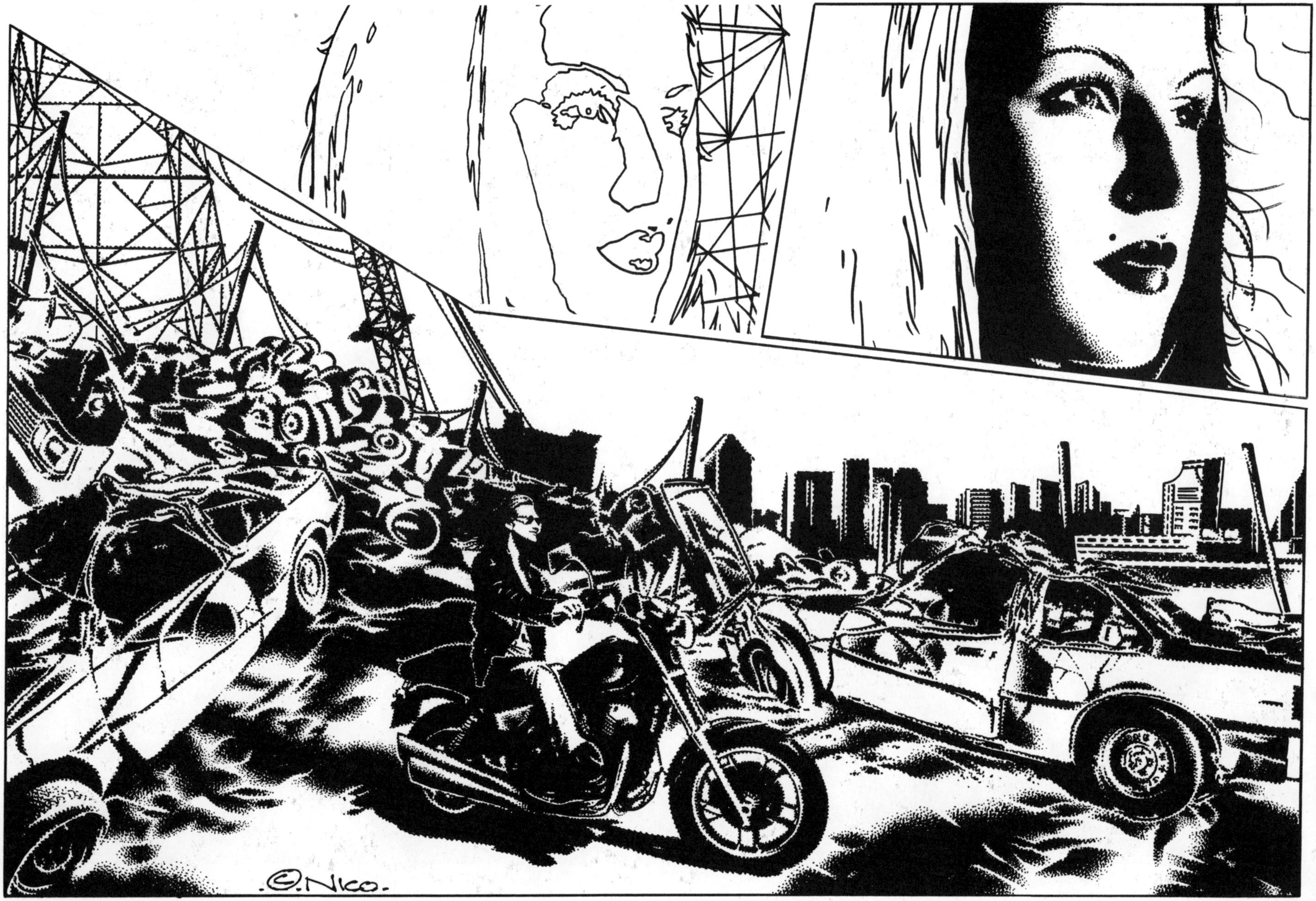
©.Nico.

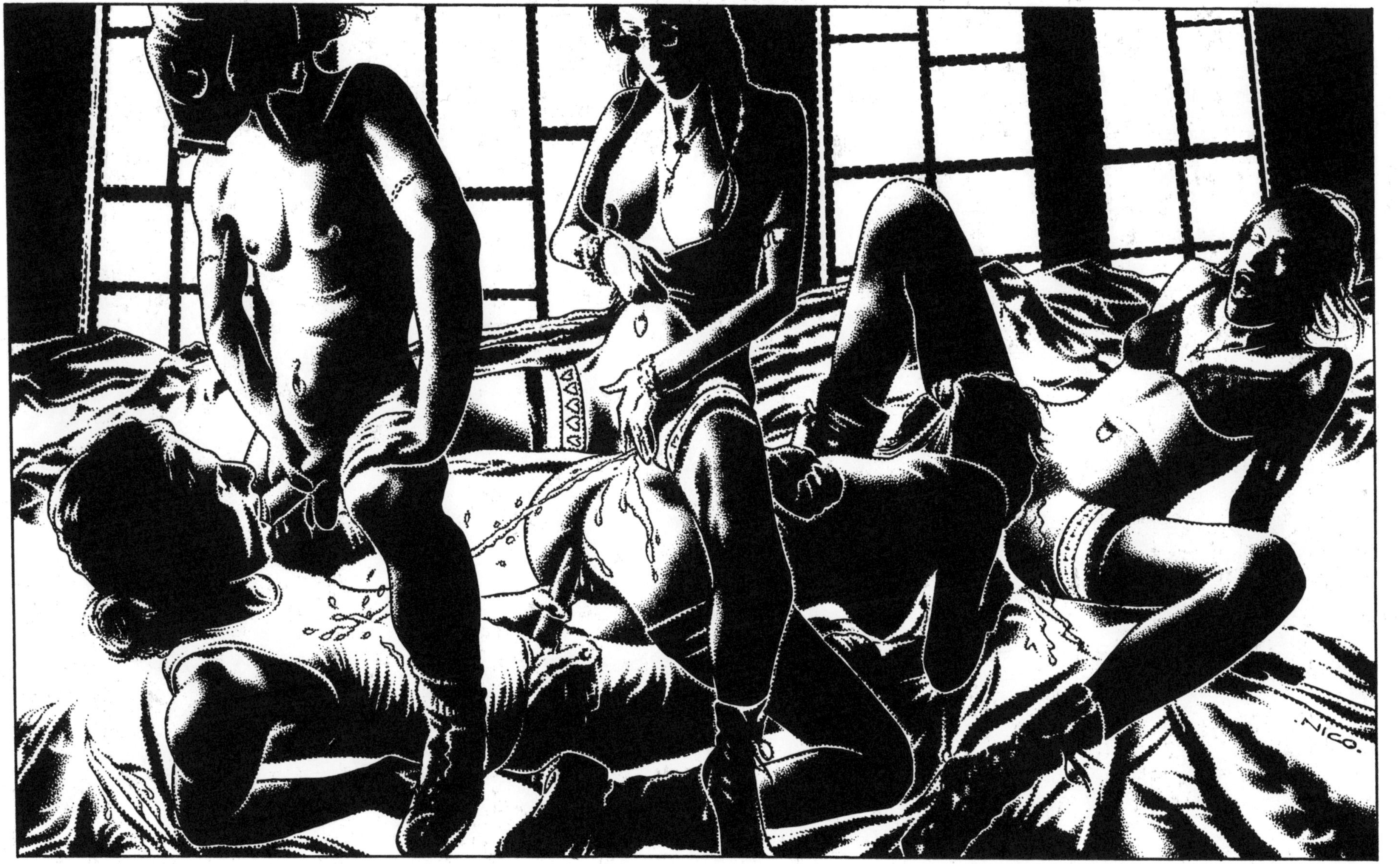
NICO.

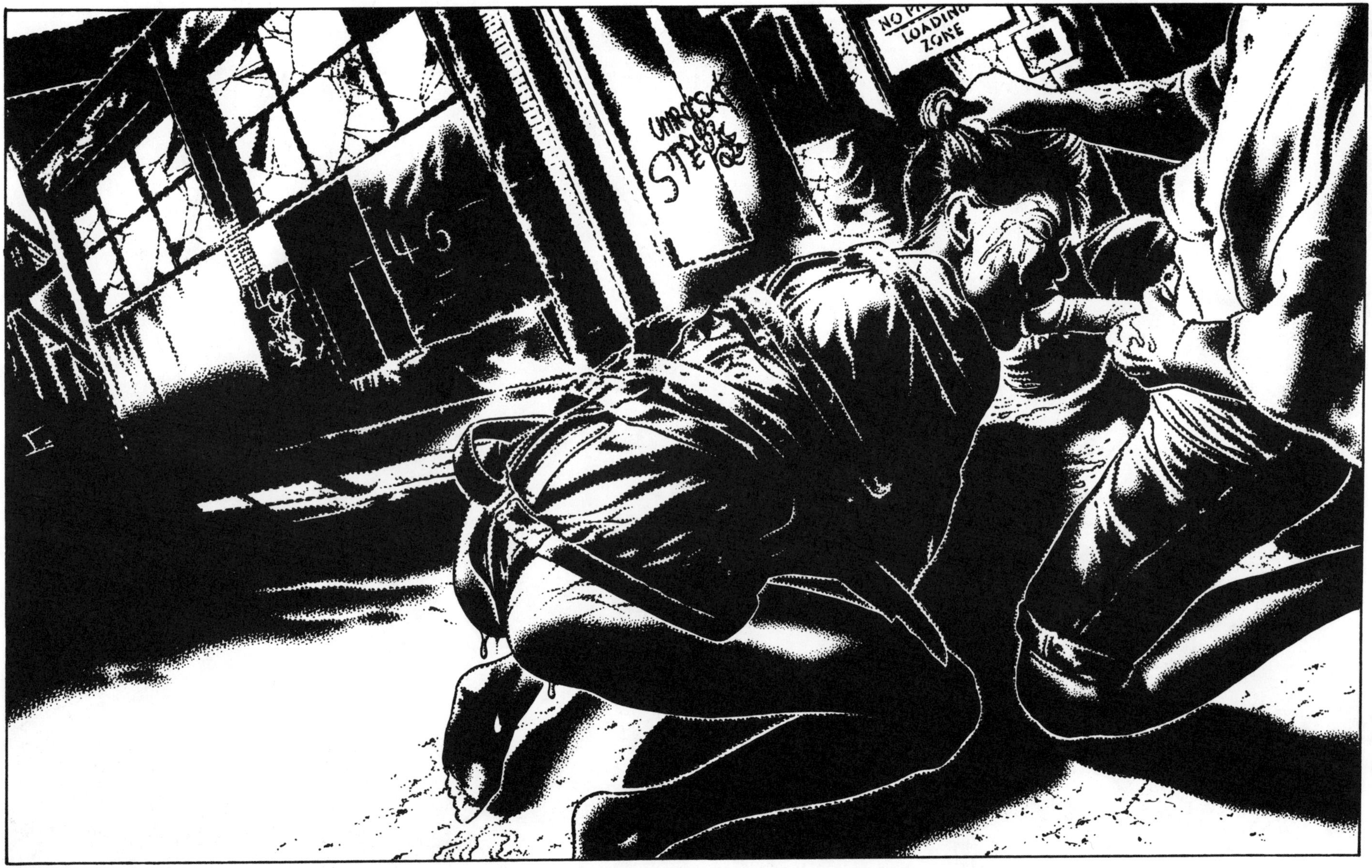
LOADING
ZONE

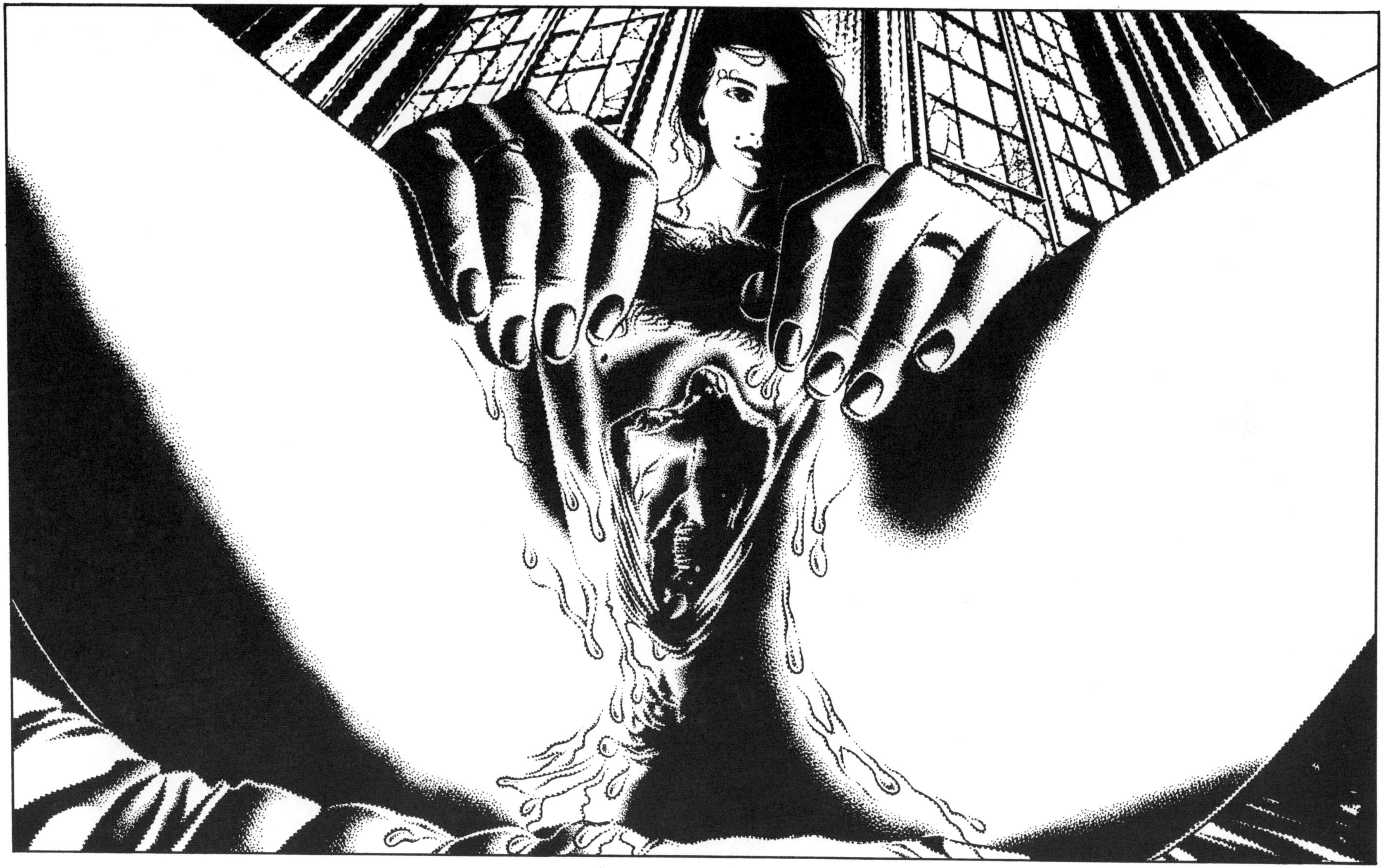

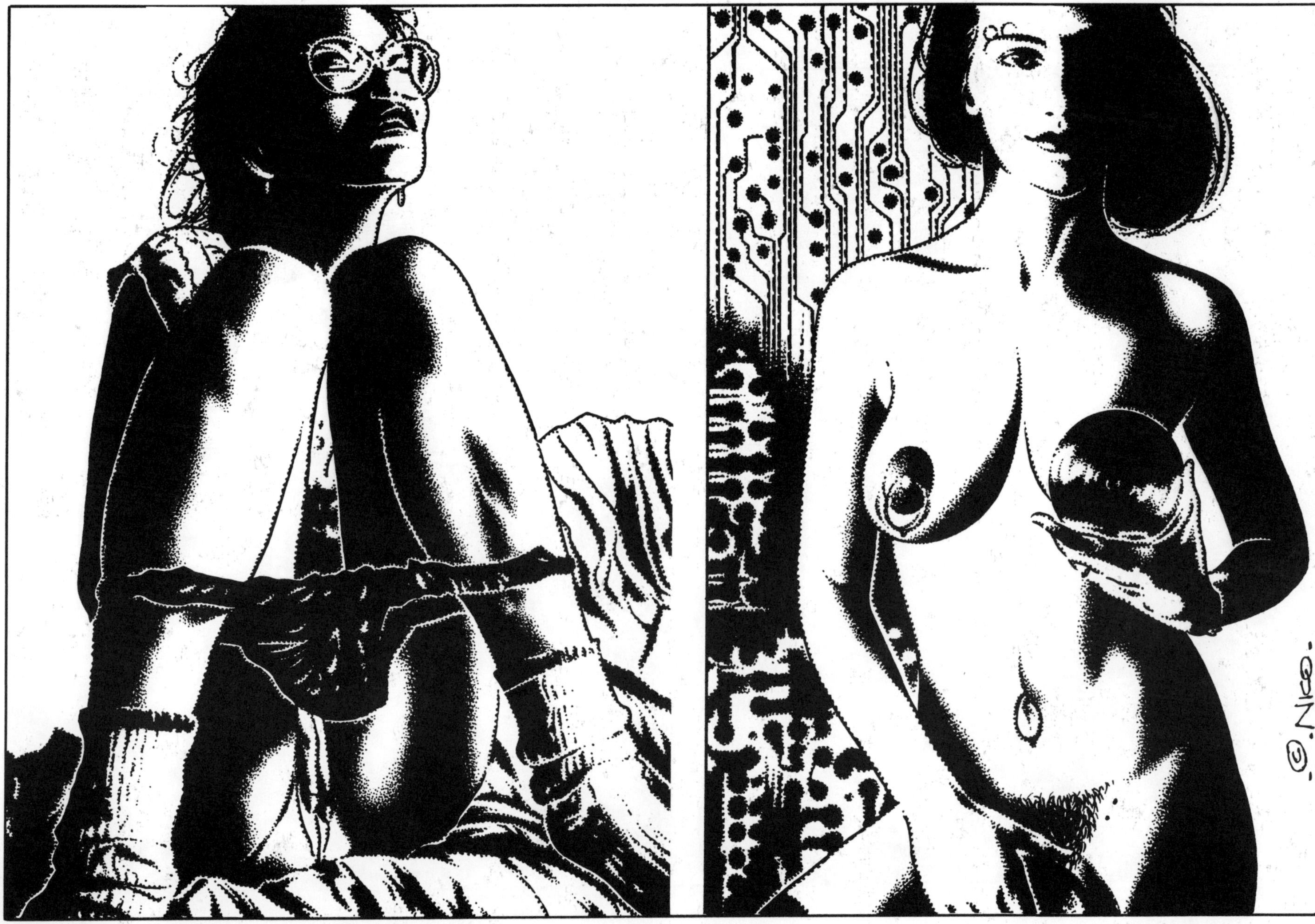
©.NIKO.

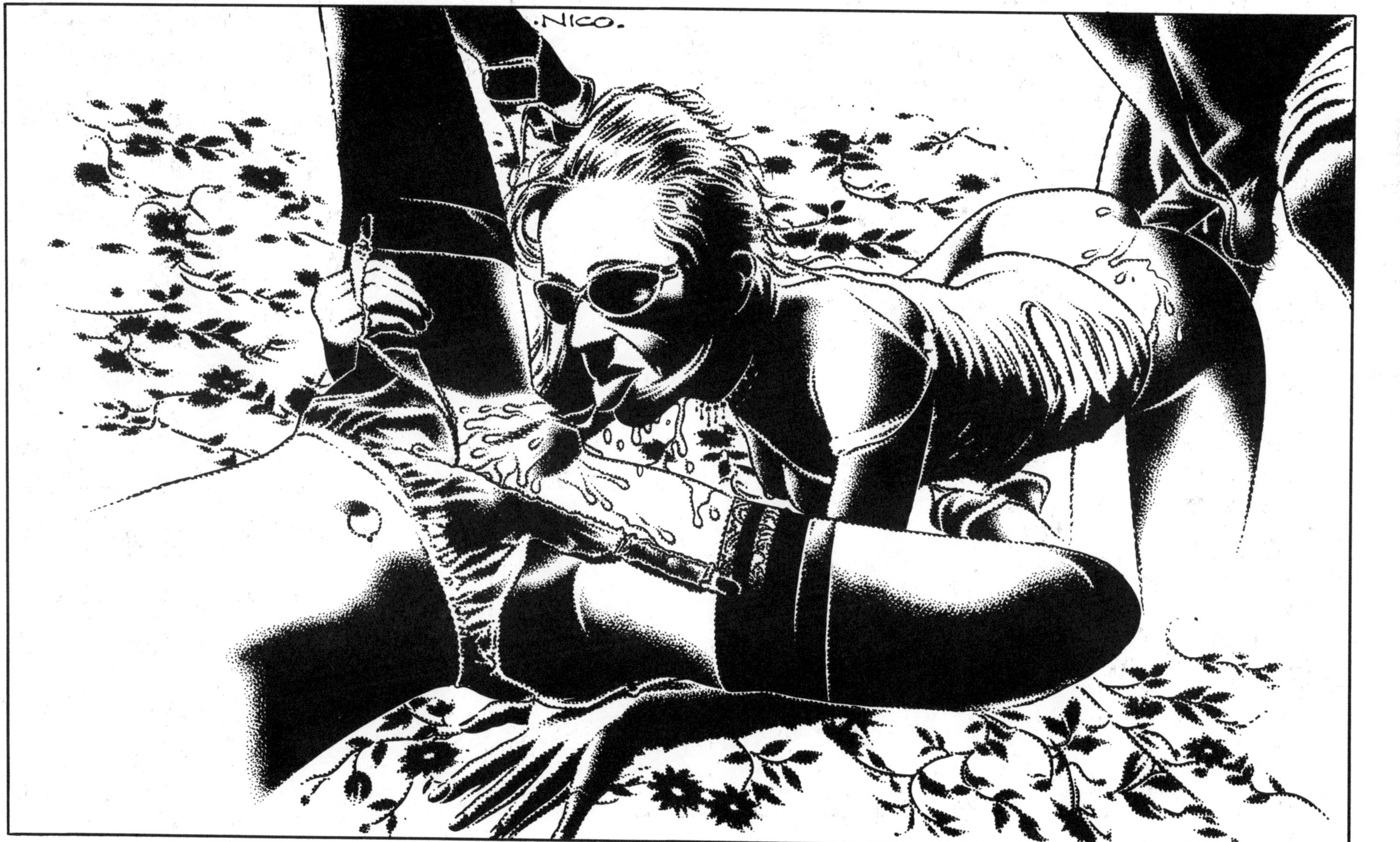
.NICO.

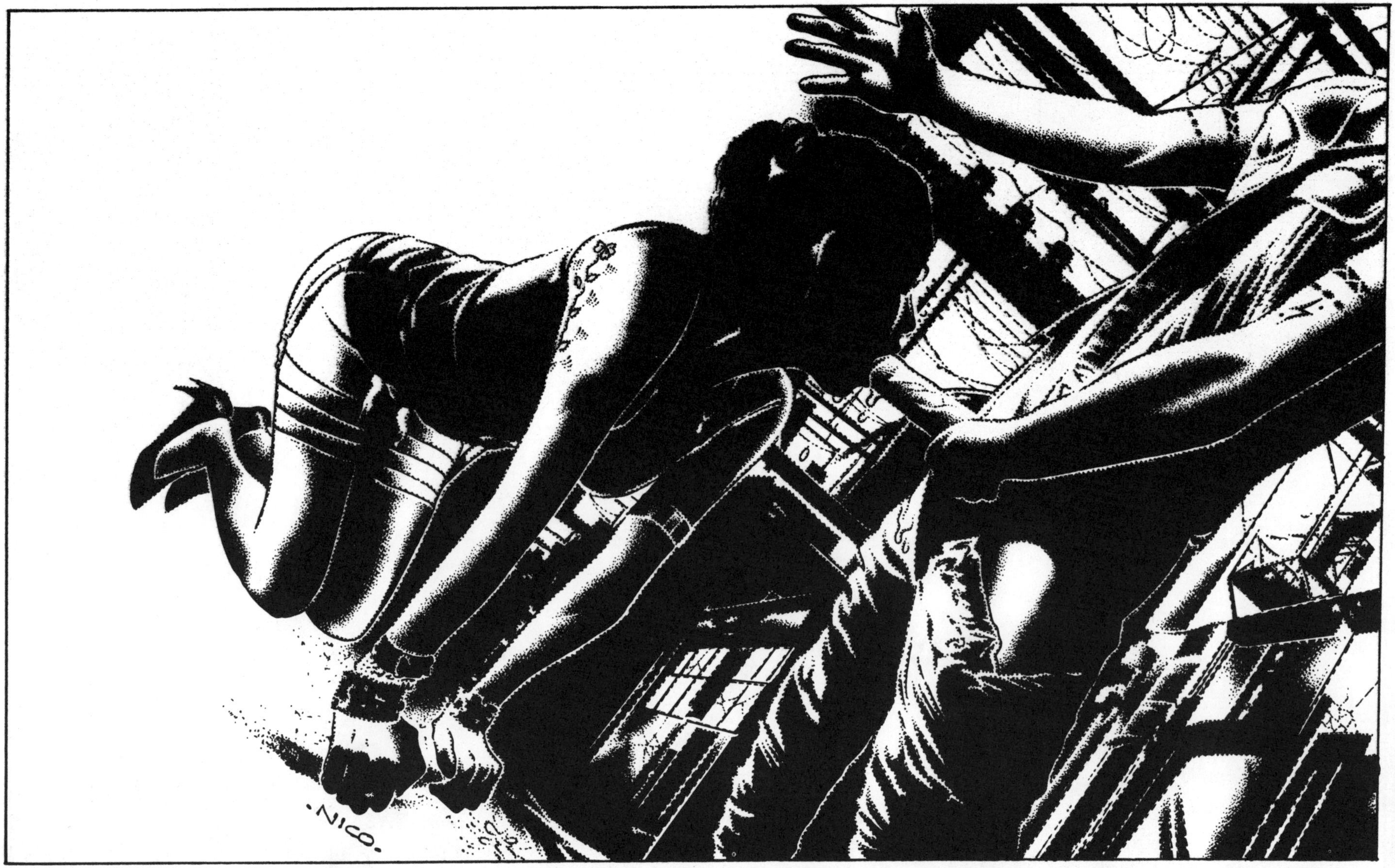
·NICO·

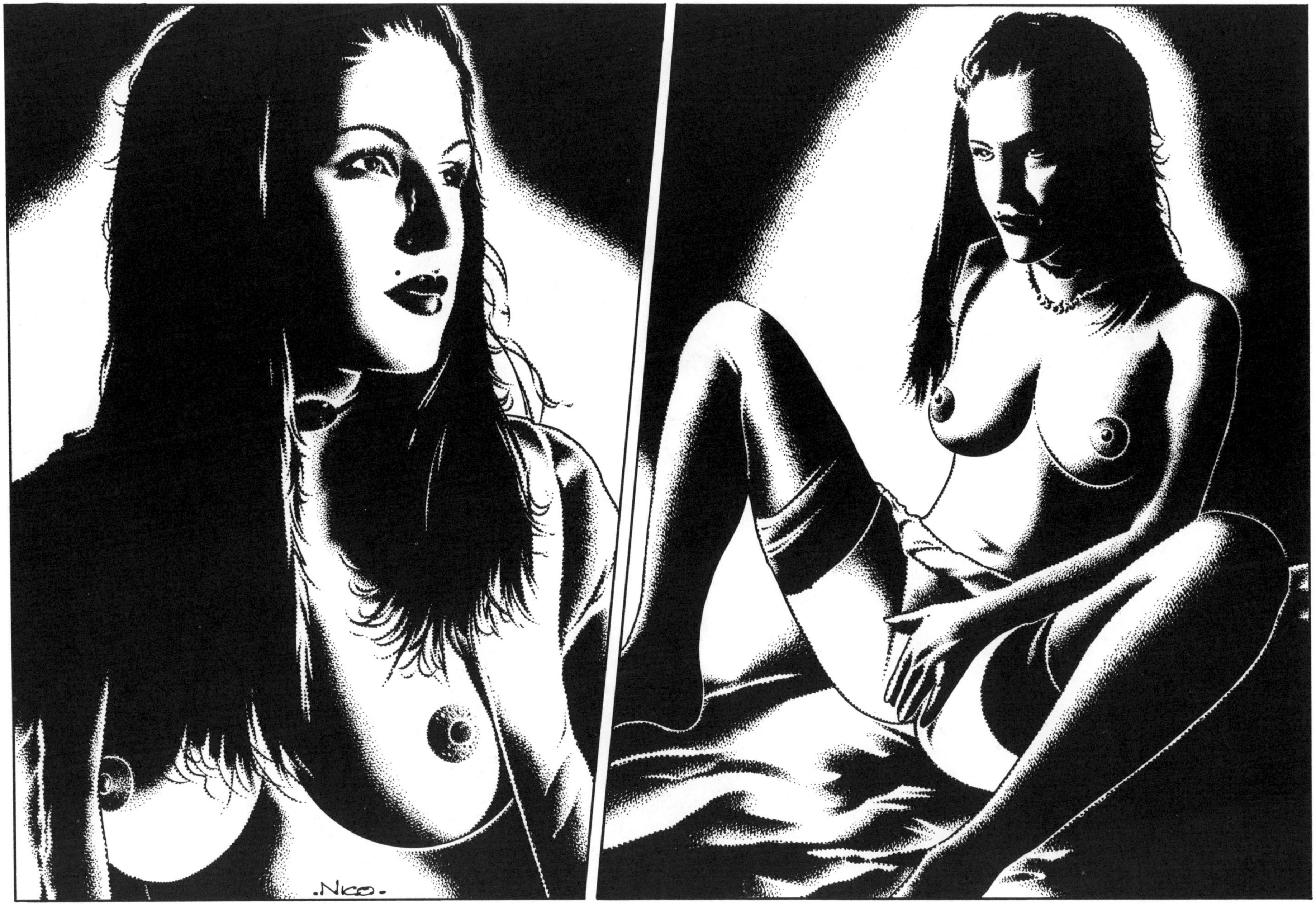
.NICO.

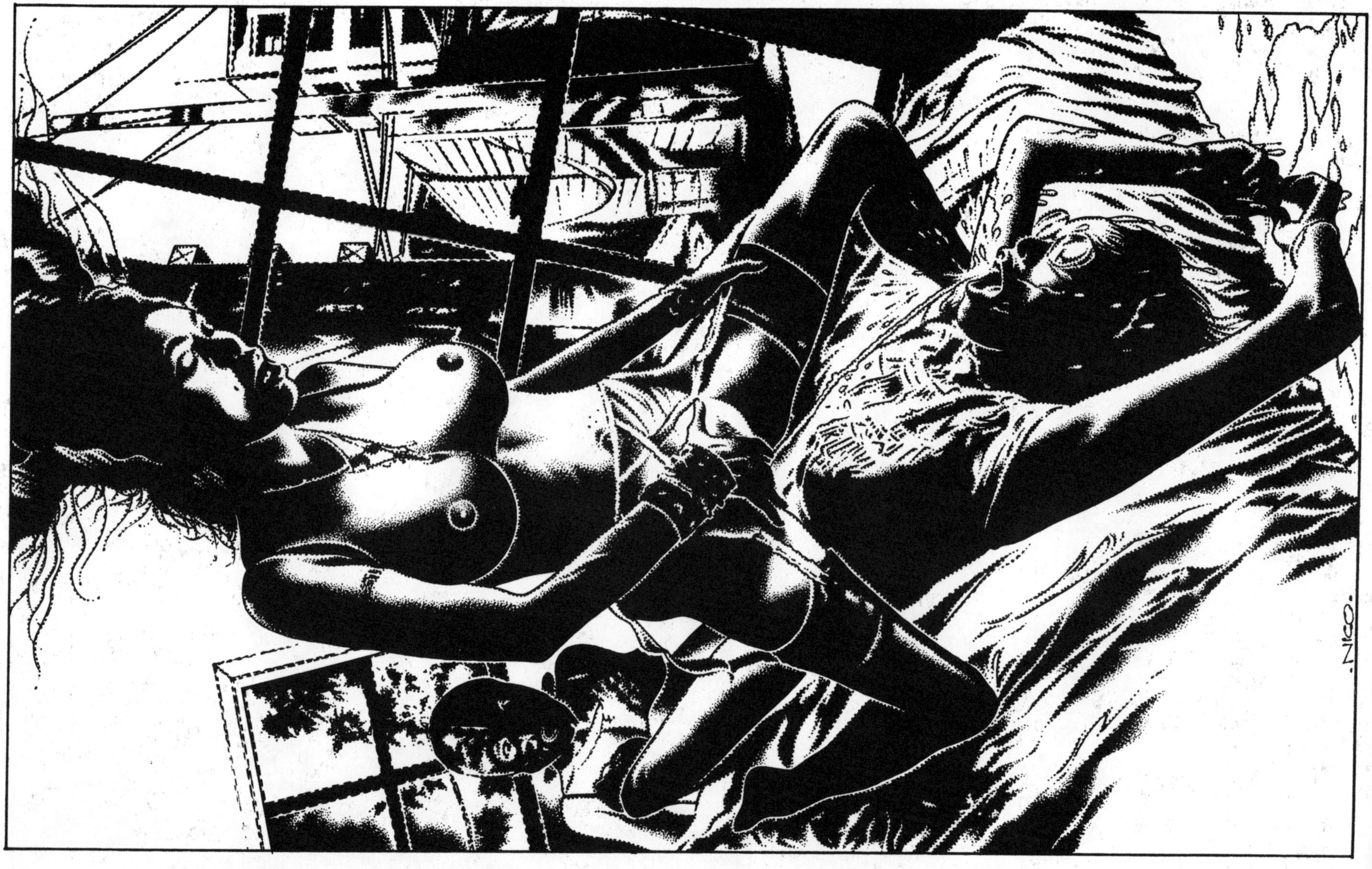

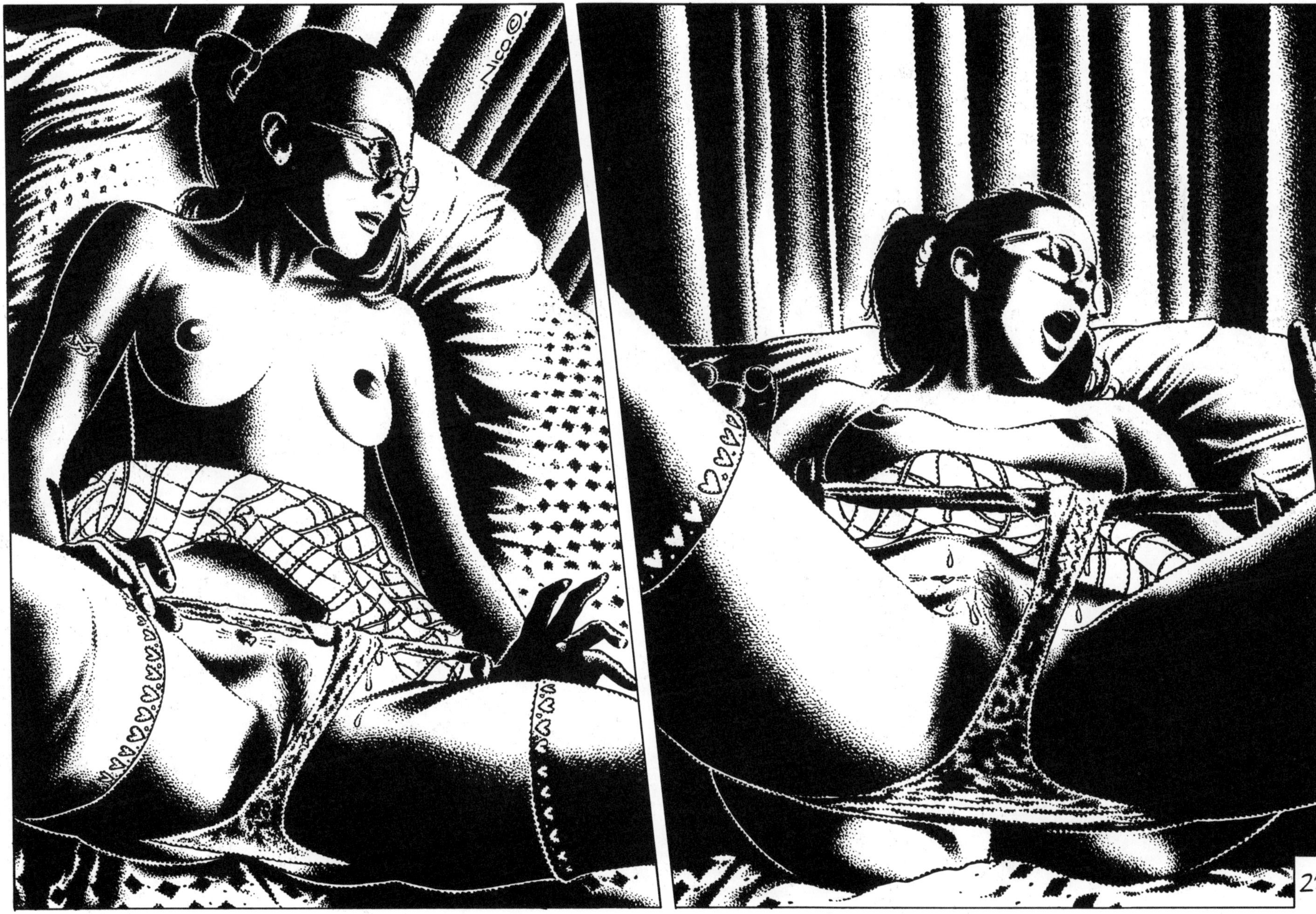
Nico ©.

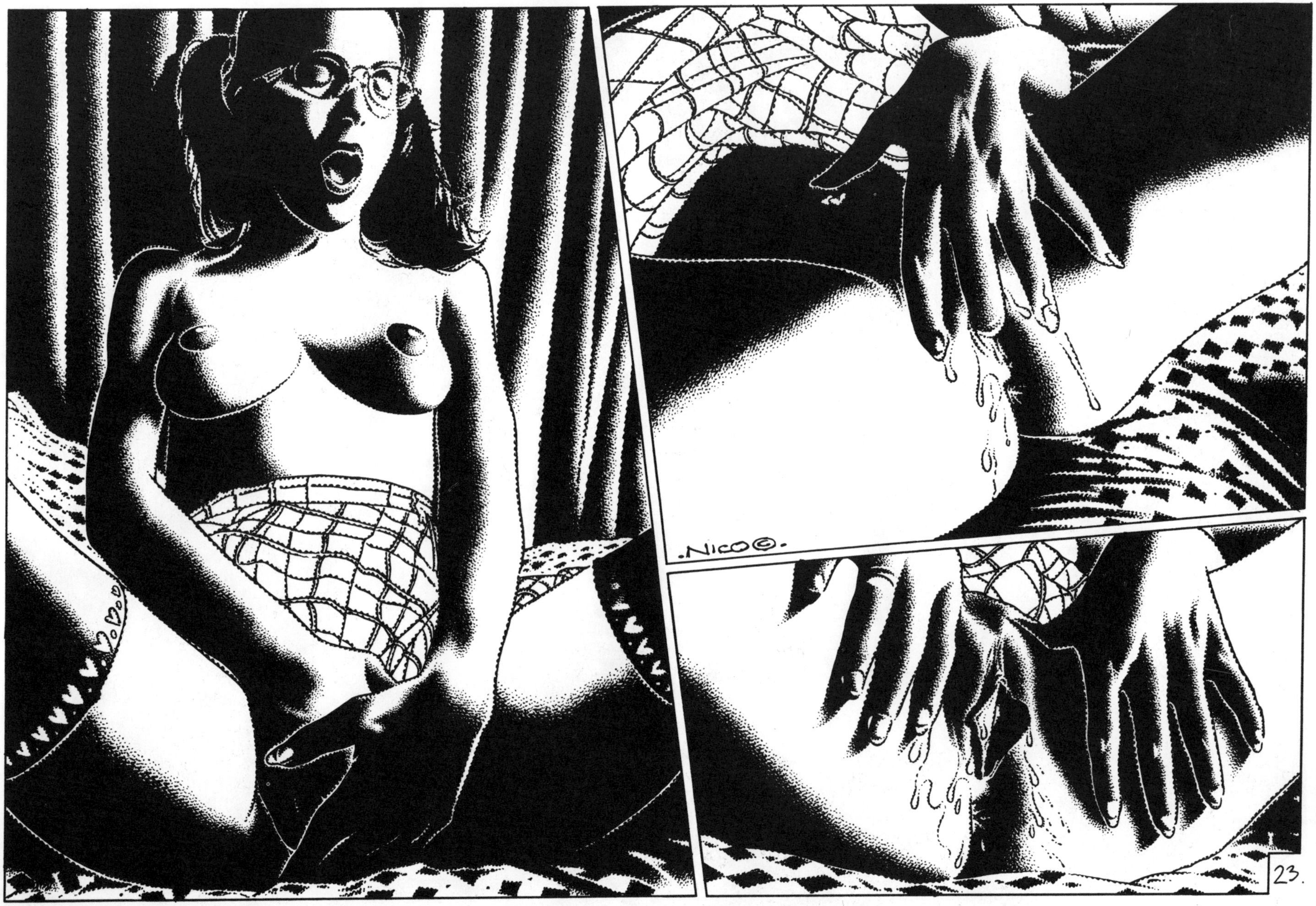
.NICO©.

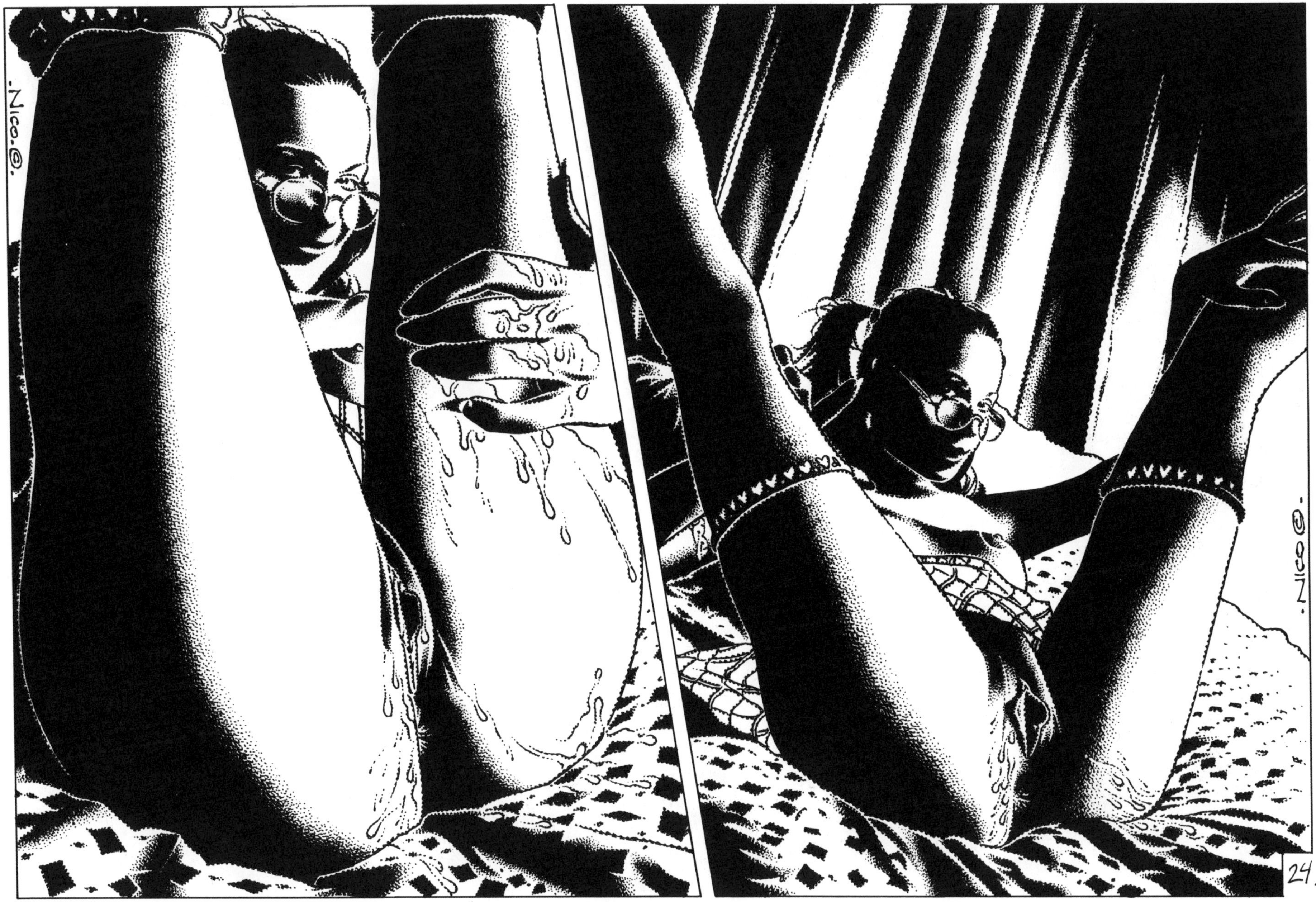

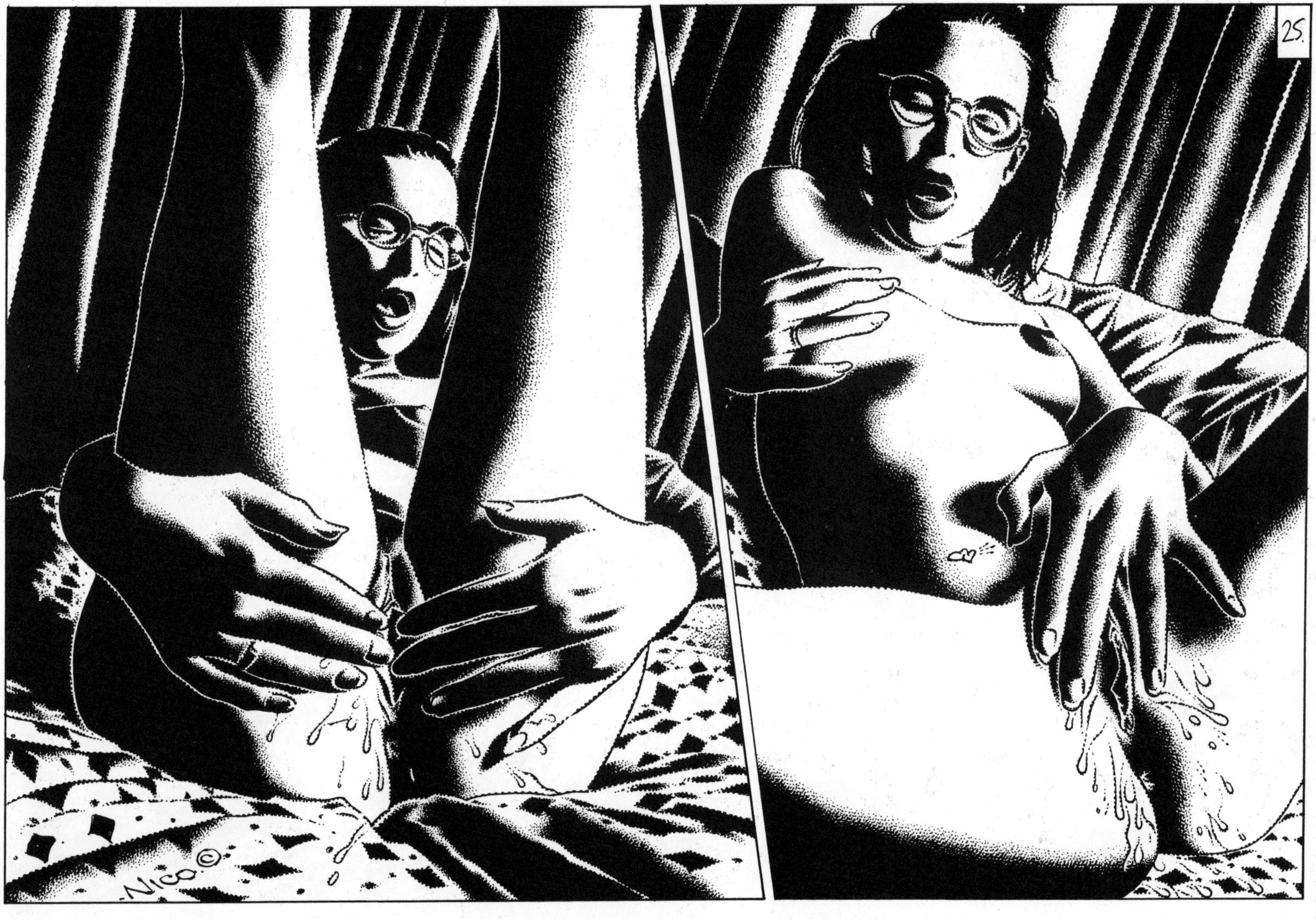
Nico ©

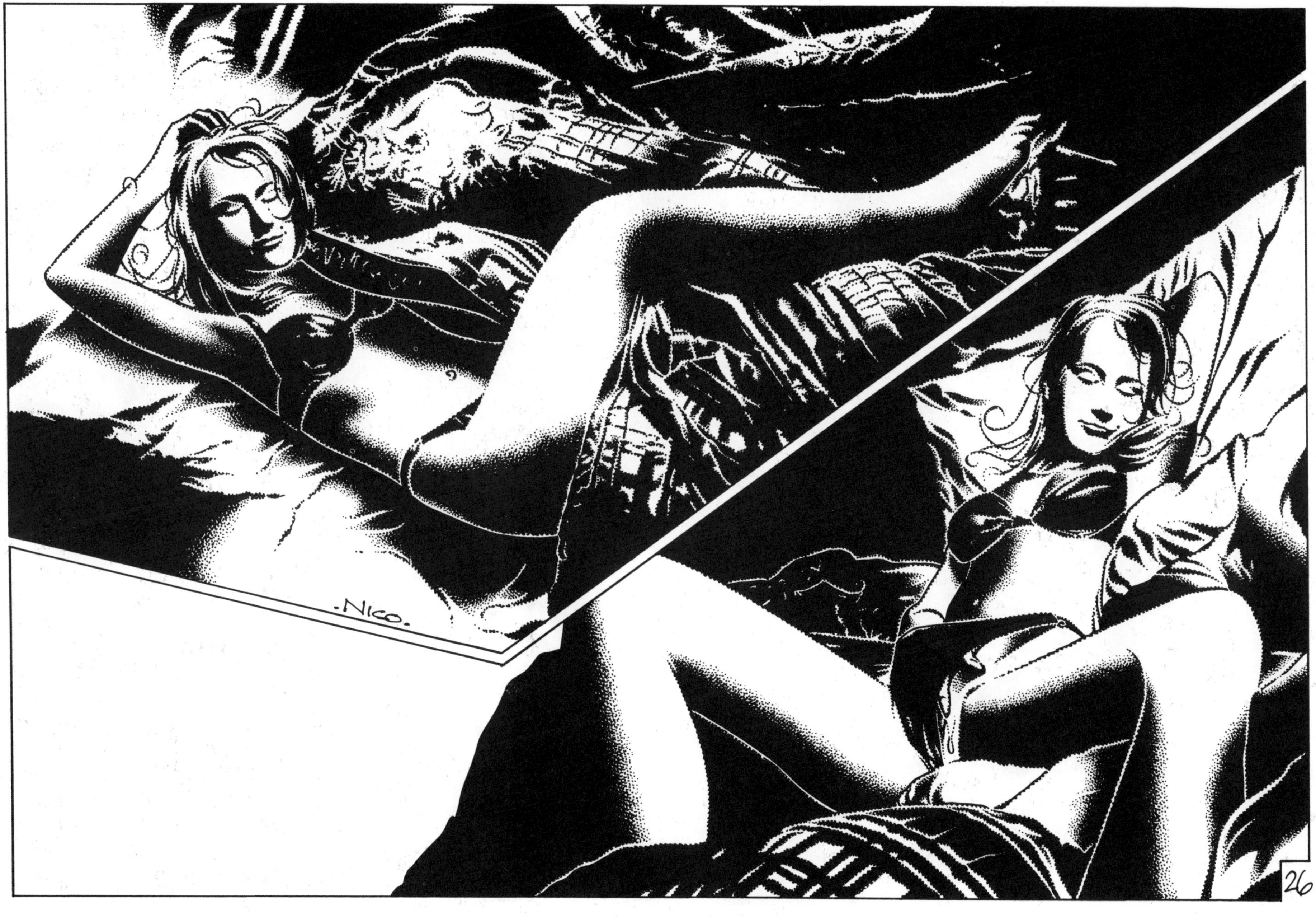
NICO

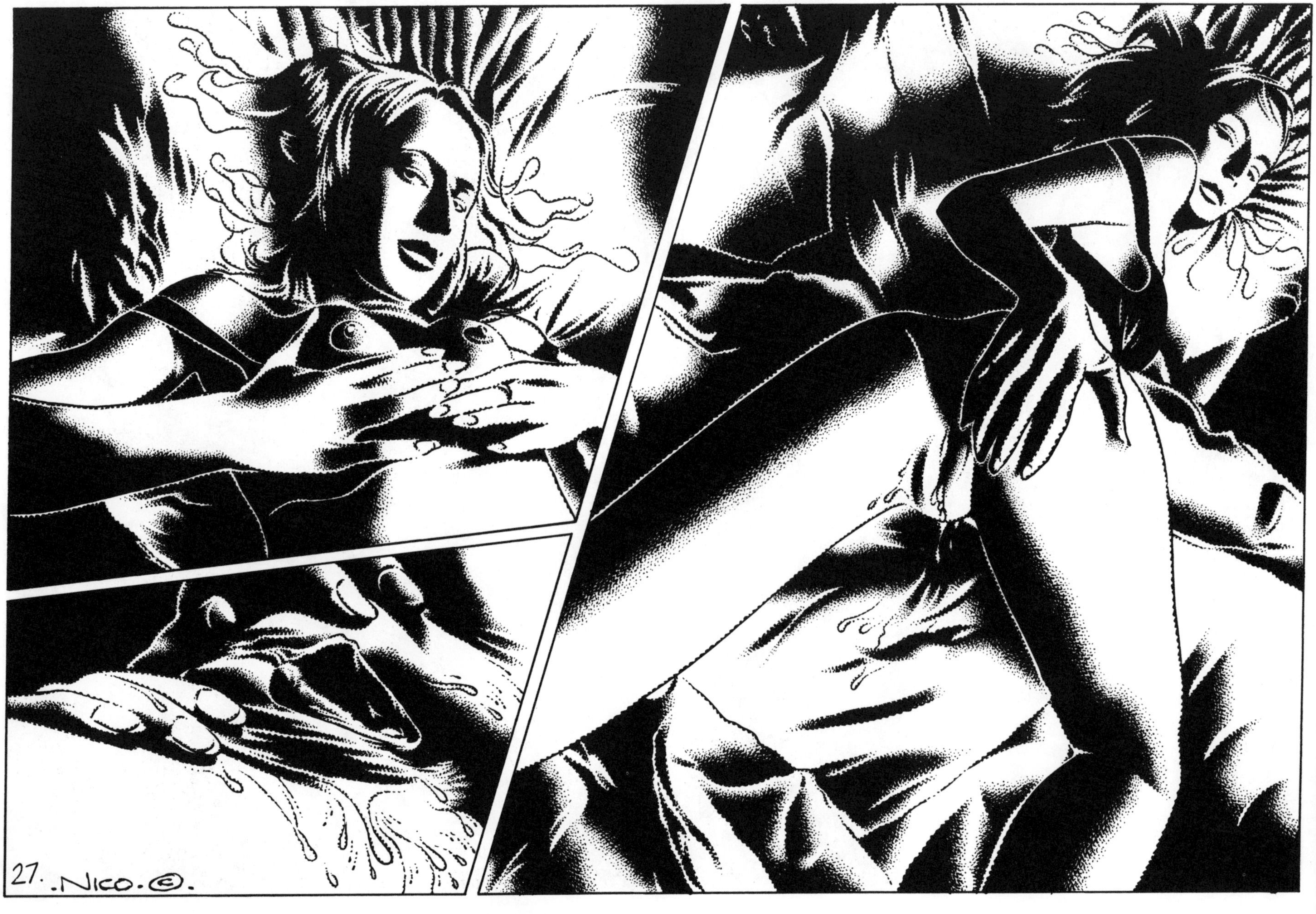
27. .NICO.©.

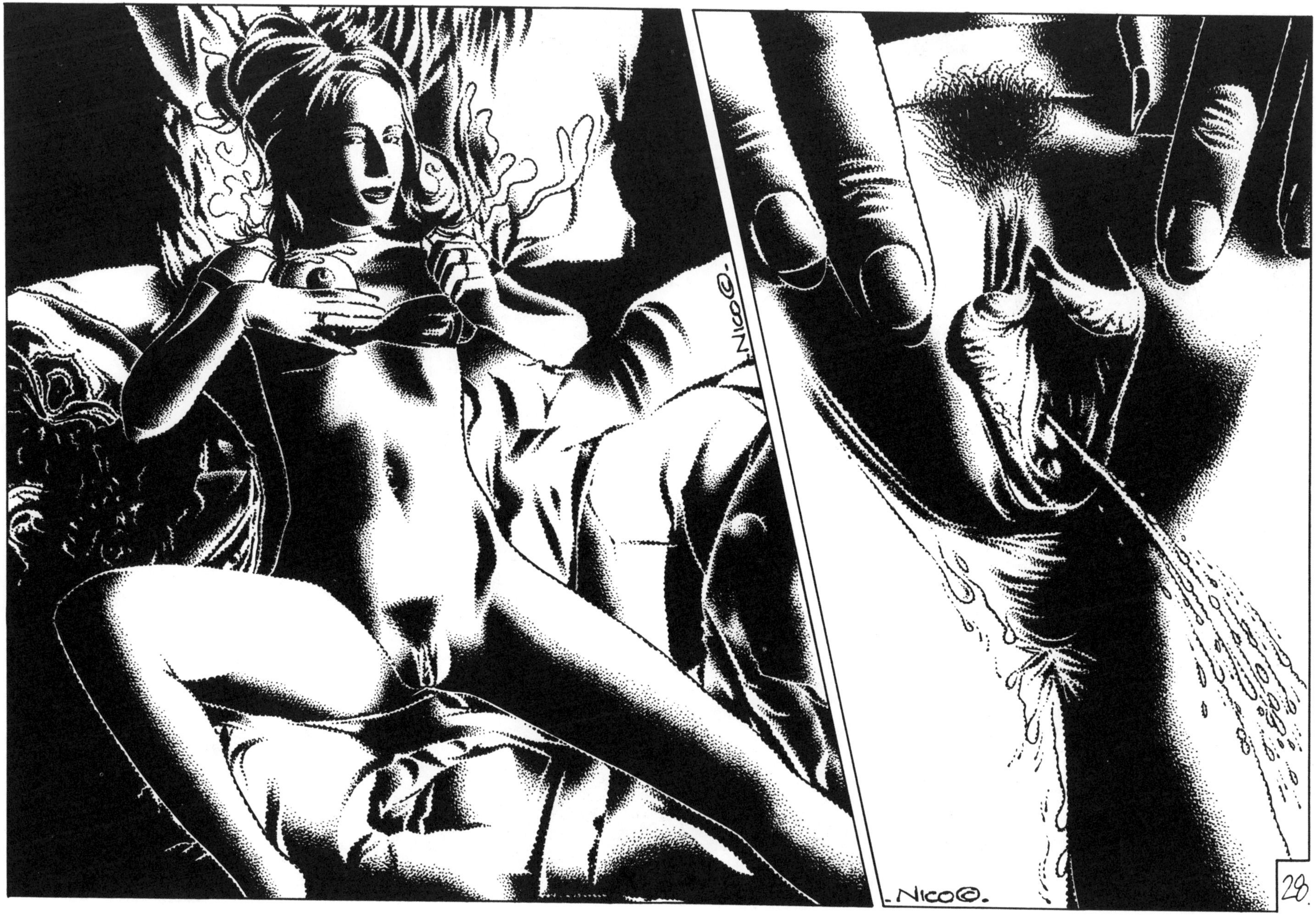
NICO©.
NICO©.

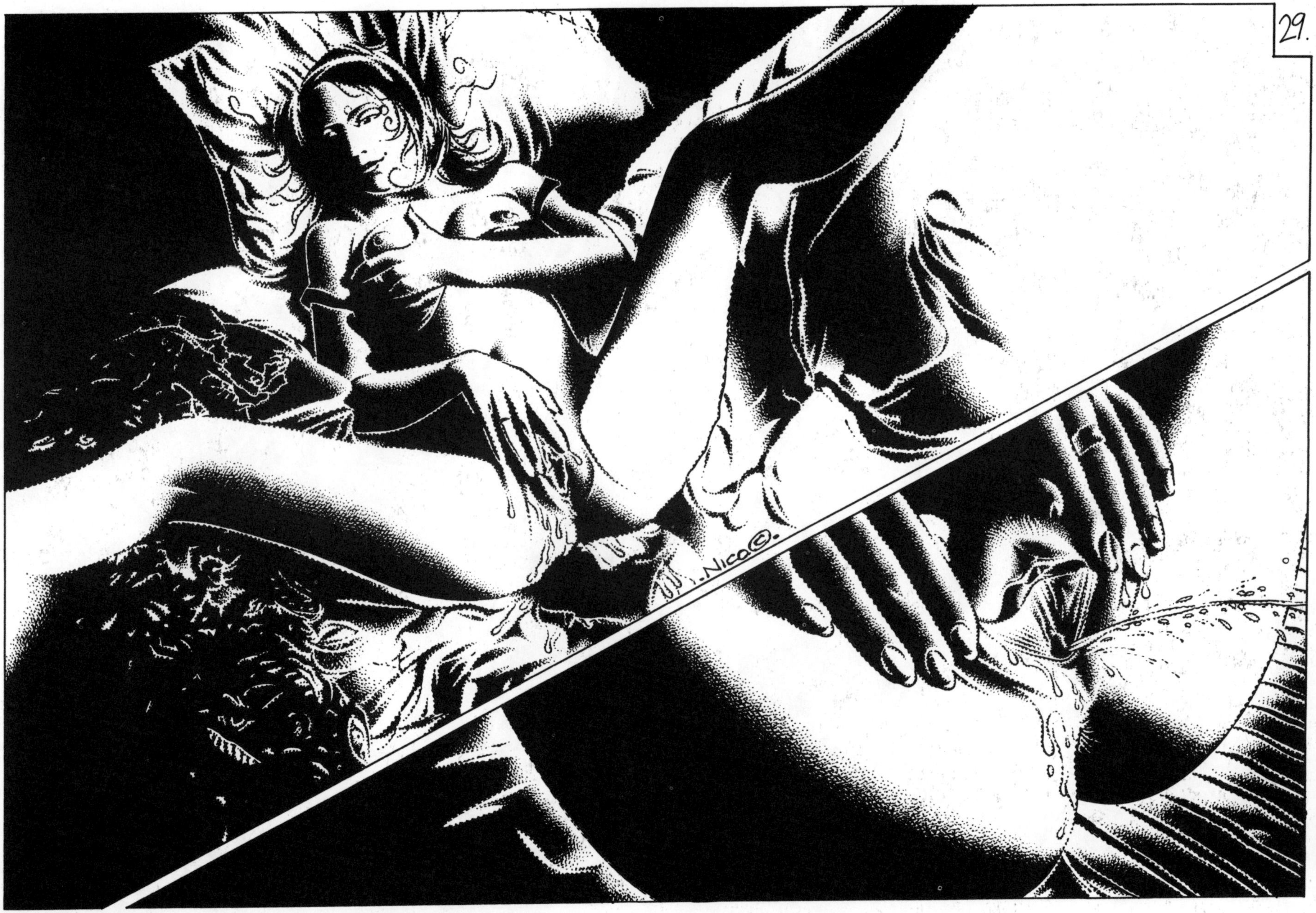
Nico©.

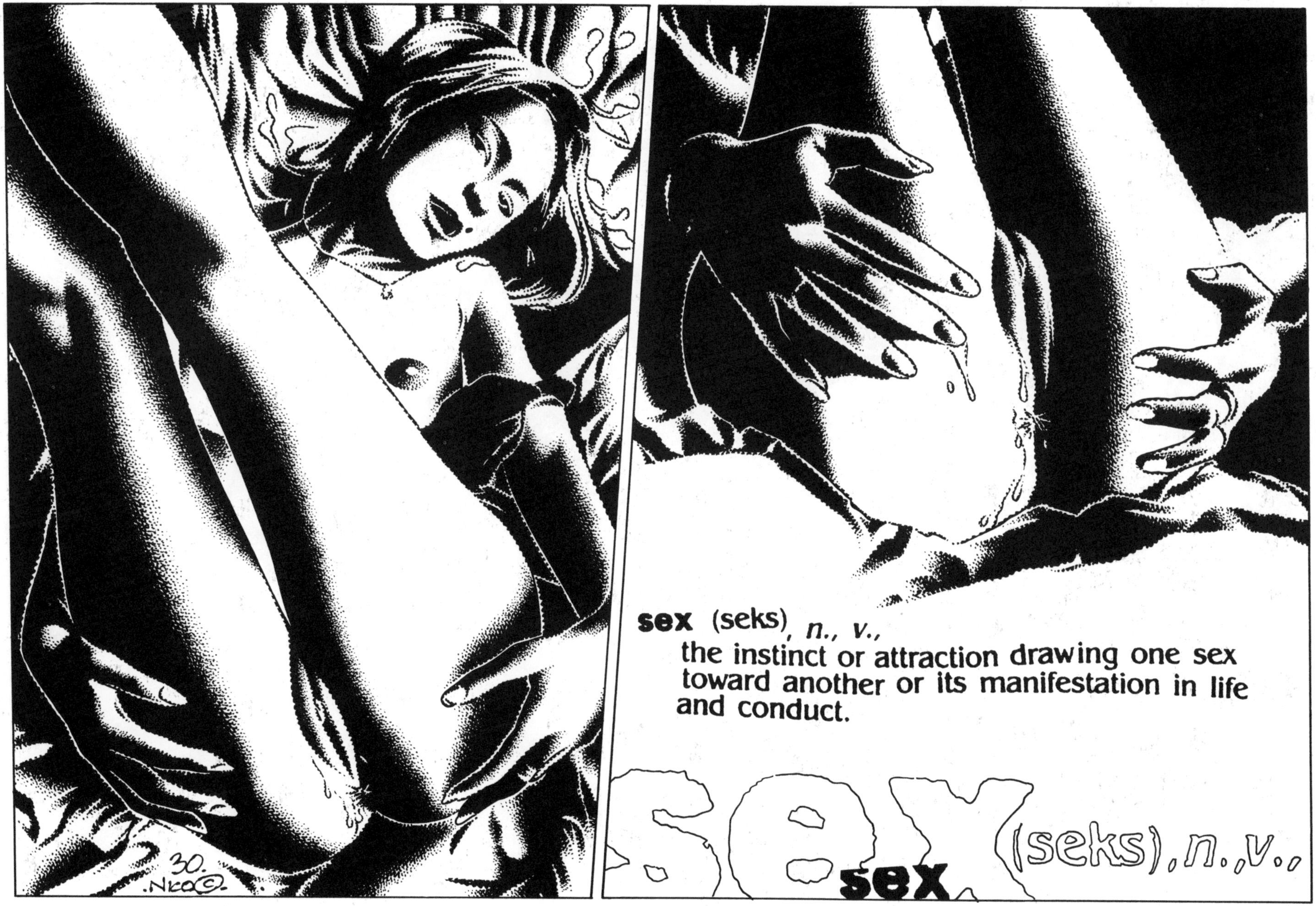
sex (seks), *n., v.,*
the instinct or attraction drawing one sex toward another or its manifestation in life and conduct.
sex
sex
(seks), n., v.,

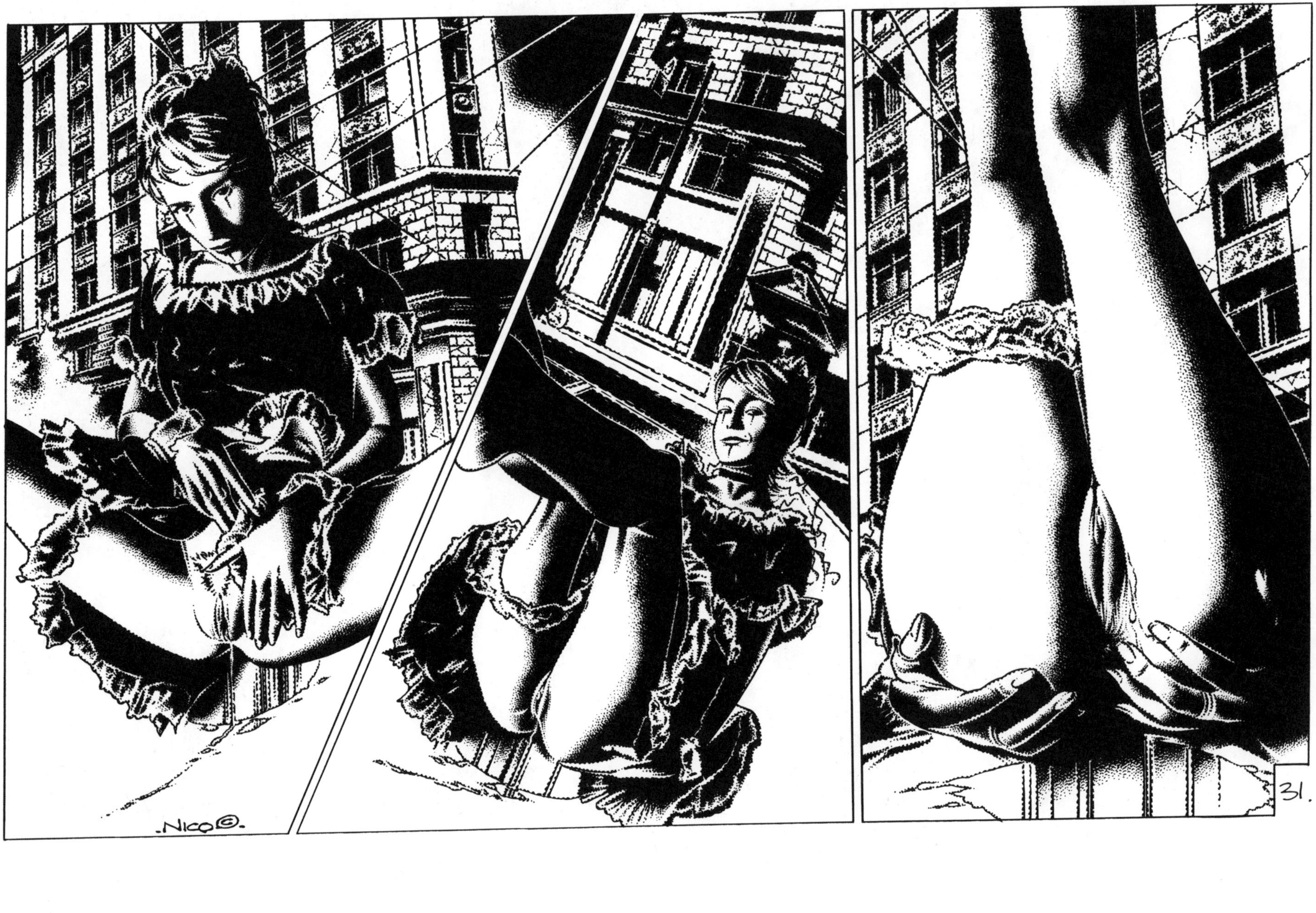
-NICO©-

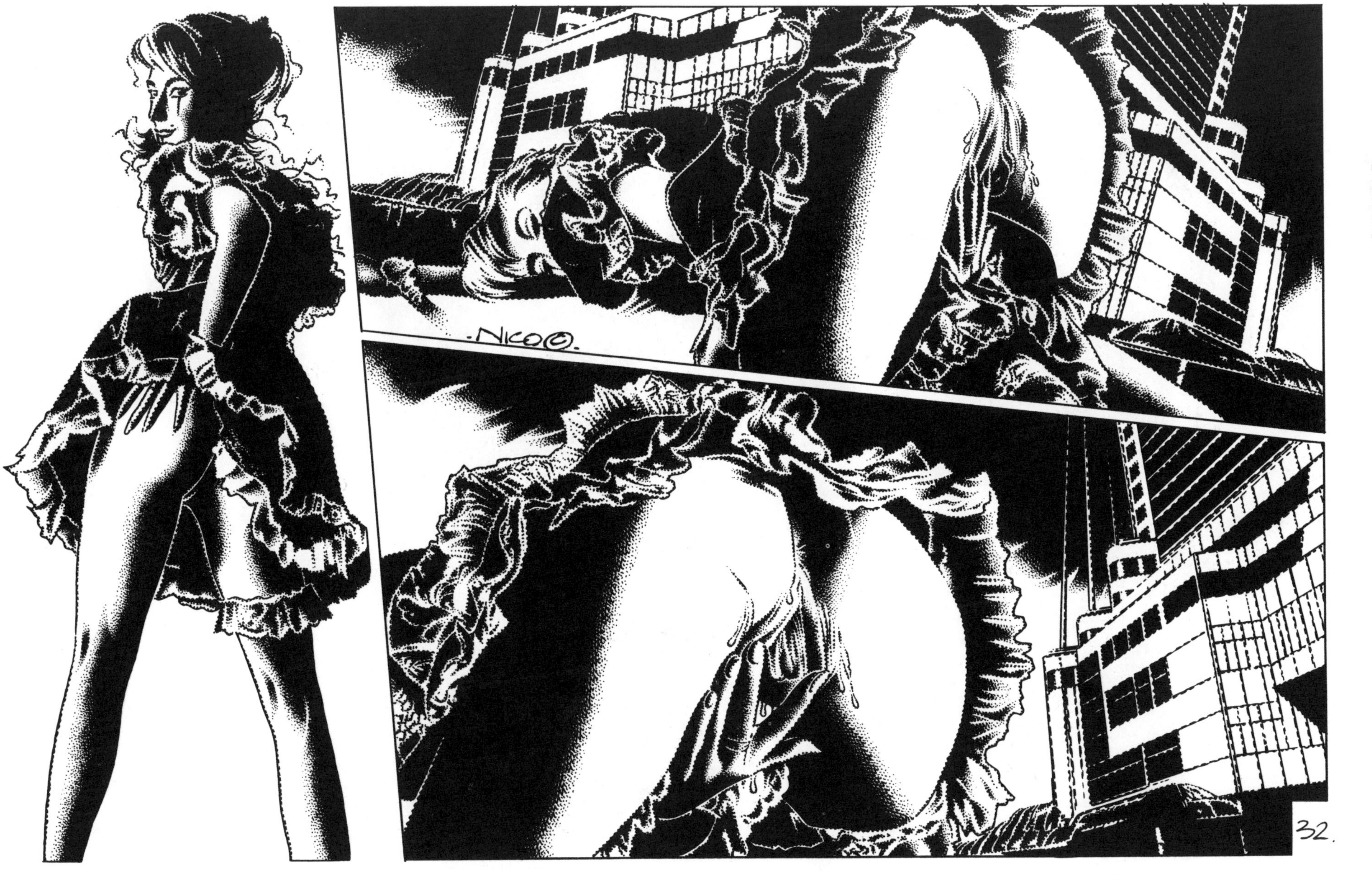
NICO©.

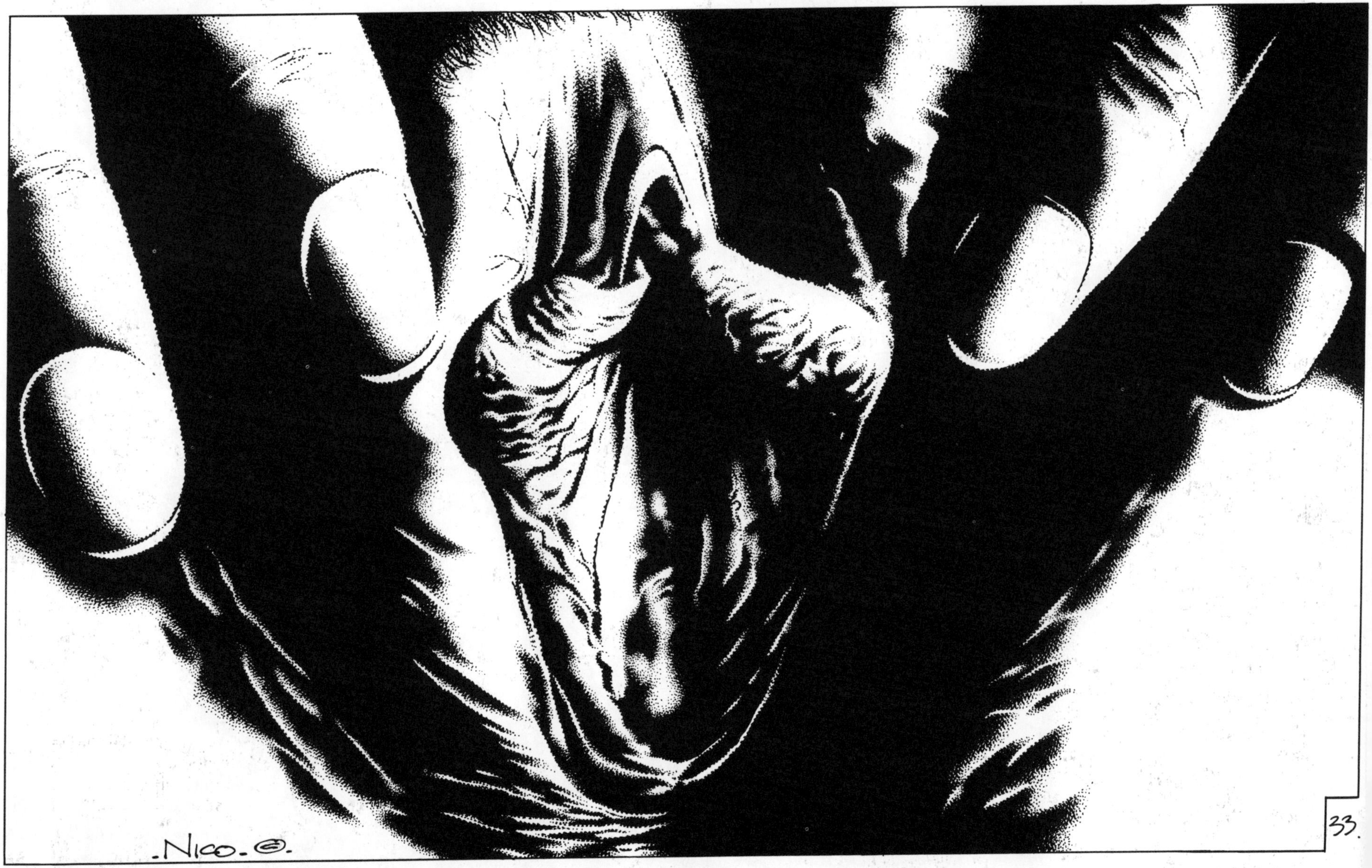
-NICO-©-

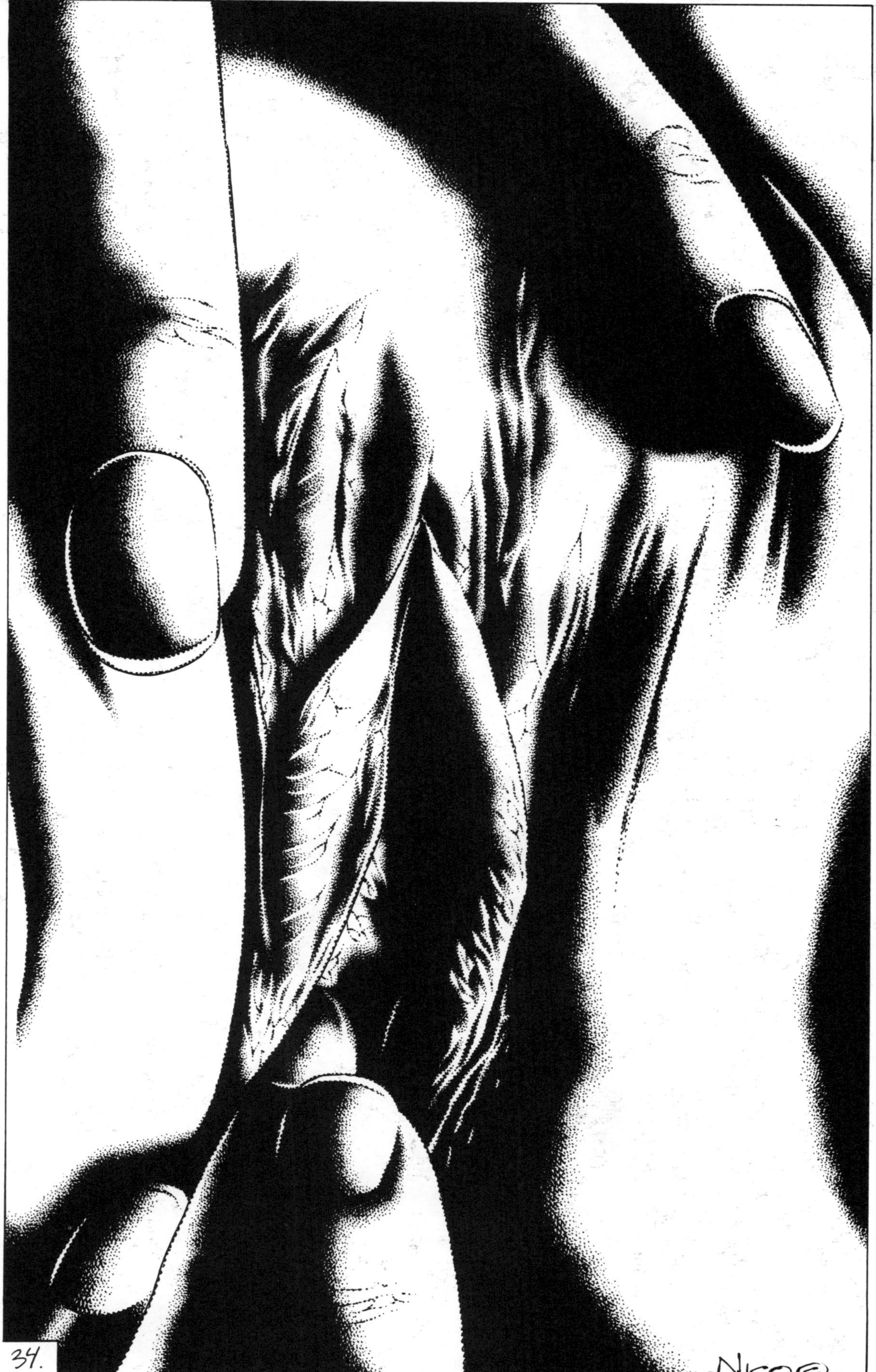
-Nico©-

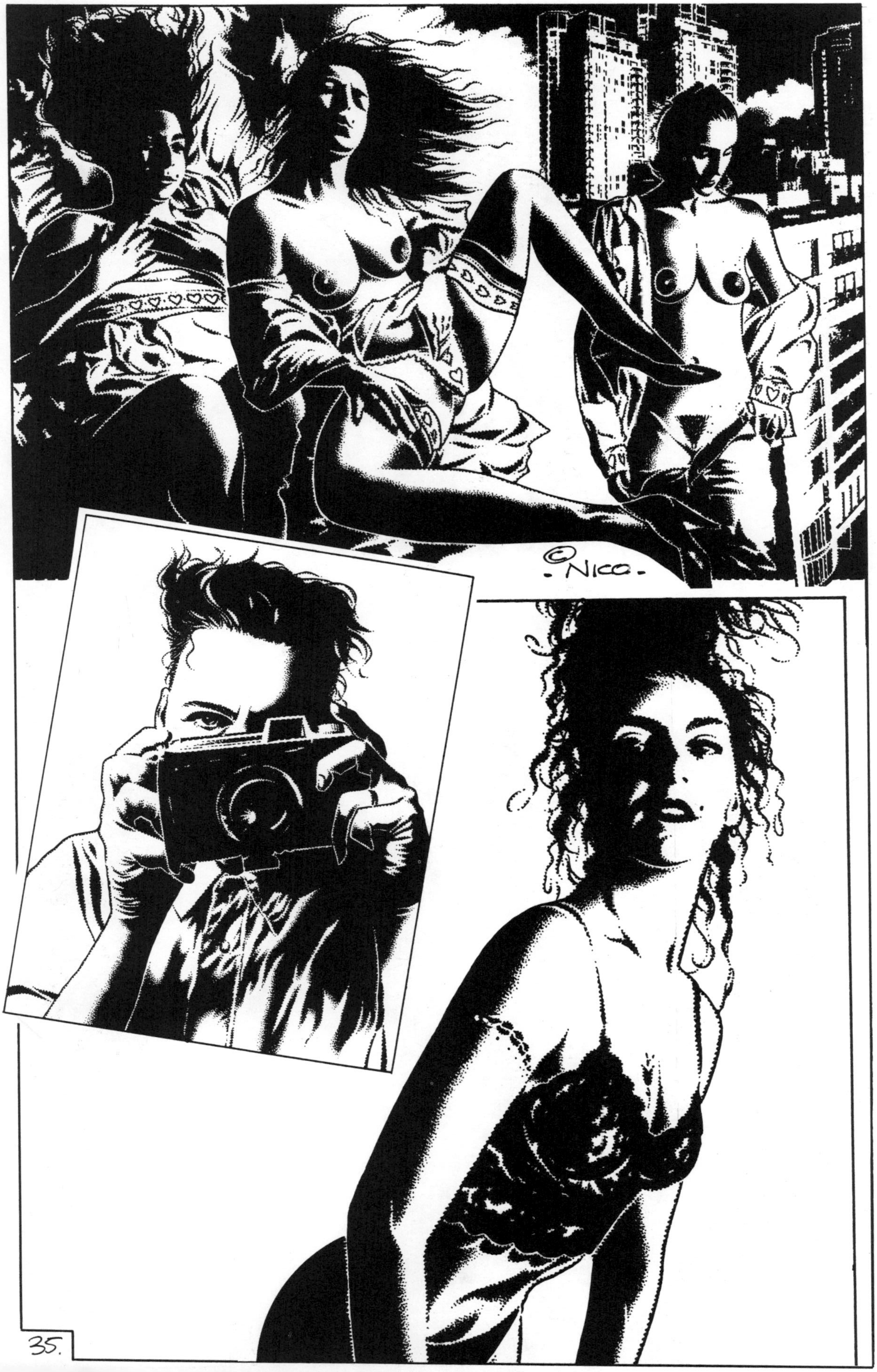
© Nico
35.